The German Influence in France
after 1870

The German Influence
in France after 1870

The Formation
of the French Republic

by Allan Mitchell

The University of North Carolina Press
Chapel Hill

Manufactured in the United States of America
Cloth edition, ISBN 0-8078-1357-5
Paper edition, ISBN 0-8078-1374-5 pbk.
Library of Congress Catalog Card Number 78-31677

Library of Congress Cataloging in Publication Data

Mitchell, Allan.
    The German influence in France after 1870.

    Bibliography: p.
    Includes index.
    1. France—Politics and government—1870–1940.
2. France—Relations (general) with Germany.
3. Germany—Relations (general) with France.   I. Title.
DC340.M64   320.9′44′081   78-31677
ISBN 0-8078-1357-5
ISBN 0-8078-1374-5 pbk.

Contents

Tables

Preface

The relationship between France and Germany, their similarities and their differences, is a theme that has fascinated me since my first experience in Europe. Scarcely a decade after the Second World War, nothing could have been more natural for a young American student than to perceive the two nations as variations of the same civilization. The cold war was in progress and Western unity was very much the vogue: the Marshall plan, the treaty of Rome, NATO, and all the rest. On both sides of the Rhine, Europeans seemed somewhat battered, troubled, often indistinguishable in the streets. The same cloud of exhaust fumes from motor scooters hung over every town. From Mont-Saint-Michel to Munich the dollar was still an almighty passe-partout, and even with a modest stipend I was able to explore both countries at leisure.

That seems long ago, but the traces remain. In part this book is therefore autobiographical. It is also the result of several subsequent years of archival work in France, Germany, and the United States. Just as any other wandering scholar, I have incurred more personal and professional debts along the way than I could hope to list. To select only a few names is distressingly arbitrary. Yet as a minimum I want to thank three French professors who offered me encouragement during the early stages of my investigation: Georges Castellan, Claude Digeon, and Jacques Droz. My gratitude is no less for the cordiality of three German historians who took me into their homes and afforded me the benefit of their advice: Josef Becker, Michael Stürmer, and Hans-Ulrich Wehler. Finally, I owe a word of appreciation to three Americans: Fritz

Stern, who allowed me to steal a look at the Bleichröder papers in his New York kitchen; David Landes, whose incisive critique led me to revise substantially several portions of my manuscript; and my colleague and friend H. Stuart Hughes, whose support has been constant over the two decades since we first met in California.

In addition, it is more than a duty to acknowledge financial assistance that has been granted by the Rockefeller Foundation, the American Philosophical Society, the American Council of Learned Societies, the National Endowment for the Humanities, and the research committees of Smith College and the University of California, San Diego.

None of the foregoing names is invoked gratuitously. All have at one time or another been important to me, and all bear a heavier responsibility for this book than they could possibly have realized. At least they have some excuse for its deficiencies.

La Jolla, California
July 1979

Introduction

For France the years after 1870 were crucial: a time of political innovation, economic adjustment, military reorganization, religious controversy, and social transition. Under the psychological burden of a lost war, the French groped unsteadily toward a redefinition of their national identity. Throughout that complex process their fledgling republic was constantly and sometimes oppressively submitted to the influence of the victorious German Reich. Indeed, it is the pivotal thesis of this study that without due consideration of the German impact in France during those years, the history of the Third Republic is incomplete and in some regards incomprehensible.

The relevance of Bismarckian Germany to the French development has, to be sure, been pointed out by numerous historians in the past.[1] But none has drawn the subject together; and most have been content to acknowledge that there was *some* German influence and then to assume that it was rather tangential. My intentions are more radical. The German question, I hope to demonstrate, vitally affected every major aspect of French public life after 1870. If so, in an important sense, the national history of France thereupon ceased; and thus the creation of a republican mentality cannot be explained in strictly French terms nor its origins traced solely from French sources.[2] In making such an assertion, of course, I do not anticipate universal assent from my friends who gather annually at the Society for French Historical Studies. Yet I shall attempt to persuade even the most confirmed francophile among them that a charming provincialism is at best suspect and at worst obsolete. If we are to comprehend the modern world, I believe, we are obliged to transcend the confinements of unicultural and unilingual history and to investigate the intricate interlocking relationships between neighboring peoples.

This is by no means to advocate a return to diplomatic history as it was practiced a generation or two ago. By now the traditional dictum about the primacy of foreign policy has surely been laid to rest. My interest here is not with conferences, treaties, ententes, and alliances; it is not a matter of "foreign relations." The point is precisely that after 1870 Germany could no longer be considered as an entity exterior to France. The Reich was a presence *within* the republic. Rather than a peripheral phenomenon, in my judgment, it was an essential component of the republic's formative phase.

As this volume is intended to be the first of a trilogy, it is important to offer some concept of the underlying principles of my work and to relate the opening study to its sequels. The most immediate and obvious problem is to define the term "influence." In order to grasp more firmly this slippery notion one might posit a spectrum composed of three segments, somewhat overlapping: *manipulation* (one nation attempting to impose certain options on another or to use another for its own objectives); *competition* (two nations responding to the efforts and advances of each other); and *imitation* (one nation seeking to emulate the admirable qualities of another). On this scale of descending directness, for example, the nature of influence would shift from Germany's frank exploitation of French military weakness to the outspoken admiration of many Frenchmen for German technique—or, to be more concrete, from the "war scare" of 1875 to the publication of Ernst Renan's *La réforme intellectuelle et morale*. These types of influence were in fact all manifest, and it would not be difficult to multiply the instances in each category. Yet by structuring a historical analysis on the basis of such a paradigm, one would risk two unacceptable consequences: losing sight entirely of the chronological sequence and ending in a labyrinth of synthetic labels (here a manipulation, there an imitation, and so on). Hence I found it wise to discard this strategy while retaining, however, its basic premise. After all, it is possible to distinguish the more direct forms of German influence from the indirect. The division is not a neat one, but it has a conceptual utility and suggests the rationale for a division of labor. The present volume treats political and economic developments. The sequels will deal first with the military and religious questions, and finally with the social question. Such a scheme should avoid the pitfalls of the alternative procedure and yet permit a sufficiently nuanced discussion of the problem.[3]

This arrangement dictates at least three methodological options that may require some justification. First, although this book is chronological, my purpose could not legitimately be to write yet another consecutive narrative of the founding of the French republic. Of those there is already a plethora.[4] But in the course of my preparations I found the history of the period far better written than researched. From my perspective the available studies display one of two shortcomings, or more often both: either they slight what may be called the German component in France; or they fail to stress the inextricability of politics and economics. Naturally, it is far beyond the scope of this work to attempt a full-scale economic history of France after 1870, a task best left to the specialists, but I have paid particular attention to those aspects that bear on the theme of Franco-German commerce: reparations, public loans, taxes and tariffs, economic growth, and the balance of trade. I have regarded these as matters not apart from but integral to political analysis. My purpose has been to show the economic context of political decisions as well as the political ramifications of economic policy and performance. This procedure might seem entirely unexceptionable were it not for the multitude of monographs that either concentrate exclusively on political events or, to the contrary, view them as merely accidental to some economic pattern.

Another corollary of my plan has been, except for a few asides, the postponement of social history to a later volume. I am fully aware that what is sometimes loosely called socioeconomic analysis has become increasingly fashionable of late, and I have no serious quarrel with those who conceive their research in such terms. But a more serviceable arrangement in my case, I concluded, was to open my account with an examination of the decision-making elites in both countries, thus confining the discussion at first to the more direct and manipulative examples of German influence in France. To be sure, the role of the popular press, of public opinion, and of mass electoral participation conditioned the behavior of elites. Yet the broader and less immediate impact of Germany on the French people can best be dissected under a different optic. My hope is therefore that each volume will perform a distinctive function and be judged accordingly, although they are of course intended to be reciprocally informative.

Finally, it seemed prudent to omit intellectual history almost entirely. The most compelling explanation is simply that the major portion of such an undertaking has already been expertly accomplished by Claude Digeon. Later contributions by other scholars have thus far added only confirmation to his luminous portrayal of four generations of French writers who responded to the "German crisis" between 1870 and the First World War.[5] Rather than to recapitulate Digeon's findings, it appeared to me only sensible to adopt his central thesis and to begin with the assumption that there was indeed a crisis in French thought. Then the question still remains: what was to be done? Granted the intellectual disorientation in France, in other words, what practical difference did Germany's influence make in the organization and operation of the republic? That is the problem to which I have addressed myself.

Admittedly, this book is marked by a *fureur de l'inédit*. Whenever and wherever possible I have returned to the sources. Although the amount of secondary literature is truly colossal, I soon discovered that I could not rely on historians whose vantage was far different from mine, who had limited their research to a single nation, or who were primarily concerned with "international relations." The great published document collections that formerly nourished diplomatic historians proved particularly problematic. Their editors, however learned and skillful, paid only marginal attention to my principal concerns, and they consequently utilized a criterion of selection unsuitable for my purposes.[6] There was, as a result, no alternative to a fresh search of the foreign office archives in Paris and Bonn. Beyond that, I have attempted to gather whatever unpublished papers I could locate in both public and private holdings. In the process, I have read much that was worthless and doubtless overlooked some things essential. Still, I am hopeful that even the specialist will share my delight in uncovering much that is new, or that corroborates previous assumptions, or that just strengthens our suspicions. Some readers who are already well informed may choose to vault Chapter 3, unless they wish to examine in detail German perceptions of French politics in the early 1870s. But since perceptions often became policy that later bore on France's internal affairs—as I have tried to illustrate in exploring the *seize mai* crisis of 1877—this is a topic that I could not afford to omit.

In this regard, I cannot fail to comment on the extraordinary richness of German archives for the internal history of France after 1870. There are at least four pertinent reasons: (1) German officials had daily contacts with their French counterparts in order to deal with a wide range of domestic matters, all of which, along with supporting documents and statistics, were ordinarily reported in detail to Berlin; (2) German representatives at all levels were professionally trained and linguistically equipped to a degree that made them highly competent as observers and, as a rule, far superior to the French stationed in Germany; (3) not only in government and in political circles, but also among bankers, businessmen, journalists, and even military officers, the Germans were able to develop an extensive network of personal contacts and secret agents with access to important information; (4) above all, from Bismarck to the lowliest clerk in the Paris embassy, German diplomatic personnel realized the indivisibility of foreign and domestic affairs and remained aware that sound policy toward another nation requires an intimate familiarity with its public mores and procedures. Therefore, though one could not hope to write a reliable account from the German documents alone, they nonetheless constitute an indispensable source for the history of the Third Republic.[7]

Although an abstract model can barely suggest the complexity of the problem at hand, it might perhaps be useful to illustrate the varieties of evidence which have been most relevant for this volume. One may choose any banal incident of the 1870s—for example, a French cabinet crisis accompanied by a sudden drop on the Paris Bourse and the rumor of an impending monarchist coup—and inquire as to the stages through which it was bound to pass. We would discern that the trail began in France, then led to Germany, and finally turned back to France again:

1. *Information.* German reports about French affairs came through official or unofficial channels, often both. The importance of the former, and particularly the role of the German ambassador in Paris, should be underscored in this regard. Envoys such as Arnim and Hohenlohe were not merely diplomatic mannequins. They directed a staff of experts, screened and analyzed intelligence reports, conferred at length with French administrators and politicians, presided over a press bureau, and communicated incessantly with Berlin. They also maintained touch with the Paris underworld of agents and counter-agents whose services were irregularly rewarded, by one or more governments, in relation to their demonstrated reliability. Although records of these cloak-and-dagger dealings are infuriatingly fragmentary, they are nevertheless essential. True, by far the greatest amount of German information was gathered by the embassy from publications, public records, and direct contacts with French officials. Yet the record is incomplete without the counterpoint of private agents, especially those supplied by Bismarck's banker, Gerson von Bleichröder, who were privy to banking and business circles in France and who were sure to gain a hearing in Berlin denied to less well-recommended informants. In addition, one needs to consider as a significant and autonomous source the dispatches of Germany's thoroughly expert military attachés in Paris.

2. *Policy Formation.* Clearly it was the German chancellor who had the decisive word in all matters concerning France. But since Bismarck never returned to French soil after leaving Versailles in 1871, he was largely dependent on the sorts of information just indicated. Of course, he could also consult personally with French diplomats in Berlin; but that was not his inclination and he seldom made use of the opportunity. Since Bismarck as a rule remained aloof, rarely socializing in Berlin and often secluded at his Varzin or Friedrichsruh estate, it was actually his staff that was the hub of activity—except on those special occasions when the chancellor himself suddenly arrived to take command. Whatever the prove-

nance or content of memoranda concerning France, therefore, they ordinarily passed through the foreign office in the Wilhelmstrasse before being forwarded to Bismarck or an appropriate government agency. Thus the internal correspondence of underlings such as Bülow, Radowitz, and Herbert von Bismarck assumed more than routine importance. There was also some input from other quarters: the Kaiser (from whom sensitive information was frequently kept), Moltke and the military staff, journalists, cronies, or occasionally a Reichstag deputy. But these were episodic. For two full decades after 1870, German policy was conceived by Bismarck and executed by his faithful subalterns; and fortunately we are able to follow their activities in substantial detail.

3. *Implementation.* The technical means by which Germany could exert direct pressure on the French republic were several. By mail, telegraph, or special courier, a diplomatic dispatch was the most frequent and rapid method of communication. Instructions dictated in Berlin could be repeated in Paris or Versailles within hours. More oblique routes were also available: an editorial in the official or semiofficial German press, a reprimand to the French ambassador in Berlin, an admonition by some military authority, a public statement in the Reichstag by the Kaiser or chancellor. Such instances of attempted German intimidation, to one degree or another, can be amply documented and placed in a comprehensible pattern. But the subject is not thereby exhausted. Since the essential problem of this study is to determine precisely how Germany affected the internal development of France in the republic's formative years, we must also attempt to establish a seismographic record of the impact of German policy. Official and personal correspondence of French political leaders has been accorded first priority in this volume on the grounds that they were the most vulnerable to German threats, the most sensitive to cajolement and innuendo. The cast of individual French characters, a few dozen in all, may seem remarkably small for a nation of nearly forty million. But these were the republican decision-makers: presidents, premiers, and ministers; some parliamentarians and politicians; ambassadors and attachés; high military officers; and a few spokesmen of commercial, banking and industrial interests. If we are to estimate the intensity of direct German influence in

France, these elites should provide the clearest echo. Beyond them, the reverberations were perceptible but more diffuse and less distinct.

With all proper regard to the objective political and economic circumstances that shaped the character of the French republic, one cannot fail to observe how often a decision crucial to an entire people finally rested on nothing more substantial than the disposition of two or three persons. Throughout, I have sought to achieve a fair balance between what Pierre Renouvin once called "les forces profondes" and the irreducible factor of individual choice and action.[8] I have not suffered from any illusion of definitiveness. Yet I have tried to keep a "total history" as my objective, however unattainable, in the sense of considering my subject in all of its important facets. My purpose will be served if these volumes add to a comprehensive understanding of the early years of the Third Republic and also provide a basis for further studies of the Franco-German confrontation that has dominated western Europe ever since.

*The German Influence in France
after 1870*

Chapter 1

The Improvised Republic

The Birth of the Republic

France may have been destined to become a republic. After 1789 there was a certain internal impetus that seemed to carry the French nation inexorably toward a republican form of state. The democratic tendency of the Revolution was not to be denied in the nineteenth century; and one regime after another that attempted to contain it was swept aside. Viewing this spectacle in retrospect, one might even conclude that republicanism was the natural reflex of the French people. By no means does it appear inappropriate that France was the first great European polity to constitute a republic as its permanent mode of government.

Yet much can be said to the contrary. The republic tradition in France was far from being unified or omnipotent. Both of the republican experiments before 1870 ended in disarray after brief and troubled tenures. Moreover, as Tocqueville among others perceived, French democracy derived strength from an egalitarian surge that also sustained its dictatorial opposite. The Napoleonic mystique was scarcely less potent than the thrust of republicanism. Nor could monarchy be discounted as only a quaint relic of the old regime. Whether in a Bonapartist or a royalist guise, the possibility of a constitutional dynasty remained for France a plausible option. Hence there was nothing inevitable about a republic. Such an assumption betrays the most common of historical fallacies: mistaking what came to be for what had to be.[1]

But these conjectures are inevitably fanciful; and they do not pose the essential question of this study. We are concerned here to

know not only how France became republican but, more specifically, why it became a particular kind of republic after 1870. The
peculiar characteristics and remarkable longevity of the republican system in France are not to be explained by a generalized view
of the subject. Necessarily, we must enter into the details of the
formative decades if we wish to search out the reasons for France's
unique development.

One of the idiosyncracies of the Third Republic was that it
both began and ended in the midst of a military defeat administered by Germany.[2] Since medieval times there had been no precedent for a Teutonic domination of western Europe, despite the
best military and diplomatic efforts of the Habsburg monarchy.
Indeed, most of the history of modern France until 1870 can be
satisfactorily explained without any special reference to the territories beyond the Rhine. With hardly a mention of Germany one
could comprehend the onset of the French Revolution, the appearance of Napoleon Bonaparte, the failure of the Restoration and
July monarchies, or the replacement of the Second Republic by
Napoleon III. Throughout, Germany was ordinarily an object of
French policies and actions, not vice versa. If we make exception
for Blücher's charge at Waterloo, in fact, there was no important
instance of direct German influence on the course of France's internal affairs before the 1860s.[3] Politically disunited and economically undeveloped, Germany remained for the French a distant
land, less a reality than a myth. The French image of Germany had
changed very little from Tacitus to Madame de Staël. Supposedly,
there existed two Germanies, the warriors and the philosophers,
both off in some dark forest. The truth mattered little, because
l'outre Rhin did not impinge significantly on France until the sudden humiliation of 1870.[4]

The inglorious end of the French Second Empire is a story in
itself, a tale often told. Simply put, the Bonapartist regime was
a victim of its own dynamism. It had presided over an era of
extraordinary public activity and economic expansion. But the
fault of its virtues was an excessive adventurism which eventually
brought the emperor and his people to grief.[5] The immediate origin of the war with Germany, so far as the French were concerned,
was a curious combination of defensive intention and offensive

comportment. Under severe internal pressure from liberal reform-
ers, with the gloss of dynastic prestige already badly scratched,
Napoleon could hope at best to maintain the status quo. France's
political paralysis during the Austro-Prussian conflict of 1866 and
the embarrassment of unrequited territorial demands thereafter
had made the imperial coterie eager not to appear duped again.
Still, the alliances which Napoleon III sought, and imagined he
had secured, were mainly designed to deter German unification, a
policy regarded in Paris as a vital interest of the French nation.[6]
The same was true of the initial maneuvers against a Hohenzollern
candidacy for the Spanish throne: the French objective was to
block Prussian expansion. Yet, as with many a slipping power, bad
nerves and hawkish advisers prevailed. What began as an exercise
in diplomacy ended in a rash attempt to inflict a defeat.[7]

The episode of the Ems dispatch has been recounted a thousand times. Suffice it to observe that the French challenge did
Prussia an incalculable favor. No one appreciated that service more
than Otto von Bismarck. Weeks before the declaration of war he
had noted that "politically our position would be vastly improved
by a French attack."[8] And so it seemed in July 1870 to nearly
everyone in Europe from Karl Marx to Tsar Alexander. Why
Louis Bonaparte then chose to ride out to the eastern front and to
risk capture was best known to himself and perhaps to his wife. In
any event, his surrender along with Marshal MacMahon's army at
Sedan apparently resulted from a personal impulse, born neither
of necessity nor of foresight. It proved to be an act of considerable
importance, since a vacuum of leadership was thereby created well
before anyone could have anticipated.[9]

The proclamation of a French republic on 4 September was
one of those melodramatic occurrences to which Parisians had
long been accustomed. It was more reminiscent of 1851 than of
1830 or 1848, accompanied by much commotion but relatively
little violence in the streets of Paris. With the emperor already
gone, after all, there was virtually no one willing to struggle for
dynastic principle. The inception of the republic was thus received
on its merits: with some enthusiasm, much caution, and a general
recognition that the provisional regime could easily be remade
or undone by subsequent events. The new leadership was mostly

drawn from the ranks of the former liberal opposition. Many of their names were well known if not universally admired. But this was in no sense a popular government, being neither the object of widespread public adulation nor the chosen representative of the common people. There was nothing of sans-culottism and little of jacobinism about it. The new leadership had no program except, somehow, to preserve the honor of France in the face of a calamity. As advertised, this was a government of national defense. France thereupon became a republic ad hoc, through an improvisation in that desperate hour when the German military forces were already moving to surround Paris.[10]

Bismarck and Thiers

At the time when the French republic was proclaimed, it was by no means certain who would emerge to lead it. To the first public documents of the new regime twelve signatures were affixed: Arago, Crémieux, Favre, Ferry, Gambetta, Garnier-Pagès, Glais-Bizoin, Pelletan, Picard, Rochefort, Simon, and—as military governor of Paris and provisional president of the government of national defense—General Trochu. One name was conspicuously absent. Adolphe Thiers had chosen to support but not to join the collective leadership, just as he had once advocated but not participated in the banquets of 1848. Whatever the motive, his instinct proved to be sound. Within a few months his name would head the ministerial list and, far more than any of the original dozen, he was able to help shape the initial character of the republic.[11]

The haphazard process through which Thiers gained the French presidency is not explicable apart from the exigencies imposed by German prowess—not that he was, from the German perspective, a logical choice at the outset. The first recorded reaction of Bismarck to the news of 4 September was jotted in a note to his wife: "In Paris a republic, at least a provisional regime of republicans. I couldn't care less (*Mir Wurscht*)."[12] From his official and private correspondence it is obvious that the chancellor had in fact no clear notion about the potential support of the Paris regime. Deprived of any regular dispatches from the French capital, Bismarck was dependent on messages routed through neutral capitals or intercepted from French couriers attempting to cross German lines. He was consequently forced to speculate inconclusively at first about the possible fate of the "rather socialistic" leadership of the new republic, to wait and see "whether it lasts, how it develops." He preferred in any case to let the French "stew in their own sauce" for a while, correctly anticipating that discord among them would not be long in surfacing.[13] The initiative of the first republican foreign minister, Jules Favre, who obtained an audience with the chancellor at Ferrières on 18 September to discuss the possibility of an armistice, was thus foredoomed to futility.[14]

Meanwhile, Bismarck tightened the second string in his bow. From Sedan, Napoleon III had been transported across the Rhine to a comfortable seclusion at Wilhelmshöhe. There he was accorded deference befitting royalty since, as Bismarck confided to his son Herbert, "a well treated Napoleon is *useful* to us." The French should be kept in doubt about chances of the emperor's return: all the better to promote their bickering. Reports had already reached German headquarters of some street fighting in Paris; and, Bismarck observed with a certain schadenfreude, "we don't have the assignment of uniting them against us."[15]

There is no reason to take these private remarks at other than face value. Then and for some time to come, the chancellor regarded restoration of the imperial dynasty as a serious alternative to the provisional republican government.[16] It is impossible, of course, to say exactly what use he expected to make of Napoleon himself; but at a minimum he could hope to obtain a personal endorsement for one of three alternatives which he considered between October and the end of the year. The first was to recognize the claim of Napoleon's young son, who was hurried into an English exile by the formidable Empress Eugénie. Such a regency would have both the advantages and the disadvantages of dynastic continuity, a mixed blessing in the midst of war.[17] A second possibility was to resuscitate the imperial administration, specifically the *conseils généraux*, which were abolished by a decree of Gambetta at the beginning of November. This could be done only after sweeping away the republic altogether, something that depended on military decision as well as political calculation.[18] The third alternative was obviously the one taken most seriously by Bismarck: to recall the Corps législatif. The lower house of the imperial parliament had scattered without ever being officially prorogued. It might be convened for the two specific purposes of opening peace negotiations and organizing national elections. The choice of a definitive form of government for France could thereby be deferred. The chancellor speculated, none too hopefully, that the Corps législatif might provisionally authorize the government of national defense to act on these matters in the name of the French nation. Yet even this ideal solution, as Bismarck recognized, depended finally on locating "a suitable personality" to take the political initiative. And the plain fact was that the imperial entourage had no such individual to offer.[19]

Il n'y a que vous, cher Monsieur Thiers. This exclamation by Albert de Broglie in mid-October 1870 was but one among literally hundreds of such letters sent by both prominent and ordinary Frenchmen during the months of that autumn.[20] The proximate reasons for Thiers's emergence as the first citizen of his nation are well known and may be briefly summarized. Before the Second Empire began he already had one full political career behind him. An instigator of the 1830 insurrection in Paris, he had twice served as premier under the July monarchy. During that time, as many had occasion to remember in 1870, he had personally supervised construction of the city's exterior fortifications. After being called at the last moment in an unsuccessful attempt to rescue the Orleanist dynasty in February 1848, he was forced to play a relatively minor role during the Second Republic. Even so, he was considered important enough to be arrested by the Bonapartist police during the 1851 coup d'état and kept under strict surveillance. Thereafter he employed some years of enforced retirement to complete the multivolumed histories of the French Revolution and the Napoleonic Consulate which earned him a European reputation exceeded perhaps only by Leopold von Ranke. His second political career coincided with the liberal phase of the Second Empire in the 1860s, when he reappeared in parliament as a principal critic of Bonapartist foreign policy, particularly the dangerous inconsistencies of French diplomacy in the German states. When the war of 1870 came he was, at the age of seventy-three, uniquely qualified and situated. He was the only national figure equally well recognized for his opposition to Bonapartism, his service to monarchy, and his cooperation with—without membership in—the provisional government.[21]

Thiers had one other important and indeed indispensable qualification: his acceptability to Bismarck. Had he been among the original signators of 4 September, this might not have been the case. He would then have been associated with Jules Favre's foolish assertion two days later that the government of national defense would cede "neither an inch of our territories nor a stone of our fortresses."[22] Ironically, it was Favre who provided Thiers with the final rung to prominence by commissioning him to make a grand tour of European capitals in search of neutral sympathy and, if possible, support. From a diplomatic standpoint, Thiers's mission was less than a stirring success. Frankly disappointed by the polite reserve of the Gladstone government and "the coolness which England has displayed toward us," Favre evaluated the response in London with some bitterness: "We had a right to expect better than that." When Thiers reached Vienna, he found much the same correct formality. The atmosphere in St. Petersburg was more cordial, but Bismarck's highly placed contacts at the tsarist court were able to assure him that Thiers would receive no more than encouragement to resume negotiations for an armistice.[23]

This situation coincided with Bismarck's fondest wish. His own travails with William and the Prussian general staff need not detain us here. The chancellor himself spoke darkly of "an intrigue . . . of women, archbishops, and academics," but his real problem had been the lack of a suitable negotiating partner to represent France. Now Thiers appeared in Versailles, armed with a *laisser passer* that had been arranged with Bismarck by the Russian chancellor Gorchakov, and thereby gained recognition as the "suitable personality" who was lacking. Thiers was appropriate above all because any truce signed with him was sure to be honored by the neutrals and was also likely to be accepted by William and his military advisers. The conflict would thus be moved back to the diplomatic sphere, where Bismarck was the acknowledged master of detail and would have no rival for his monarch's ear.[24]

The failure of the talks between Bismarck and Thiers in the

first week of November did not alter the logic of the situation. Privately, the chancellor confessed that he had little hope that an immediate accord could be reached. But it was not because he doubted the intentions of his interlocutor. The difficulty was simply that Thiers was not yet master in his own house and could not deliver the unanimous consent of his colleagues in Paris and Tours: "They want to have everything and to grant nothing."[25] There was nothing to do but wait for the German armies to break the French will to resist. Once that was accomplished, the rest followed. By the middle of December, Paris was helplessly besieged, the military issue elsewhere was all but decided, and Gambetta's frantic efforts began to wane. In January 1871 the armistice was finally concluded, and elections for a National Assembly to meet in Bordeaux were set for 8 February.[26]

Among the candidates, Thiers's name was chosen in twenty-six departments and easily led all the others. If the Assembly was overwhelmingly reactionary, it had first of all a mandate for peace —which was under the circumstances a euphemism for capitulation. Thiers was the single common denominator between the French Assembly and the German chancellor; and both were more than willing to allow him the responsibility of accepting German terms in the name of France. The full implication should have been perfectly clear: Thiers represented not only a policy of fulfillment toward Germany but also a de facto option for the republic; one reinforced the other. Officially, Thiers's policy, advertised as the "pact of Bordeaux," was to leave unresolved the definitive form of state. But the practice was to be a republic by default. Accordingly, government letterheads were henceforth set in bold type: **République Française.**[27]

The Price of German Consent

The terms of the provisional peace between France and Germany, embodied in the treaty signed at Versailles on 26 February 1871, stipulated some essential principles of agreement but left several practical issues unsettled. The German annexation of Alsace (excluding Belfort) and part of Lorraine (including Metz), the promise of 5 billion francs in reparations payable within three years, the withdrawal below the Loire of all French military units other than the Paris garrison of forty thousand men, the establishment of the initial boundaries of German-occupied territory, and the obligation by France to provision the military force stationed there—these were the general results of cruel negotiations conducted by Bismarck with Favre and Thiers. But many of the details remained to be specified, such as the mode and timing of the financial installments, the coordination of German evacuation procedures, the precise amount of maintenance expenses for German troops, and the future commercial relations of the two nations and of both with Alsace and Lorraine. To regulate such matters and to prepare the draft of a definitive settlement, negotiating teams were designated to meet in Brussels immediately after ratification of the Versailles document by the German emperor and the French Assembly.[28]

Therewith the French were forced to their knees. The succeeding decade would eventually bring a perceptible relaxation of Germany's hold. But for the time being, the victor held the fate of the French republic in a tight clench. This was a humiliating reality which the Bordeaux Assembly could neither ignore nor evade. All the protests, lamentations, and demonstrative exits of its members could not alter the intractable necessity of capitulation to German demands. Moreover, the advent of the Paris Commune was to confirm rather than to alter this situation by stripping away virtually the last shred of the republic's independence and exposing it to an elaborate procedure of German blackmail.

The primary psychological motivation of the Paris insurrection was a suspicion of collusion between the German government and the predominantly royalist Assembly in Bordeaux. The charge of treasonous complicity with the Germans had already been brought against Thiers by Gambetta, rashly, before he withdrew into a self-imposed exile in Spain. Then similar stories circulated in the capital, where scattered symptoms of impending violence had been evident for weeks. True, no hostile demonstrations of note occurred during the ceremonious display of German military power on the first day of March, when thirty thousand Prussian troops paraded down the Champs Elysées. But the atmosphere was heavy with menace; and reports of minor disturbances continued to accumulate.[29] The members of Thiers's cabinet present in Paris, chief among them Favre, were becoming more apprehensive by the hour. They determined that three courses of action were necessary: (1) the Paris garrison ought to be strengthened at once; (2) the Bordeaux Assembly should openly declare support of the republic while announcing the intention to transfer its seat to Paris in the near future; and (3) the government must move at the first opportunity to assert authority over the city by requisitioning the mobile artillery pieces parked in the potentially volatile sections of Belleville and Montmartre. Each of these assumptions requires some amplification.

Insofar as possible, the new regime hoped to deal with public disorder in Paris by itself, without requesting the Germans for any more military assistance than permitted by the preliminary peace agreement. But at the Hôtel de Ville there had already been one shooting incident involving insurgent national guardsmen, and the republican ministers were visibly unnerved by the possibility of worse to come. On 4 March, Favre wrote directly to Bismarck: "Paris is threatened by a serious collision." Perhaps embellishing his account for effect, he described the sporadic incidents of violence, the theft of munitions, and the activity of agitators in the city. Since General Vinoy, Trochu's successor as military commandant, had only one division under arms, he felt helpless to preserve order and had requested that reinforcements be dispatched from Bordeaux. Would Bismarck command that the French troops be allowed to pass?[30] It was a request that the chancellor had no reason to refuse, especially as some German forces were already being evacuated from Paris forts on the left bank. On the following day Thiers received a telegram in Bordeaux which permitted "the passage by railway of troops destined for Paris."[31] This was one of the last of Bismarck's acts before leaving France for the final time in his life. And it was to be, more importantly, the first of many favors accorded to the Thierist government by Germany during the three months of that spring. Without such favors, as everyone realized, the republic might not survive.

At the same time a struggle was developing within the French government over the fate of the Assembly. "You reproach me . . . for thinking only of Paris," Favre wrote to Thiers; "I reproach you for abandoning it to itself and thereby exposing it to accidents that may destroy and dishonour your work." To undercut the rumors of a royalist plot in Bordeaux, Favre demanded that Thiers and the Assembly move immediately to Paris, or at least provisionally to Versailles. Otherwise, he would resign rather than remain party to "a phantom government" in the capital. His military advisers there, while counseling prudence, nonetheless thought the situation "impossible to tolerate for long"; and, Favre added, "I am altogether of their opinion."[32] In reply, Thiers assured that he regarded Paris "as the final goal." But he was under heavy pressure from conservative members of the Assembly to keep at a safe distance from the threat of insurrection. He therefore preferred Fontainebleau, quickly accessible from Paris by rail, yet easily defensible. Thiers thought Versailles was too much of a risk; besides, it was still infected by the Prussians and by typhus. Meanwhile, the arrival of military reinforcements from the west would be sufficient to strengthen the government's hand in Paris. "You will be able to reestablish order little by little if a combat does not take place, or at once if a battle is fought." Thiers agreed that they should temporize and not use force unless provoked. But "if we are reduced to a fight, it must be vigorous and decisive."[33]

Favre remained unconvinced: "I consider it absolutely impossible to govern if the Assembly is at Fontainebleau." The choice of Versailles was therefore essential. If Thiers could not assert leadership to that extent, Favre advised, "I would tell the Assembly to choose another government." To avoid a catastrophe the Assembly would need to act promptly and, in addition, to declare its intention to cooperate loyally with "the experiment of the republic." If not, an insurrection would surely occur, and France's financial credit would be ruined. The result, Favre offered as his clinching argument, was then bound to be that "the Prussians would take revenge at our expense and this time invade us completely."[34] Subjected to such an unrelenting barrage of dire warnings from Paris, Thiers decided to confront the Assembly. With an eloquent and urgent oration he was able to obtain a vote for the transfer to Versailles.[35]

If this could be considered a victory for "the chief of the executive power" in Bordeaux, it did little to dampen radical agitation in Paris. Favre and his colleagues consequently determined that the time had come "to execute the laws." Six newspapers were suppressed "which every day preach assassination." Furthermore, "we have decided to have done with the redoubts of Montmartre and Belleville," Favre informed Thiers on 11 March, adding the hope that "all this can be done without an effusion of blood."[36] Both men were fully conscious of the gamble they were taking. On the next morning Thiers wired his approval, leaving it to Favre to choose the opportune moment for the seizure of the cannons, offering only his judgment that "the sooner it can be done, the better." That telegram was, in effect, a blank check.[37]

Without the indulgence of the German military command, this crucial decision would have been totally infeasible. Not only were armed French troops permitted to pass through the German lines; their number began to swell beyond the limit of forty thousand men fixed in the preliminary peace. "The concentration of seventy thousand men in Paris and around Paris might occasion some difficulty with the Germans," General Suzanne warned Thiers. He also noted that the Prussian authorities were "remarkably informed about everything" and had already commented on the violation of the treaty. Not that they intended an admonition; to the contrary, the French were also promised the return of twelve thousand additional chassepots, more than the quota allowed.[38]

In return for German patronage, however, the Thiers government was required to accept the most stringent interpretation of the Versailles agreements. Favre complained bitterly that "the Prussians are abusing their power to falsify the conventions and constantly to impose new expenses on us." He was referring to the demand that France pay "at horribly exaggerated prices" the total cost of provisioning all German troops, including those being evacuated, not just the cost of supplying the army of occupation.[39] This was but one problem of many concerning the relationship of French civilian officials and German military personnel in the occupied territories. Just before his departure from Versailles, Bismarck had issued instructions that as much leverage should be applied in these matters as might be useful in negotiation. These orders were now followed. Despite Favre's feeling that the Prussians were "continuing to be intolerable," he returned to German headquarters at Ferrières on 4 March and struck a bargain: the French would accede to the German demands if Thiers regained control in the occupied departments of civil administration, post, telegraph, rail service, and the local police force.[40]

The deal was hardly optimal for the republican leaders. With it they accepted both the maximum expense and the full responsibility of keeping order in the eastern territories. Yet the alternative seemed infinitely worse. Bismarck had explicitly threatened to interrupt all evacuation procedures until the German terms were met, something that Thiers could not contemplate. To rid French soil of the foreigner and to regain national autonomy represented for him "our great interest, for which we have sacrificed everything."[41] But in reality the sacrifices had only begun.

The Paris Commune and the Frankfurt Treaty

Despite all the signs of warning, the volatility of the situation in Paris was seriously underestimated by those charged with political responsibility. "I believe that with fifty gendarmes and perhaps less," Favre wrote to General Vinoy, "the Prefect of Police might easily prevail." This was only a few days before the incident of the cannons at Montmartre on 18 March. Once the insurrection had begun in earnest and government officials had hastily withdrawn to Versailles, there was still total confidence among them that the conflagration could be quickly extinguished. Apologizing for the temporary disruption of communications to General von Fabrice, the German commander at Rouen, Favre glibly expressed the expectation "that order will be promptly reestablished and that our common interests will not have to suffer a delay." Much later, in his memoirs, Favre explained the reason for his sanguinity. Even if the communards should be successful in standing off the army of Versailles, they would soon be crushed by the Germans. The Commune was therefore bound to fail, since the population of the city would naturally refuse to be led into "an inevitably disastrous adventure" by a militant minority.[42] All one can say in hindsight is that Favre's logic was impeccable. But neither logic nor the Prefecture of Police can always prevail in Paris.

In several important respects, the onset of the Commune

confirmed rather than altered the existing circumstances. First of all, it further increased Bismarck's capacity for extortion. He at once informed Favre through Fabrice that he expected prompt and complete execution of every obligation undertaken by the French government. Moreover, no French troops should approach German lines or forts still occupied by German troops. If the Versailles regime could not contain the uprising, the German military command would find it impossible to remain passive.[43] Meanwhile, in the occupied territories, stricter measures of curfew and censorship were imposed, and some garrisons were demonstratively strengthened.[44] From this time forward, the French were incessantly pounded from Berlin with remonstrances that they were failing to act with sufficient vigor, that they were deliberately stalling the negotiations in Brussels, and that they were biding their time merely in order to gather the nucleus of an army which might later be used to resume hostilities against Germany. Denials were received with polite coolness. Versailles was simply informed that no further active cooperation by the Germans could be expected until the terms of the preliminary peace settlement and the Ferrières agreement were fulfilled and a definitive treaty was signed.[45]

The Commune consequently reduced the Thierist republic totally to the role of a supplicant. The French were dependent on Germany's tacit (or at least unpublicized) indulgence for gathering of military intelligence, transportation of troops, release of war prisoners, and stockpiling of weapons and munitions. They requested, and obtained, permission to raise the ceiling of the Versailles army to one hundred thousand men. In return, they were forced to offer repeated assurances that "our engagements will be kept." But this exchange fully satisfied neither German demands nor French needs. By the last week of April, the Commune still reigned in Paris virtually unmolested. Bismarck continued to complain of the unreliability of the French in financial affairs and to insist that they must "to a certain extent place themselves in our hands." Although he wished to avoid the appearance of doing so, Thiers in reality had no choice but to comply.[46]

Paradoxically, these circumstances also served in some respects to strengthen Thiers's position against his political opponents and thereby to confirm the republic. There was a very real threat, after all, that the internal order of France would collapse altogether. Besides Paris, reports arrived of insurrectionary activity in Lyon, Marseille, Toulouse, and elsewhere. These were accompanied by pleas from prefects and local officials that the Assembly's intention to uphold the republic be publicly reaffirmed.[47] The result was to paralyze the royalist opposition to Thiers in Versailles. There was, to be sure, no absence of acrimonious debates. But Thiers did not fail to remind the Assembly of his own indispensability in dealing with the Germans, "for it is impossible that these negotiations be conducted by another authority than that of the executive power itself."[48] Nor did he hesitate to exercise his authority by choosing loyal prefects and by appointing Marshal MacMahon to assist him in directing the siege of Paris. He also intervened personally to demand that the Assembly reverse itself on a municipal law which it had just adopted; animated and rhetorical, he openly threatened his resignation and then put the issue squarely to the deputies: "Yes or no, do you want order? That is the whole question." For the time being, while there was mutiny within and the foreigner stood in force without, the answer could not be in doubt. The Thierist republic thus survived.[49]

Both the French cabinet and the Assembly were irritated by a rumor of negotiations between the German military command and the Commune. The suspicion of direct contact was not ground-less, though it proved to be inflated. Soon after the insurgency in the capital began, the commander of the Third German Army Corps, General von Schlotheim, formally cautioned the commu-nards to remain at a distance from all fortifications held by his troops. To this warning the central committee of the national guard in Paris responded that "the revolution" had "an essentially municipal character" and in no way threatened the German armies. Simultaneously, a French translation of Schlotheim's message was printed which quoted the general as promising to maintain an "attitude amicale" toward the Commune. The sensation caused by this phrase in Versailles was such that Fabrice was moved to issue a denial of any German recognition for the rebellion, point-ing out that "friedlich" was properly translated as "pacifique," not "amicale."[50]

Yet the fears were not altogether allayed, and in early April Favre compounded them by confirming a story that the insurgents had once again contacted German authorities. He naturally minimized the importance of the fact and insisted to the Assembly that the Versailles regime was recognized as "solely legitimate" by Germany.[51] No doubt this claim was accurate. Unknown to him, however, Bismarck's interest had been aroused by a direct appeal from the Commune's new war minister, Gustave Cluseret, who requested an interview. After obtaining permission from the very reluctant Kaiser, Bismarck dispatched an affirmative response. On 26 April, Cluseret met with a young foreign office attaché from Fabrice's staff, Friedrich von Holstein. This was the only recorded meeting of the two parties, and it was inconclusive. Cluseret offered a half billion francs in return for German impartiality, abstention from a blockade of Paris, and the sale of some arms. Holstein claimed that the first two points were not a serious problem but that the third would violate a German pledge of neutrality.[52] In reality no such pledge existed—or, if it did, the Germans had already violated it in their attempts to buttress the Thierist republic. Either Holstein was less than candid with Cluseret or he was astonishingly ignorant of the policy that Bismarck was directing from Berlin and Fabrice was executing in France. So far as can be confirmed, the chancellor's only purpose in opening direct contact with the Commune was to establish a source of information. Although it cannot be absolutely disproven, the hypothesis that Bismarck in any way abetted the Paris insurrection or that he provided it with captured French weapons is highly implausible.[53]

If Bismarck refused to collaborate with the Commune, he was more than willing to exploit it. Barely a week before the Cluseret interview, he had sent off two telegrams to General von Fabrice expressing his impatience with the siege of Paris. As Fabrice put it, "the Prince is becoming nervous." Were the army of Versailles not up to the task, the implication was clear, the Germans would soon be compelled to seize the military initiative themselves. Very possibly this was only a bluff. But it was one which the French had to take seriously. On 24 April, Bismarck was informed that a French assault was ready; all it required was German permission for government troops to use the northern railway into Paris from St.-Denis.[54] The chancellor's reply was evasive. He would need to consult with the Kaiser and with General von Moltke, he said; and considering "the present level of our confidence in the intention of the [Versailles] regime," approval for an attack through German lines was "not likely." Fabrice was instructed to tell the French "in ultimatum form" that a written pledge to meet German terms was necessary before any active cooperation would be forthcoming.[55]

Favre could not conceal his exasperation. Three weeks earlier, he claimed, he had offered to travel to Berlin to settle all outstanding questions and to sign a definitive peace treaty. Bismarck had ignored this suggestion and had continued to badger the French, accusing them of harboring "a sort of *arrière pensée* . . . of preparation to resume the war." Versailles was in fact ready to do as the chancellor wished, on two conditions: that permission be granted to pass via St.-Denis, and that Germany require the communards to withdraw far from the exterior fortifications of Paris. "It is thus up to Prince von Bismarck to make known whether he accepts or rejects these two conditions." Clearly the time for a bargain, if ever there was to be one, had come. Consequently, a meeting was arranged in Frankfurt for 6 May.[56]

The course of the confrontation—one cannot really speak of negotiation—between Bismarck and Favre is too familiar to require recounting here. Both men were eager to reach a quick settlement, but Bismarck would do so only at his own price. It was an uneven contest. At the first sign of French recalcitrance the chancellor again resorted to accusations and threats. "He feels his greater strength," Favre lamented to Thiers, "and he will abuse it to the utmost." Bismarck was especially keen on securing a commercial agreement, a most-favored-nation clause; and he demanded a "correction" on the Luxembourg-Lorraine frontier near Thionville, which, as Favre was aware, "would deprive us of very rich iron mines indispensable to our industry."[57] For the latter concession, France would receive an extension of the Belfort enclave in Alsace. Favre could delay but not refuse. He was convinced that the existence of the republic was at stake: "The convention will save Paris and maybe France, for if Prussia intervenes she will perhaps restore the Empire." Thiers was no less inclined to pay Bismarck's price, and on 8 May he telegraphed his concurrence.[58]

It is worth noting that, whereas Thiers and Favre had accepted the preliminary peace in Versailles on 26 February "representing France," the delegation of three headed by Favre signed the Frankfurt treaty on 10 May "in the name of the French republic."[59] On paper the republic had been secured. It had yet to survive in the streets of Paris. If the army of Versailles failed, it would not be Bismarck's fault. He instructed Fabrice to close a complete blockade of Paris, to allow French government troops to cross German lines, and to order the Commune to abandon all the city's exterior fortifications. The Third German Army Corps meanwhile moved to take up position closer to the capital.[60] On 20 May, Favre met for the last time with Bismarck to exchange formal ratifications of the Frankfurt agreement. The chancellor thereupon offered whatever aid was necessary "to finish as rapidly as possible," including sixty thousand more prisoners of war. And he prodded Favre on: "It is not a party against which you are fighting. It is a pack of brigands violating the laws on which rests all of civilization." Thiers asked that Bismarck be thanked for the additional prisoners, and urged that his army should be allowed to settle the score with the Commune by itself: "Count on us, and the social order will be revenged in the course of the week."[61]

These messages revealed a mutual interest between the Thierist republic and the Bismarckian Reich that went far beyond anything apparent in the eighteen articles of the formal treaty. Both wished to crush the Commune in order to preserve a conservative conception of European society. To eliminate the threat of radicalism was no less desirable for the nascent bourgeois leadership in Versailles than for the ensconced aristocratic court in Berlin. The fanaticism of the troops which infested Paris in the last week of May was fired, consciously or not, by class interest as well as national pride. They executed their assignment with a thoroughness and zeal that surpassed anything Europe had yet witnessed. Thereby they brutally fulfilled Thiers's promise to Bismarck. Within seven days the communards literally had their backs to the wall in the cemetery of Père Lachaise. Karl Marx was correct to announce that the Commune was the harbinger of a new society; but it was that of the Third Republic.[62]

Chapter 2

The Cost of Liberation

French Finances and the First Public Loan

For the French economy the decade of the 1870s was a moment of hesitation, a period in which the thrust of the Second Empire was slowly expended. France experienced the end of an era of expansion and the beginning of a long phase of economic lassitude. That evolution was a consequence not only of the war and the resulting loss of Alsace-Lorraine but, it will be maintained here, also of financial and political circumstances after 1870, when direct German influence on France was greatest.

Economic indicators had pointed upward for most of the previous thirty years.[1] The agricultural, financial, and political crisis just before and during 1848 proved to be only transitory. Initial gains that had been registered in the early 1840s were resumed and magnified a decade later. A major impetus was provided by the vast public works projects, especially railways, sponsored by the Napoleonic regime and financed in large measure through the innovation of credit banking.[2] Although the tenure of the Second Empire was punctuated by brief economic slumps in 1858, 1865, and 1868, it was generally a time of rapid economic growth and widening prosperity. There is evidence to suggest that the French economy was already showing signs of fatigue before the war of 1870 began; yet it is important to retain the generalization that the hostilities with Germany commenced while France was still sustaining a relatively high rate of growth. Industrially and commercially France was still a developing nation and, moreover, one which possessed considerable financial capabilities in both the public and the private sectors.[3]

There is no way to estimate closely the total cost of the 1870 war to France. We can only be sure that it was of enormous magnitude and that it produced an acute financial strain, which resulted less from an absence of wealth than from its unavailability. Not the sheer lack of funds but their distribution was the main problem. The French nation had savings, but the French state did not have cash. The immediate crisis was therefore one of monetary liquidity. This problem was rendered all the more troublesome by the military circumstances which dictated that armies be raised in the southwest while the Banque de France was left isolated in Paris.

The full extent of the crisis was revealed in the correspondence (mostly conveyed by messenger pigeons) between the capital city and the temporary seat of government in Bordeaux. Cabinet members in Paris were informed shortly before Christmas of 1870 that, despite large infusions of borrowed funds, the resources of Gambetta's regime were virtually exhausted. Expenses since September had mounted to a rate of more than 200 million francs a month. Loans, credits, taxes, and miscellaneous receipts were barely sufficient to cover the debits and could no longer be expected to do so without "new and considerable resources." France could not continue, as Charles de Freycinet notified Gambetta, "to satisfy at the same time the war and the finances. . . ."[4] One of three alternatives could be chosen: to seek another major loan abroad, such as that already obtained from the Morgan bank in London; to create a new state bank in Bordeaux and print paper money at a forced rate of exchange; or to borrow an average of 8 million francs a day from the Banque de France for as long as the war continued. None of these was splendid. The first would have to be arranged at short term and high interest; the second was regarded disparagingly as "the American system" of creating fictitious wealth; and the third was complicated by the physical problem of effecting an actual transfer of funds from Paris.[5] In reality no effective solution was found, and the decision of the provisional government to accept an armistice on German terms was prompted not least of all by the financial impasse. When the war closed, the debt of the French treasury to the Banque de France stood at 928 million francs. The city of Paris owed the bank another 200 million francs and required at least 50 million more by the end of February in order to alleviate "the deplorable financial situation."[6]

This is only to begin to detail the economic woes inherited by the Thierist republic in the winter of 1870–71. The Paris Chamber of Commerce was forced to report that "the factories are idle, the shops for the most part closed, and business entirely suspended." Trade in the capital was reduced to the bare essentials of food, clothing, and military equipment.[7] The government was meanwhile deluged with requests from businessmen and property owners in the occupied territories that the payment of all debts be suspended until the commercial and financial paralysis was relieved. And no relief was immediately in sight. A fortnight before the incident at Montmartre, Thiers was informed that the liquid assets of the state were all but depleted: the treasury in Paris had no more than 13 million francs available. France appeared suddenly on the verge of bankruptcy.[8]

It was under these circumstances that Thiers was required to sign in Versailles the provisional peace treaty with its promissory note of 5 billion francs in reparations to Germany. This was coupled with a pledge from France to provide a still unspecified amount to defray the expense of quartering and provisioning the German army of occupation—a fund for which the Assembly was later pressed to vote an appropriation of 72,500,000 francs.[9] If account is taken of local requisitions and "contributions" extracted in the zone of occupation, a simple computation shows that the actual bill presented to the republic by Germany was well in excess of 6 billion francs. To this must be added the hidden costs of raising and deploying the army of Versailles during the two months of the Commune, a task for which the Germans provided logistical but no financial support.

In one sense, Germany unquestionably did France a favor by imposing such staggering demands. From London the French ambassador, Albert de Broglie, wrote that "the financial exigencies of Prussia have caused and are still causing here a veritable scandal." Not only English bankers but also the Gladstone government were inclined to assist in the reestablishment of French solvency. If Broglie's hopes for an "alliance of credit" with England were overwrought, there were certainly those willing to buy up part of France's foreign investments.[10] This possibility was explored by Charles de Rothschild on a special mission to London in February. The disadvantages were clear. Not only would the house of Rothschild claim a handsome price for its services, the attrition of the French portfolio would mean less interest from the state's foreign assets with which to meet the spiraling public debt. Yet in the short run there seemed little choice but to proceed. In all, about 2 billion francs were eventually raised in this manner.[11]

The first signs of optimism, which soon proved quite excessive, appeared in early March. After a conference with Minister of Finance Auguste Pouyer-Quertier, the governor of the Banque de France, Gustave Rouland, exclaimed to Thiers with "great joy" that "we are preparing a combination . . . which could assure in 1871 the liberation of our soil" and thus "chase the Prussians *financially* as soon as possible."[12] Rouland's objective but not his confidence was shared by Thiers. He was willing neither to deplete French holdings in foreign investments nor to risk irritating Bismarck by convening a formal conference of international financiers in London for the purpose of restoring French credit. France should tap her own resources while avoiding gestures that might prove "more harmful than useful." His own priorities were clear: "Let us obtain the evacuation . . . and when we no longer have the foot of the enemy on our throat, then we shall see."[13]

But what financial device, beyond the liquidation of some foreign assets, should be employed? It is difficult to trace precisely the emergence of the scheme to float a public loan or to fix the exact date of its adoption by Thiers. The apparent reasons for risking a loan and for doing so at once had already been discussed between Pouyer-Quertier and Rouland in connection with the "combination" they planned in order to hasten the German evacuation. Apart from the obvious desirability of that objective, Rouland offered Thiers two justifications—one technical and one political —for prompt action. First, interest rates on domestic loans had been at their lowest level in decades during the past three years, ever since the crash of the Crédit Mobilier in 1868; hence, investment capital was presumably available if provided a lucrative place to accumulate. Secondly, there was reason to attempt a public loan before the Assembly could clamor for a full accounting of "our miseries and our embarrassment." It would be better to gamble while Europe "*guesses* our difficulties but *does not know them at bottom*." To promote the loan, Rouland assured, the government need only display its desire to liberate French territory by the end of 1871.[14]

These lines were written only a few hours before the onset of insurrection in Paris. If a final decision for the loan was reached at that time, it remained without practical consequences for the next ten weeks.[15] Not until the Paris Commune was finally crushed did the rumor begin to spread again in financial circles that a huge public loan was imminent. Although the French government later claimed that there was inadequate time to establish relations with foreign bankers, especially German, this can scarcely have been the case. Nearly three weeks before the public subscription was opened in France, Pouyer-Quertier had received a request from the Bayerische Handelsbank to arrange a similar and simultaneous operation in Munich, Augsburg, Stuttgart, Mannheim, and Frankfurt. This message was accompanied by assurances of "complete success."[16] That the request was refused can only be ascribed to a political decision, the reasons for which had already been indicated by Thiers in rejecting the proposal of an international conference in London. To deal with German banks, especially those south of the Main, without Bismarck's formal consent would only invite the chancellor's wrath and possible reprisal. On the same grounds, the appearance that the loan was unduly beholden to English and other foreign banks was also undesirable. An offer from the Morgan bank to serve as an agent for the subscription in London was consequently declined.[17] More than anything else, this political decision explains the origins of the useful myth that France was largely dependent on her own financial resources and that the nation was rescued from bankruptcy by French peasants and petits bourgeois who drew hidden caches of gold from stockings under their mattresses.

Despite the presumed availability of foreign capital, then, Thiers chose to resort to a unique financial manipulation. Pouyer-

Quertier was instructed to arrange a guarantee for the *second* billion francs of the public loan with a financial consortium headed by the Rothschilds. In return, the Rothschild group was assured of a major share of the total loan, an amount of 60 million francs beyond the 2 billion authorized by the French Assembly on 21 June. An additional fee of 21 million francs was made payable (whatever the outcome) to the consortium, which meanwhile assumed exclusive rights to public subscriptions abroad, specifically including those in London, Berlin, and Frankfurt. The success of the loan was thereby ensured, but at a price more dear than anyone cared to admit.[18]

Yet the "colossal result" which Pouyer-Quertier could exultantly report to Thiers within hours after the subscription opened on 27 June was more than the French had dared to hope for (see table 1).[19] There could no longer be any question of France's ability to meet the immediate obligations to Germany set by the treaty of Frankfurt. The liquid assets heretofore lacking were henceforth available at call. The many smaller subscriptions gathered in the towns and hamlets of France, even if not financially indispensable, were a heartening sign of political confidence in the republic. Perhaps most encouraging of all, the response from abroad indicated that far more capital could easily be generated there if required. Reports to this effect arrived from Venice, Brussels, Basel, Florence, Frankfurt, and elsewhere. In Copenhagen alone, to cite one instance, 3 million francs in French bonds were pledged within a day, and had time permitted the establishment of

Table 1 | The First Public Loan, 1871

	Number of Subscriptions	Capital Pledged (in francs)
Paris	16,525	2,498,440,000
Departments	292,838	1,264,654,000
Foreign	22,543	1,134,460,000
Total	331,906	4,897,558,000

Source: Adolphe Thiers, *Notes et souvenirs de M. Thiers, 1870–1873*, p. 195.

offices throughout Scandinavia, "the subscription could have been very considerable."[20] This meant that the success of any future bond issue was virtually guaranteed. As it was, a proportional reduction of 55 percent was necessary to trim the total capital pledge to the maximum admissible sum of 2,250,000,000 francs; in other words, less than half the money offered to the French government could be accepted at a net interest of 6 percent.[21]

Two days later about one hundred thousand uniformed French troops led by Marshal MacMahon paraded past the grandstand of the Longchamps raceway. The military review had been scheduled a fortnight before and then several times postponed, ostensibly because of inclement weather. Possibly the delay was actually due, as one German observer supposed, to the reluctance of French generals "to show their poorly equipped army to the world."[22] But it seems more likely that Thiers had correctly anticipated that his nation would soon have something more pleasant to celebrate than the eradication of the Paris Commune. No doubt a moment of jubilation was in order. But no Frenchman could forget that the Germans still occupied fortresses on the right bank of Paris and thirteen departments to the north and east.

The German Occupation

By the time the treaty of Frankfurt was signed, the German armies had already occupied some parts of France for nearly ten months. Until early March 1871 the military administration of captured French territories was under four governor-generals located in Strasbourg, Nancy, Reims, and Versailles. Then, once the armistice was in effect and Bismarck had departed for Germany, the entire command in France was awarded to General von Fabrice, whose headquarters were in Rouen. After the definitive peace was concluded in May, Fabrice was replaced in turn by two men: General von Waldersee, who established a diplomatic position in Paris as Bismarck's personal chargé d'affaires, and General von Manteuffel, who assumed supreme military authority at first in Compiègne and later, as the evacuation began, in Nancy.[23]

So long as the war was still in progress, the record of the occupation was spotted with ugly incidents. There were several harsh instances of reprisals for French sniping, a few executions of convicted murderers, confiscations and requisitions, some arbitrary arrests, and threats of taking hostages. Yet, as a rule, the conduct of German troops was restrained and correct. Bismarck even found occasion to complain that the military administrators seemed bent on shielding the French population as much as possible from the effects of the war and suggested that they should instead be made "to feel more keenly their misery" in order to exert more pressure on French political leaders to conclude a rapid armistice.[24]

But the cessation of hostilities by no means brought the discomforts of the occupation to an end. Local incidents continued to occur, strict disciplinary measures were enforced, and the intensity of French protests if anything began to mount. To deal with these, the Germans temporarily instituted a special commission to investigate the more nagging problems and complaints. Its deliberations revealed that both sides were interested in regularizing administrative and judicial procedures in the occupied zone.[25] Bismarck was in fact willing to restore control of civilian affairs in the German-held departments to the French bureaucracy—provided that the French agreed to pay the maximum sum demanded to provision German troops. This was the substance of the accord signed at Rouen on 11 March. When Favre's objections to the high price were ignored by German officials, he felt it necessary to consent anyway, "in order to avoid requisitions and executions" and also simply "because they demand it."[26] Besides the financial terms, the agreement had one notable advantage for the Germans: henceforward, French authorities could be held to account for any untoward behavior among the populace. Germany kept part of the bargain by withdrawing its civilian administrative corps from the occupied departments and allowing French prefectures to be reinstated. But the military command reserved and occasionally exercised the right, in the case of further incidents, to announce "more severe measures for the maintenance of security" or to strengthen certain garrisons.[27]

Although a recitation of the daily episodes that occurred in the occupied territories would be tiresome, their cumulative significance should be emphasized. The retention of a clearly superior military force in France gave Germany immense leverage in every negotiation, the last word in every dispute. French failure to meet the precise terms of the reparations settlement could, in the language of the Frankfurt treaty, be compensated "by levying taxes and contributions in the occupied departments and even outside of them."[28] Any French newspaper editorial construed as harmful or insulting by German officials could be, and frequently was, made a subject of admonition at the highest political level. The same was true of every quasi-political organization considered to be dangerous by the Germans. A single incident, however insignificant, could serve as a pretext for recriminations, momentarily upsetting every reasonable political calculation and providing Bismarck with an opportunity to douse the French with what he himself described as "a cold shower." The result was to force the Thierist republic repeatedly into the stooped posture of an inferior.[29]

To gain some concrete notion of the shock produced within the French government by a menace from Berlin, we may reconstruct one such brief occurrence. On 16 June, Foreign Minister Jules Favre received a "most unexpected telegram" from Bismarck. Therein the chancellor claimed that French troops had just taken up positions near Romainville, not far from Paris, in an area reserved to the German army of occupation. He admonished Favre that the Germans would open fire on the French lines precisely at midnight unless the troops were withdrawn at once. All German evacuation procedures, at the personal command of the Kaiser, would be suspended. Although he knew nothing of the affair, Favre wired back immediately that there must be a misunderstanding: "I beg Your Eminence not to interpret it otherwise. I also beg you to countermand any aggressive orders that might be disastrous for our two countries." He then informed Marshal MacMahon of Bismarck's ultimatum and requested that an officer be detailed forthwith to the scene of the trouble.[30] This MacMahon did, while simultaneously instructing General Ladmirault to have all troops in the vicinity of Paris and Versailles return to their quarters. Neither of the two military leaders could offer the slightest explanation for the alarm. Thiers was also aroused and naturally seconded MacMahon's instructions for withdrawal.[31] Yet by eleven o'clock in the evening, Favre still had no report from Romainville. He telegraphed to Bismarck once more, out-lining the action taken and imploring the chancellor "to believe that we have but one concern: the strict execution of our engage-ments." Thereupon the deadline passed quietly; and on the next morning, Bismarck simply informed Favre that he considered the matter closed. By then the investigation at Romainville revealed that there had indeed been a minor altercation there, but it could be attributed to "the excessive sensitiveness" of some Prussian officers and "a lack of tact" by their French counterparts—hardly a casus belli. After reviewing the evidence, MacMahon could find no sufficient rationale for "the error committed by the great chancellor [or for] the objective which he had in mind."[32]

The historian has less difficulty. According to the terms of the Frankfurt settlement, full payment by the French of the first half billion francs in reparations was to be completed within thirty days after the termination of the Paris Commune. But by 11 June the transfer of funds had not yet begun, and Favre was moved to request a delay. Angered and suspicious that a dangerous precedent might thereby be set, Bismarck expressed his determination to refuse any concession in a communiqué addressed to Waldersee in Paris; this note was drafted on 14 June but was not sent until forty-eight hours later, on the same day as the incident just de-scribed.[33] Given the timing and the uniformly threatening tone of Bismarck's dispatches, there can be no question of a coincidence. Romainville was, rather, a paradigm of how German pressure could be applied to manipulate the French and subdue them to the conqueror's will.

Understandably, the central aim of French policy was "to obtain as promptly as possible our liberation and the evacuation of our territory."[34] At the same time the French found reason to believe that the Germans, too, were interested in speeding the pace of reparations payments as a quid pro quo for advancing the date of total military withdrawal. If the occupation was, as Favre said, "intolerable" for France, it was far from comfortable for Germany. There were reports from German agents of a rise in anti-German feeling since the success of the public loan and, in Paris at least, still more talk of revenge than before. If most of the French seemed largely indifferent, organized groups of agitators were beginning to appear. The French press and the citizenry of the occupied departments were becoming bolder in dealing with German authorities. The result of this adversity, in turn, was a constant irritation of German officers, as well as some signs of sagging morale among their troops—all providing fodder for the German press, where daily editorials began to urge that the soldiers be brought home.[35] As a matter of fact they were being returned to Germany at a rapid rate. The troop level of more than half a million men at the time of the Frankfurt treaty in early May had already been reduced to about sixty-five thousand two months later, with an armed force of another forty thousand stationed just across the new border in the "Reichsland" of Alsace-Lorraine.[36] The French chargé in Berlin, the Marquis de Gabriac, picked up the rumor that the occupation might terminate altogether as soon as the first 2 billion francs in reparations were paid; but no one could be certain, as he observed, so long as "the lion of Varzin continues to slumber."[37]

It was to explore this possibility that the Comte de Saint-Vallier was dispatched from Versailles as Thiers's personal envoy to the current commander of the German army of occupation, General von Manteuffel. Thiers knew what he was about. Manteuffel was a francophile of long standing and an open admirer of Thiers the historian, whom he had visited in Paris a decade earlier in the company of Leopold von Ranke. In May 1871 the general had reminded Thiers of that occasion while asking and gaining a favor from him for his only son, a young military officer who had contracted typhoid fever in France. Manteuffel was thus well disposed toward Thiers and more than eager to to assist in seeking a rapid end to the occupation, which he tended to regard as something of an embarrassment.[38] But his contact with Saint-Vallier proved to be as frustrating politically as it was touching personally. Misfortune dictated that Saint-Vallier arrived at German headquarters in the midst of a controversy over the final installment in the first half billion francs of reparations. Manteuffel's cordiality could not hide his consternation at the discrepancy between Saint-Vallier's assurances that the transfer of funds had been completed and reports from Berlin to the contrary.[39] Days passed before the matter was finally settled by Manteuffel's direct appeal to the German emperor. William consented to order the immediate evacuation of three northern departments, even though the German treasury still insisted that all the money was not yet in hand.[40] This action earned Manteuffel the gratitude of the French but also the suspicion of Bismarck, who was always quick to resent anyone who circumvented him in order to deal personally with William. Here was the key to the chancellor's altercations earlier with Moltke, now with Manteuffel, and later with Harry von Arnim. As Saint-Vallier reported to Thiers, Manteuffel became aware that "Bismarck and his friends even accuse him of being *trop français*."[41] The French were nonetheless persuaded more than ever that Germany could be induced to evacuate the remaining departments altogether once the first 2 billion francs were paid in full. Whether guiding public opinion or responding to it, the French government took steps to make its hopes known.[42]

In August all such expectations were quashed. Transfer of the second half billion francs was effected in the first days of that month, a task made easier by the 325 million credited to France in payment for the German purchase of railways in Alsace-Lorraine.[43] During this transaction Minister of Finance Pouyer-Quertier had been in contact with Manteuffel; and now the two men mutually decided to consult on the next step to be taken. From their meeting at Compiègne came a seven-point accord that payment of the third half billion should be acquitted by the last day of the month, in return for which German troops should begin immediate evacuation of four more departments and the fortifications of Paris. The seventh point specified that ratification was necessary from William and Thiers. Bismarck's name was left conspicuously unmentioned. Manteuffel and Saint-Vallier were confident that the accord would be accepted, although both were concerned that the chancellor might take umbrage.[44] Justifiably so: on 13 August, Bismarck expressed his disapproval and at once took a train from Varzin to join William in Gastein. Manteuffel and Saint-Vallier were left to commiserate about this "unexpected decision" and to speculate, correctly as it proved, that "the refusal of the chancellor applied much less to the substance of the affair than to its form." Having dared to overstep his competence, Manteuffel was badly stung and humiliated by a reprimand.[45] For his part, as Bismarck undoubtedly intended, Saint-Vallier drew two appropriate conclusions: if the French wished to avoid serious friction they would need to pay "vite et beaucoup"; and they must henceforth deal directly with the man now designated by Bismarck as his plenipotentiary to conduct further negotiations in Paris, Harry von Arnim.[46]

This episode coincided with the successful attempt by Bismarck to have suppressed two of the more strident agents of germanophobia in France, the Ligue de la délivrance d'Alsace-Lorraine in Paris and the Ligue anti-prussienne in Lyon. Far from slumbering, the "lion of Varzin" was keeping close watch on the French.[47] The details need not be recapitulated here, but Bismarck's technique deserves a word of comment. As a rule, he preferred to remain inaccessible to French officials, dealing rather through loyal subordinates whose decisions were always conditional, because they were at any time subject to the chancellor's review and possible veto. Bismarck was thus able to hold a tight rein on the French without appearing at every instant to be doing so. Although it was extraordinarily successful, at least for the duration of the occupation, this procedure had two limitations. First, it meant that Bismarck himself could not intervene too frequently, lest he undermine all confidence in the authority of his subalterns. Secondly, it placed a natural restriction on the amount of direct pressure which could be exerted on the French leadership. After all, Bismarck wished to control Thiers but not to topple him. Just as Manteuffel was sensitive to the charge of being *trop français*, Thiers was vulnerable to the suspicion of being *trop allemand*. The suppression of inflammatory political groups and newspapers was a case in point. After the two leagues mentioned had been abolished and a newspaper of like mind, *Le châtiment*, closed down in Lyon, a German agent there pointed out that the anti-German agitation was being conducted instead through clandestinely printed pamphlets. When confronted by the Germans with evidence of this agitation, the new French foreign minister Charles de Rémusat pleaded the extreme difficulty of enforcing an absolute prohibition. The chancellor obviously had some sense of this when he penciled instructions on his agent's report: "Not too much zeal with brochures and details." France should be pushed but not rudely shoved.[48]

With the arrival of Arnim in Paris there was reason to think that official business would be expedited. The French privately regretted Manteuffel's fall from grace; but "in any case," Rémusat remarked, "we will be happy to find ourselves in the presence of a man in possession of the entire confidence of the federal chancellor."[49] And so it initially seemed. Arnim was given a relatively free hand to thrash out the complicated provisions of a tariff agreement covering the industrial products of Alsace-Lorraine. Bismarck was careful, however, to stipulate that the treaty was Arnim's to negotiate but not alone to conclude. The signatures of Bismarck, Arnim, and Pouyer-Quertier were affixed in Berlin on 12 October. So far as reparations payments and evacuation procedures were concerned, the game of tit for tat meanwhile continued: a separate convention was signed on the same day, which regulated payment of the fourth half billion francs in return for a reduction of the German garrison to fifty thousand troops and the release of six more departments. The only ominous note was a provision that, in case of default, the Germans retained "the right to reoccupy the evacuated territory."[50]

Within the prescribed limits of French obedience and German indulgence, a certain relaxation of tension was thus possible—not that the occupation ceased to provoke its customary round of local disputes, but incidents such as those described here would appear less critical in a general political context of cooperation. To be sure, the situation was far too tenuous, and the war still too close, to permit talk of an actual reconciliation. Yet a modus vivendi had been established by the end of 1871, which at least permitted the two nations to conduct their business in a spirit of reciprocity—assuming, of course, that the Thierist republic could continue to meet its financial obligations.

Tariffs, Taxation, and the Second Public Loan

It may be recalled that France had signed a free-trade treaty with England in 1860 and that on this basis a commercial agreement was reached two years later with the Zollverein. Thus, France and Germany already had in practice a kind of most-favored-nation arrangement before 1870. The treaty of Frankfurt confirmed rather than altered that circumstance. But the British were frankly concerned that the actual result of the peace settlement would be to create a privileged economic role for Germany and to abrogate their own claim to equality in the quota of French tariffs. London therefore let its opposition to any new protectionism be known and expressed a desire to renegotiate the earlier accord. Although he was willing to make some concession to the English view, Thiers was at the same time determined to establish what he regarded as an essential minimum in tariffs, especially for the textile industry. This was not simply a matter of national pride, he claimed; "no, it is a necessity of life and nothing else."[51]

Thiers's opinion, seconded notably by Pouyer-Quertier (himself a textile manufacturer from Normandy), was that the lack of adequate import duties on English goods had harmed French industry in the past decade and would do even more damage under the unfavorable economic circumstances of the postwar period. His instructions were consequently to omit all mention of the 1860 treaty in discussion with the English and "to await their claims on this point."[52] When these were immediately forthcoming, Thiers did not budge from his position that the absence of trade barriers was infeasible for France. The treaty with England would therefore need to be revised so as to admit "slight augmentations on certain products." In formal bargaining the French commercial delegation in London maintained that the proposed changes were not in the least intended to revive the principle of protection. But in private Thiers was more frank: "We are protectionist by conviction, we ought to be so by duty."[53]

Given the provisions of the Frankfurt treaty and the manifest ability of the occupation army to enforce it, France was in no position to adopt the same attitude toward Germany. A hint from the French that the tariff issue might still be negotiable was brushed aside in Berlin. The exceptional arrangements made for Alsace-Lorraine, noted above, were not to be regarded as a modification of the rule.[54] As early as March 1871 the German Handelstag had drafted a policy statement which the director of commercial affairs at the Quai d'Orsay accurately described as "a long list of tariff reductions which Germany wants to obtain"; and by the end of that year the German government showed no signs of relenting on such demands.[55]

Caught thereby in a tariff squeeze between powerful neighbors, the republican government continued to suffer the debilitating effects of financial constriction. The problem of obtaining liquid capital remained acute at a time when gold prices and interest rates were falling. And every delay increased the French deficit. Not only did the state have to meet the cumulative interest on loans already contracted, it also owed Germany an additional 150 million francs as interest due for the 3 billion in reparations which remained to be paid.[56] Whether for better or worse—that remains to be judged—Thiers decided on two courses of action in order to cope with the difficult circumstances just summarized. One was to beat down support in the Assembly at Versailles for an income tax and to impose instead a more stringent system of indirect taxation than France had ever known. We need not follow in detail Thiers's travail to have his program adopted by the Assembly. After obtaining a favorable vote on the Rivet law confirming his position as president of the republic in August 1871, his authority was further strengthened by republican victories in by-elections thereafter. Following a long parliamentary recess that autumn, he was consequently able to have his way when the Assembly reconvened in December. Once again he submitted his resignation and then allowed the Assembly to choose between sustaining his wishes or facing the obligations to Germany without him. In essence, his personal victory in January 1872 was also an affirmation both of indirect taxation and of moderate protectionist tariffs.[57]

The second decision was to seek an accelerated schedule of reparations payments and a correspondingly rapid conclusion of the German occupation. Thiers proceeded to advise Manteuffel of these intentions and to solicit his cooperation. Always sensitive to flattery and anxious to recoup his status as an intermediary, the general responded by forwarding the French proposition in separate letters to William, Bismarck, and Moltke. With Saint-Vallier he shared his confidence that this initiative would be fruitful ("le moment est bon"), as well as his doubts that either Armin or the new French ambassador to Germany, the Vicomte de Gontaut-Biron, would be nearly as suitable for French purposes as the practiced tandem of himself and Pouyer-Quertier.[58]

Unknown to Manteuffel, interest in a reparations deal was

already being stimulated by Bismarck's personal financial adviser, Gerson von Bleichröder. Hopeful of enjoying much the same role in a second French loan as the Rothschilds had played in the first, Bleichröder confided to Gontaut that an immediate and total evacuation was not in prospect; but a progressive withdrawal from the final six departments might be arranged, he hinted, and his bank would be able to ensure the French capacity to meet payments on an advanced schedule.[59] It seems probable that Bismarck himself was being prodded by Bleichröder, who conveniently supplied the chancellor with reports that Thiers had been approached "from various sides" with offers to support a 5 percent public loan. He also passed on the information that Thiers was meanwhile exploring the possibility of having a loan of a billion francs or more underwritten in London. In any case, by mid-April the French ambassador was able to report that Germany was prepared to open bilateral negotiations, albeit "without the assistance of foreign powers," whose direct intervention Bismarck wished to discourage.[60]

An inordinate amount of diplomatic ink was consumed in the succeeding two months before a reparations agreement could finally be signed in Versailles by Arnim and Rémusat on 29 June 1872.[61] There is little point in recounting the numerous verbal skirmishes that occurred along the way. It is difficult, in fact, to take too seriously even the most acrimonious of these, especially as the French themselves remained calm throughout. In the course of the negotiations, for example, Manteuffel suddenly received "a bad letter" from Berlin—yet another cold shower. This time it was Moltke running up the warning flag, insisting that the army of occupation take "certain military precautions" in light of "the probability of a resumption of hostilities."[62] This probability was categorically denied by Thiers, who pointed out that the French would hardly be contemplating another major public loan if they intended to fight rather than pay. Saint-Vallier agreed that they were simply confronted with one more "machiavellian ruse." The same pattern had been repeated many times before, he recalled. Whenever Germany wished to impose the terms of a treaty or accord, "we have seen the horizon suddenly darken." Bismarck became ill and aloof, upsetting the French and creating an atmosphere of uncertainty. Then, once concessions were made by France and confidence was restored, "the Prince would find himself cured as if by magic" and the affair would be closed.[63] The historian can only corroborate this version. No doubt the Germans wanted to inhibit the recovery of French military prowess and, specifically, to prevent the augmentation of Thiers's budget for the army. But there was absolutely no evidence of French preparations for armed conflict in the near future. The truth was, as German military officials well knew, that France was not remotely prepared for a military challenge. Despite all the tergiversations, then, a reparations settlement was probably never in serious jeopardy after the negotiations were under way.[64]

Once a bargain was struck, France still needed the funds to implement it. Bleichröder wasted no more than a day in sending an associate from his Berlin banking firm to Versailles to propose "a financial combination which will permit the liberation of the territory within less than two years." Gontaut gained the impression, surely correct, that this move had Bismarck's blessing and that the chancellor now wished to proceed as rapidly as possible. In early July, Bleichröder himself traveled to Paris, where he conferred repeatedly with Thiers. The two men calculated that France could expect to liquidate the entire balance of reparations by March 1874. Thiers was confident that a second public loan would be many times oversubscribed. The only immediate problem, as usual, was to amass the necessary quantity of negotiable currency. Beyond that, of course, there remained the question of how to finance the loan once it was contracted.[65]

Thiers then took his case to the Assembly. His argument was simply that there could be no hastened reparations schedule without a public loan, and no loan without more protectionist tariffs to ensure its amortization. In this way the French president was actually able to exploit the German occupation in order to defend his own financial policy against the proponents of free trade and direct taxation. He knew he could count on popular enthusiasm for the loan: "*Everyone wants it*," Rouland had confirmed, "from M. de Rothschild to the doormen."[66] No less important, the opposition was divided. Some industrialists objected strenuously to increased duties on raw materials, fearing that French goods would be priced out of the international market. But the natural ideological support of the political Left for this stance was undercut by fear that a conservative majority would override Thiers and begin to undo the republic. By playing one faction against another, again submitting his resignation and seeing it refused, Thiers managed to emerge with his program virtually intact. It would require several more months of haggling before the Assembly adopted nearly all of its separate tariff proposals; but the vote of 309 to 261 on 26 July gave Thiers, in effect, the most crucial majority of his presidency.[67]

We may defer a discussion of the political ramifications of this development and concentrate here on the financial consequences. The first was to clear the agenda for the public loan of 3 billion francs which was opened two days later. The success of the first loan and Thiers's continuing mastery of the Assembly gave every assurance of a bonanza. The government's confidence was such that recourse to an expensive guarantee of the final billion was this time considered unnecessary. Yet even the most sanguine predictions fell far short of the extraordinary response (table 2). Anticipating an oversubscription, many banks and individuals apparently offered several times the amount they intended to invest. In the end the government was able to accept only 7.88 percent of the capital pledged.[68] An obvious difference from the first loan was the substantial participation of foreign banking houses. The subscriptions of German banks alone would have been sufficient to cover the entire loan eight times over; and they constituted nearly

Table 2 / The Second Public Loan, 1872

Number of Subscriptions		Capital Pledged (in francs)
Paris	34,324	13,252,455,931
Departments	792,340	4,513,445,566
Foreign	107,612	26,050,195,054
Total	934,276	43,816,096,551

Source: "Note sur l'emprunt de 3 milliards," Bibliothèque nationale, Paris, NAF 20641.

twice the pledge from within France. Such an observation need not denigrate the willingness of the French themselves to invest, but it necessarily places the matter in a less quaint context than stockings under the mattress.[69]

To evaluate properly the implications of Thiers's financial arrangements one needs to examine the French budget for 1873. From a total appropriation of about 2.4 billion francs which Thiers requested from the Assembly, well over half was inscribed under the rubric of public debts and endowments. Less than a billion francs were left for distribution among the various branches of the state's administration, and nearly half of that amount was allocated to the Ministry of War for rearmament and reorganization of the shattered French army. On the other side of the ledger, the annual income for 1873 was estimated at close to 2.5 billion francs. But the state deficit for 1872 was approaching 200 million by the end of the fiscal year; and there was no indication that new revenue from tariffs and other indirect taxes would reach the optimistic projections of 9.5 million and 20 million, respectively.[70] The truth was that every calculation depended on two essential conditions— political stability and commercial revival—neither of which was assured. France was in reality an uncertain nation living far beyond its.means with an economy already heavily mortgaged.

Diplomatic Isolation and Military Evacuation

The elation in Paris was understandably great. If the second loan was a better indication of available credit than of actual wealth, its success had nonetheless provided a remarkable demonstration of national and international confidence in France's future. Yet internally the Thierist republic was far from secure; and abroad it remained as isolated as before.

From the outset the republican regime ordinarily displayed a realistic grasp of both these facts. France would need to maintain "a great spirit of moderation," Jules Favre had admitted a few weeks after the treaty of Frankfurt, since "the moment of initiative has not yet come for us."[71] But there was one exception. As much as anyone, Favre had been emotionally shaken by the Paris Commune, which he blamed on "deserters and foreigners" who were agents of atheism and communism. In detailed instructions to France's diplomatic envoys throughout Europe he elaborated a conspiracy theory of history in which the International was compared to "a vast freemasonry" enveloping the entire continent. Initially, his proposal was to promote "an exchange of views" about measures to be taken by the governments of Europe, explaining that this was to be "not a persecution but an inquiry." In particular he sought to interest Germany, the nation he considered most contaminated by radicalism, in hopes of stirring some mutual or parallel action.[72] The first reports from Berlin indeed indicated a reciprocal concern; the German regime, he was led to believe, would provide "full cooperation in all measures which might be necessary to combat such a formidable scourge." The only problem, it seemed, was that England remained unwilling to join in any formal agreements. Favre felt encouraged nonetheless and vowed that he would not abandon "the idea of an international conference" to deal with the widening threat to the European social order.[73]

Bismarck had his own ideas on the subject. The encouraging words to Favre had been transmitted, as usual, through functionaries at the Wilhelmstrasse. The chancellor himself had neither spoken nor assumed responsibility for them. Instead, he took up the question in the late summer of 1871 with the Austrian chancellor, Count Beust. He then advised the French that each government should decide on its own program of social legislation and subsequently inform other governments of such action taken.[74] Favre's campaign thereupon expired in embarrassed silence. His successor at the Quai d'Orsay, Charles de Rémusat, was no less convinced that the European nations should take "energetic measures for their own defense and for the protection of the social order." But he abandoned altogether any ambition to organize an international congress and imitated the posture already assumed in Berlin. Insofar as the form of Favre's original suggestion was concerned, the whole affair was quickly forgotten.[75]

To conclude that Bismarck was unalterably opposed to an anticommunist witchhunt would be misleading. But his dominating motive was, we know, to prevent France from again becoming "capable of an alliance (*bündnisfähig*)." For this purpose a red scare emanating from France could not be more convenient. Rather than be permitted to lead a crusade against the International, therefore, the French republic was to be displayed as an object lesson and a menace. We need not follow the path by which this rationale led through a tripartite conference at Berlin in September 1872 to the formation of the Three Emperors' League in 1873. Nor should its importance be exaggerated. The object of Bismarck's diplomacy was not so much monarchical solidarity as mutual acquiescence in the military verdict of 1870, including the German annexation of Alsace-Lorraine. Primarily the League thus had the negative effect of rejecting in advance any French initiative to gain support for a status quo ante bellum. Given the demonstrated prowess of Germany's military machine, French revenge was a most dubious cause for Austria and Russia to espouse in any case, League or no. Whatever the actual degree of solidarity among the three eastern empires, then, France's isolation from them was unmistakably ratified.[76]

The French were left to cover their impotence with the fig leaf of optimism. Thiers regarded Austria and France as natural allies who "ought to practice an alliance without professing it." The consultations between Bismarck and Beust at Gastein, and the rumors of Tsar Alexander II's desire not to be excluded, were upsetting; but the president considered it doubtful that Bismarck's "manner of making love with Austria and Russia can last for long." Yet his greatest fear remained that the monarchs might sign a formal territorial agreement, which, as Rémusat admitted, would strike another blow "to our dignity and to our liberty of action in the future."[77] When no such proclamation was forthcoming, Thiers was immensely relieved: "Now this Berlin crisis has passed, and as well as possible." He even put a good face on it, claiming that the only consequence of the Three Emperors' League was a rapprochement between Austria and Russia, "a result rather favorable than unfavorable for us."[78] Yet the truth was unquestionably less flattering. For the time being, it was vain for France to look eastward for aid and comfort.

Of the traditional European pentarchy, then, only England remained to account for. There the admiration for Thiers's success with the second loan was mixed with concern about his advocacy of protectionism. Yet French negotiators were hopeful of obtaining a commercial treaty which would be "in some sense a counterpart of the reunion of the three emperors in Berlin." Once again, Thiers professed complete optimism that "our political, diplomatic, and financial affairs are going well."[79] But as the bargaining proceeded, English resistance to higher tariffs stiffened; and by late October 1872, Thiers had to concede that the news from London was "hardly satisfactory." In reality it was the news from Berlin that had sapped French strength. Since Thiers could not afford to alienate the English, his only possible allies, he instructed his agents to make whatever concessions were necessary. The resulting accord was "not as protectionist as I would have wished it," he allowed, "but acceptable for the present."[80]

Thus, for France everything continued to hinge on the relationship to Germany. No foreign agreement, no domestic arrangement could be wrested entirely free from the German grip on French public life. Of this fact the occupation was a constant reminder. Unfortunately for everyone concerned, the amount of friction in the occupied territories had not been reduced in ratio to the number of departments evacuated. Indeed, the mechanics of withdrawal produced new strains. Since the German troop level had been set at fifty thousand men by the accord of 29 June, the question arose whether occupation forces leaving the progressively liberated departments would be concentrated in those still under General von Manteuffel's command or transported out of France altogether. Germany's insistence on the former procedure loaded an increasing burden on the easternmost provinces for the provisioning and billeting of troops. This provoked a predictable outcry that the population of a few departments was being martyred for all of France. Try as it might, the Versailles government was incapable of tamping down such protest sufficiently to suit German authorities, who continued to issue stern rebukes.[81]

As the band of occupied territory narrowed, another problem added to the aggravation. By special agreement, individuals in the annexed portions of Alsace and Lorraine could exercise an option to retain French citizenship and, if they so chose, to move their belongings across the new national border by the first of October 1872. As the deadline approached, activity in the frontier areas became more frenetic. Groups of refugees began congregating in the occupied departments adjacent to their former homes, creating a new wave of unrest with which local gendarmes were hard pressed to cope. Nettled by German complaints about public disorder, the French government was finally forced to command the arrest of young agitators and their temporary internment in neighboring departments to the west.[82] These difficulties were compounded by the activity of various organizations formed to deal with the refugee problem. Some of the agencies were legitimate, others were not. Anti-German leagues and publications, though officially banned, were able to thrive clandestinely as never before. By adding to this psychic toll an estimated average of 3,400,000 francs a month required of the French to defray maintenance costs of the German garrison, one can readily comprehend the growing sense of urgency in France to liberate the remaining departments at the earliest possible date.[83]

The Germans had their own reasons. They were learning that military occupation is never a pleasant affair, even and perhaps especially when it is close to home. Their discomfort over the distressing incidents of every day increased as their duties began to include the interrogation and sometimes the apprehension of Alsatian refugees. Crowded conditions in temporary barracks were adversely affecting the morale of German soldiers, and alcoholism among them was increasingly prevalent. Relations with the local population also deteriorated visibly as the months passed, a phenomenon ascribed by Saint-Vallier to the recent arrival of German officers' wives, who were keenly sensitive to signs of hostility encountered in the shops and streets. The greatest sufferer of them all was Manteuffel, forever wounded by insults in the Parisian press and even more so by the disparaging epithets of those German military officers who considered him too lenient toward the French.[84]

Yet the issue was more than injured feelings. In the autumn of 1872, Germany was already beginning to feel the first seriously negative economic repercussions of the postwar years. The initial sense of concern was shared in Paris, where there was conjecture that trouble in the German financial market might bear on transaction of the second public loan because of the heavy subscription by German banks. In turn, difficulties with the loan would, of course, subsequently affect the French capacity to maintain an accelerated schedule of reparations. Reports from French consular officials, in response to an inquiry from Rémusat on 4 October, differed as to the extent of the crisis. Some thought it seasonal or temporary; others, very serious and likely to worsen. Yet all agreed that the basic cause was, as the most knowledgeable of French diplomats in Germany put it, "the fever of speculation" that had swept the Reich since the latter months of 1870.[85] The intoxication of victory, the undisciplined creation of joint-stock companies, and the promised infusion of French capital had served to overheat the economy. Consulted by a French official in Berlin, Bleichröder himself confirmed this analysis and indicated that active German participation in the French loan was only one manifestation of a more general phenomenon. Personally, though he regarded the disturbance as an unavoidable consequence of excessive speculation in Germany, Bleichröder did not believe that a serious crisis was imminent. Yet he was hopeful that his government would take measures to reduce the flow of financial adrenalin, since, as he commented wryly in a private note to Bismarck, "it did not make a good impression" to tolerate such circumstances at a time when France was "with great facility" acquitting a debt of 3 billion francs within a year.[86] From this we may draw without distortion the unstated conclusion that Germany's economic sanity required an early termination of the unsettled economic conditions. The corollary followed: a rapid completion of reparations payments and evacuation procedures.

Although the curious role of Harry von Arnim will subsequently require more complete explanation, it should also be mentioned in the present context. The Arnim affair was an elaborate mosaic of *petite histoire* and *Grosse Politik*. In one light it was a personal rivalry of the German ambassador with Bismarck and Manteuffel, in another a clash of political principles. Suffice it here to single out Arnim's astonishing suggestion that the Germans should deliberately stage a coup d'état in France before the end of the occupation, cutting short Thiers's attempt "to organize and electrify revenge against Germany" and replacing him with a more conservative leadership. The chancellor's rejection of this scheme was quick and categorical. Before William, Bismarck accused Arnim of false premises and self-contradictory conclusions.[87] Given their antithetical views, it is a wonder that one of the two did not resign at once. Instead, the matter was allowed to fester for nearly a year before Arnim's eventual dismissal and disgrace. In the course of that time, Bismarck's heretofore pragmatic support for the Thierist republic hardened into an intractable dogma of German national interest. Along with the other political and economic motivations for reaching a satisfactory conclusion to the reparations question, therefore, the chancellor's jealous defense of his entire French policy against Arnim must be counted as an important contributing factor.[88]

Only the technicalities remained. Although the documentation of the ensuing negotiations is particularly copious, the gist of them may be simply stated. There were two basic proposals: Thiers's suggestion that the German occupation should be terminated by June of 1873 in return for a French commitment to begin payment of the final billion in reparations at that time; and Bismarck's demand that German evacuation of the final four eastern departments not commence until after the complete liquidation of the entire French debt. A far more elaborate scheme submitted by Arnim, based on the principle of gradual evacuation for gradual payment, was at first dismissed out of hand by Bismarck on the suspicion that his ambassador was distorting reports and withholding information from Thiers.[89] A graduated schedule was nonetheless adopted, even though Bismarck preemptively removed the matter altogether from Arnim's hands. Once a final complication had been resolved—whether the last remaining German garrison should be maintained at Belfort or Verdun—a convention was signed in Berlin on 15 March 1873 by French ambassador Gontaut-Biron and Bismarck. It provided that all financial transactions be concluded by 5 September and that all German military forces be evacuated from French soil within a fortnight thereafter. The liberation was at last in sight.[90]

What had it all cost? By some reckonings the total expense to France of the war, the Commune, and the liberation was in excess of 15.5 billion francs.[91] But this is not to estimate the disruption of industry and commerce nor to include the physical damage to agriculture. Confronted with losses of such magnitude, most of them unavoidable, one might well hesitate to criticize the republican regime for its financial efforts. Under humiliating and trying circumstances not of his own making, Thiers had conducted the affairs of state with remarkable tenacity. Throughout, he managed to keep two central objectives in view: restoration of order in his nation and freeing France from the occupying armies of the invader, whatever the cost. No historian who has studied the record can withhold admiration for his fidelity to this policy of fulfillment; nor should one, for reasons sufficiently analyzed, underrate the psychological advantages that an early evacuation brought to France. As it was, the last German soldier was due to cross the frontier eighteen months in advance of the originally scheduled date. To persist in obtaining an early release of the hostage territories undeniably required both vigor and political courage.

Yet it is not alone Thiers's ability but also his judgment that must be questioned. The great public loans, successful as they were, had the paradoxical liability of perpetuating the temporary shortage of state assets. By contracting massive debts at high rates of interest, Thiers had in effect paralyzed more than half of the entire national budget for years to come. The result was to limit financial appropriations which, precisely at the moment of greatest opportunity, might otherwise have been employed to encourage a genuine reform of French institutions. The elevation of indirect taxes may also have abetted a slackening of French industry, because they were "the most inimical to economic growth of all forms of taxation."[92] These measures cannot therefore be dissociated from the mediocre performance of the French economy during the succeeding decades; and they were also not unrelated to the fairly lamentable record of the Third Republic in social legislation. The parsimonious expenditures for reform all too faithfully reflected a basically unsympathetic attitude of those who governed, starting with Thiers, toward the underwriting of public welfare. If Thiers may be credited with a patriotic achievement, then, he must also bear the serious charge of "economic reaction perpetuated under the guise of fiscal necessity."[93]

The price paid for liberation was political as well as financial. There was a notable disparity between Thiers's comportment toward German authorities and his treatment of the French Assembly. In his behavior with Bismarck in particular, he established a pattern of servility that his successors would later find difficult to alter. Precedents of obedience were set which, once Thiers was gone and the occupation concluded, were to remain as an exacting standard applied by the Germans to the conduct of other French statesmen. Of course, a slow erosion of direct German pressure on France inevitably occurred; but it was a process surely not facilitated by the example of Thiers's initial eagerness to please. This attitude contrasted markedly with the imperious manner assumed by the first president in thwarting his parliamentary opposition. The persistent claim to indispensability and the repeated threats of resignation were more nearly Bismarckian than republican. By resorting to such means, Thiers raised justifiable fears of a personal consulate, tarnished the image of the presidency, and actually nourished a climate of political instability that his policies were intended to dissipate.

Chapter 3

The Political Alternatives

The Monarchists

Several schemes have been proposed to account for the complex political structure of the early Third Republic. Entire schools have formed to defend theories that the ideological spectrum should properly be divided into two or three segments.[1] Other analyses of French parliamentary life have often posited the existence of four groupings—Right, Right Center, Left Center, Left—each composed of several factions, whose combinations provide the fodder on which political science thrives.[2] But the central concerns here are necessarily more specific than the development of a general model of French politics. They are, first of all, to identify those political formations which, at a given time, actually had some prospect of obtaining and exercising authority in the French state; and secondly, to determine the extent of German influence on the performance of each of them in French internal affairs. By applying these criteria to the 1870s we may appropriately set the number of political groupings at five.

The monarchist cause was by far the oldest and most self-defeating of them all. After the indignities of revolution in 1848, the Second Republic, and the Bonapartist coup d'état in 1851, the future of monarchy in France hardly seemed promising. Yet nothing is so conducive to political idealism as a safe distance from the responsibility of decision; and for Legitimists and Orleanists alike, the Second Empire was a time of alienation, opposition, or exile. Their leaders were consequently free to dream of a reunited lineage that would one day be restored to the French throne, a vision which to this day has never totally vanished.[3]

As briefly as possible we may reconstruct a summary of the monarchist travail. The first effort to effect a fusion of the royal branches developed in November 1853, when, at his Austrian exile in Frohsdorf, the Bourbon Comte de Chambord received an Orleanist delegation. Although no record of the conversations was made public, conjecture had it that unification of the two houses was a *fait acquis*. But there was evident skepticism at the European courts as to the significance of such an event. Not only was the imperial regime of Napoleon III thought to be securely established; the extent of reciprocal commitment among supporters of the royal families was dubious. As the Duc de Broglie was heard to remark, an alliance of French princes "would only produce five more Legitimists."[4] Still, the attempted reconciliation was not allowed to languish. In the late spring of 1855, Chambord greeted another Orleanist caller, this time the Duc de Montmorency, who brought fresh tidings of devotion from members of the junior branch. This meeting aroused more skepticism among those best placed to judge. The Prussian legate in Paris, Paul von Hatzfeldt, believed that if the Legitimists were actually given a choice between perpetuating the Bonapartist dynasty or replacing it with an Orleanist monarchy, most of them would favor the former. The Orleanists were meanwhile prepared to pledge fealty to the heirless Bourbon pretender only on two conditions: that he espouse the tricolor and that he adopt a constitution. Neither was acceptable to Chambord. By January of 1857, Hatzfeldt therefore articulated the consensus of European diplomats that "the fusion, which had never been solidly established [and] which has been gradually weakening for some time, is now officially buried."[5] Occasional rumors persisted in the following decade—the most bizarre concerned a plot allegedly hatched by the Austrian emperor and a Prussian general to depose Napoleon III in favor of Chambord— but in reality the fusionist campaign was marooned in Frohsdorf.[6] For our purpose the evidence is thus adequate to support two conclusions: that the so-called white flag controversy already divided French monarchists before 1870, and that German observers were well apprised of that fact when the war began.

Although a disaster for France, the military conflict (as he saw it) was literally a godsend for Chambord, who was sure that a golden chance for a restoration had been created by Sedan. The capture of Napoleon III and the inexorable retreat of French armies meant that the political fate of the nation temporarily rested in Prussian hands. What the course of history had not bestowed on Henri V might now conceivably be granted by a *deus ex germania*. After several days of fretting, Chambord packed his bags and set out to offer his country "my arm, my blood, my life." He meanwhile composed a letter, dispatched from Switzerland on 1 October, addressed to "my brother and cousin," the king of Prussia. This was nothing less than an appeal for William's intercession to restore the Bourbon dynasty. If the language was befittingly elevated, the message was unambiguous. It spoke of the "wisdom of princes," of "sacred duty," and of "noble instincts," which stood in contrast to the "faults of the Second Empire" and the "sinister plots" in Paris. On the principle of hereditary monarchy alone rested the destiny of Europe and the future of France, a nation that now wished "to close forever the era of revolutions." Chambord's petition was thus directed as much to Germany's self-interest as to William's monarchical pride, just as Talleyrand had pleaded the case of legitimacy in Vienna a half century before. "I am therefore ready," he concluded, *"if my country calls me."*

The italicized phrase is one of the few in the letter underlined with a heavy pencil. The pencil was Bismarck's, and it is probable that his annotations were made before the pages reached William. We know that the letter was first sent to the Countess zu Sayn-Wittgenstein in Düsseldorf with explicit instructions to forward it to William "as directly as possible and under the seal of strictest secrecy." In an envelope addressed to Bismarck, along with a brief word of explanation from the countess, it was then relayed by courier to Versailles and handed directly to the chancellor. Not until the next day, 10 October, did Bismarck pass on the lady's note "with its enclosure" to William.[7]

These details are essential to explain why a Willy-Henry correspondence never materialized and how Bismarck managed to intervene with the intention of discouraging Chambord's candidacy to the French throne. The only response from Versailles was an acknowledgment to the countess from Bismarck that his monarch had "gladly received" the communication and was touched that Chambord had "turned to him in full confidence." But, the chancellor continued, "if the king does not personally and directly reply, His Majesty hopes that the Comte de Chambord will appreciate the considerations which require such reticence of His Majesty for the time being." Despite its oblique phrasing, Bismarck's answer was no less transparent than Chambord's inquiry. A restoration of the Bourbon line, as the pretender himself had noted, depended on the expressed desire of the French nation; until that was forthcoming, "any pressure from abroad could only disturb, not advance, the development in this direction." Germany must therefore remain scrupulously impartial in France's internal affairs and "refrain from any interference."[8]

The pious tone should not obscure the political reality. The contention that German policy was simply to allow events in France to take their natural course was not even a half-truth. Far too many instances of direct German pressure, consciously applied, testify to the contrary. It was untypical of Bismarck to allow matters within his power to drift unless his purposes were thereby served, or at least not obstructed. Since he did not consider it in the German interest to encourage French unity under the banner of a Catholic monarchy, he had no reason to endorse Chambord nor to allow William to do so. The evidence here and later scarcely suggests that the chancellor saw his role in the choice of a successor to Napoleon III as that of a disinterested observer. He actively opposed the monarchist cause in France, whatever the color of its flag. Indeed, his preference, if anything, was probably for white. More flexible in France and more popular abroad, the Orleanists were likely to be a greater danger to Germany than the Legitimists. Bismarck feared not so much Chambord, whom he thought a fool, as the possibility that fusionism would soon spawn an Orleanist successor.[9] By intercepting the letter to William, then, he identified himself as an active opponent of any monarchist restoration.

So Chambord remained in exile, hovering on the borders of France. The Orleanist family proceeded otherwise. Two of them, the Prince de Joinville and the Duc d'Aumale, had obtained election as deputies to the Assembly. The right to claim their seats was in doubt, however, unless the parliament rescinded laws barring them from all political activity. While the verdict was awaited, they permitted their interest in resuming negotiations with Chambord to be known.[10] It was this threat of a revived fusionism that clinched the marriage of convenience between Thiers and Bismarck. Although he disapproved of validation of the Orleanist mandates, Thiers lacked a majority in the Assembly to prevent it. He was also formally bound by the "pact of Bordeaux" to deal impartially with royalists and republicans. His public stance was therefore a grudging neutrality; but his private view, of which he made no particular secret, remained that "there is nothing possible *for the time being* but the republic."[11]

This circumstance drew from Bismarck an unequivocal endorsement of the Thierist presidency. Four days before parliamentary debate on the seating question opened, the chancellor sent instructions to General von Fabrice, copies of which were distributed to diplomatic missions at the major European courts and to provincial capitals in Germany: "Since the regime headed by M. Thiers has concluded the definitive peace with us, it lies in our interest and in our international situation to recognize only the present French regime, so long as another does not develop from it by legal means which assures the execution of the peace treaty and the maintenance of the current relations between the two countries in the future." The memorandum added explicitly that Germany would reserve the right to withhold recognition from any new form of political leadership in the French state. Should such a change occur without prior German approval, the army of occupation, "which stood in France in the winter," might be fully reconstituted within a fortnight. Although this unsubtle admonition did not hinder the Assembly's vote to seat the Orleanist princes, it did represent a formidable obstacle in the further path of French monarchism, and it provided Thiers with a crucial advantage that he could later exploit in sustaining the republic.[12]

Holding the trump of German support would have been worth far less to Thiers had his conservative opponents only agreed on a single strategy. But the fusionist campaign continued to sputter. Rumors placed Chambord near Bruges, where he was supposedly expecting a visit from the Orleanists.[13] Instead, he moved capriciously. Arriving in Paris at dawn on 2 July, Chambord made an incognito tour of the city by cab and met with a few of his supporters in private. To them he declared his refusal to "abdicate," that is, to make a fusionist compromise on Orleanist terms. He then traveled to his family chateau in the Loire where he signed the stunning manifesto pledging his immutable allegiance to the *drapeau blanc* of Henri IV. No act could have done the republic a greater favor; and none judged its significance more astutely than Thiers: "Now I am free from all reproach; henceforth no one will be able to deny that the true founder of the French republic is M. le Comte de Chambord. Posterity will speak of him as the Washington of France."[14]

Bismarck was not less well served, since the manifesto spared him any further necessity for direct intervention to discourage the fusionist cause. Chambord's intransigence was discouragement enough. From Paris Waldersee reported "the termination of the nearly forty-year struggle of the Legitimist party for the throne of France." German agents were unanimous in regarding the manifesto as an act of "political suicide" which would debilitate Chambord's following and increase the stability of the Thierist republic.[15] Not that German interest in the monarchists thereafter slackened. Secret reports continued to supply Berlin amply with information and speculation. Apart from Thiers himself, and perhaps Gambetta, the most carefully watched personality in France was the Duc d'Aumale. In the absence of an accord between the royal families, the German assumption was that the Orleanists would be forced to seek power by parliamentary maneuver. This was, after all, a possibility left open by Bismarck's directive in behalf of the Thierist regime ("so long as another does not develop from it by legal means"). If the Orleanists could successfully rally all moderate factions in the Assembly, Aumale might yet be elected to succeed Thiers to the presidency. The restoration would then be only a matter of time.[16] But this was only conjecture. The splintering of monarchist factions, republican victories in by-elections, and the consolidation of Thiers's position by the Rivet law—these were the operative facts of political life by the end of 1871.

One complication in gauging the German role in regard to the monarchists was the ambassadorial performance of Harry von Arnim. The earliest known contact between Arnim and the royalists was in November 1871, when he requested Bismarck's permission to meet privately with Aumale. The chancellor expressed no reservation so long as the contact remained "without political prejudice."[17] Yet obviously it did not. Henceforth, Arnim's reports began to denigrate Thiers as a man whose failing health and revanchist inclinations made him unworthy of German confidence. Aumale was portrayed, by contrast, as a "sympathetic personality" who enjoyed broad support in the Assembly, who was thoroughly conciliatory toward Germany, and who merely lacked a bolder and more unified party behind him. Arnim thus advocated the view that Aumale was the pivotal political factor in France: "In the event of Thiers's death, the greater part of the president's parliamentary contingent would switch" to Aumale. Yet even the ambassador was dismayed at the Orleanists' failure to advance their cause in the Assembly during the spring session of 1872.[18] In turn, since the alternative strategy was simply not working, this failure encouraged a revival of fusionist agitation by the following autumn. French rightists were "conscious that they are presently incapable of founding another political order," the German attaché Wesdehlen observed in August, "and they sadly concede that the restoration of the monarchy sought by them can only be the sequel of a *fusion*."[19]

The sense of urgency in the monarchist camp was heightened in September by the publication of an open letter in the Orleanist *Journal des débats* by a prominent conservative and family friend of Thiers, Jean Casimir-Périer, who announced his defection from royalism to the republic. The reason given was that the apparent failure of the fusionists to rally sufficient popular or parliamentary support had "nullified reasonable hope for a monarchist solution." There was also evidence that Casimir-Périer was not an isolated case. Thus, by the beginning of 1873, as Arnim had to admit, the longevity of the Thierist republic was increasingly enhanced by "the sterility and impotence of the monarchist parties."[20]

In later years royalist historians would never tire of repeating that the Third Republic was a creature of Bismarck's foreign policy. Since it suited Germany to keep France isolated from the European monarchies, especially from Catholic Austria, the chancellor imposed a republican form of state on the French nation. He then employed Thiers as a willing tool of his grand strategy and prevented the monarchists from claiming what was rightfully theirs.[21] But the record examined here shows only two instances of Bismarck's direct intervention to inhibit the monarchist campaign: the interception of Chambord's petition to William and the blunt warning of reoccupation should Thiers be suddenly upset by a coup d'état. Both came very early in the day, and neither was demonstrably preemptive. The real saboteurs of the restoration were the monarchists themselves, who attempted the art of the impossible: fusion without unity. Legitimist intractability and Orleanist ineptitude provided Germany with an almost effortless solution to the problem of retaining France as a compliant vassal until the full payment of reparations was assured.

The Bonapartists

No political formation was so obviously and profoundly affected by the war with Germany as the Bonapartists. After Sedan the same men disappeared from sight who, only a few months before, had conspicuously defended the emperor's program during the final plebiscite of the Second Empire. Their disgrace was so complete that few Bonapartist politicians dared to enter the improvised elections to the Bordeaux Assembly in February 1871. Consequently, the *appel au peuple* went virtually unheard by a nation still deafened by the discharge of Prussian cannonry. In all of France the Bonapartists managed to gather barely one hundred thousand votes and to elect only nineteen deputies; of these four were from Corsica and three from the political fiefdom of a local notable in the Charente-Inférieure. Apart from these few exceptions, the mighty had everywhere fallen.[22]

Yet the imperial party was far from a negligible factor in the formative period of the Third Republic. The essential ingredients of Bonapartist aspiration were one part Napoleonic myth, one part residual loyalty among those who had prospered during the Second Empire, and one part lingering hope for German support of a "return from Elba." We have already noted that, precisely because of its disgrace, the Napoleonic dynasty remained for Bismarck an attractive alternative to the French republic. Even after signing the armistice agreement with Thiers, the chancellor was still keeping Napoleon III as "Tell's second arrow," an alternative "en cas que."[23] In March the emperor was permitted to leave his comfortable captivity at Wilhelmshöhe and to join Eugénie in exile at Chislehurst, on the outskirts of London. The more optimistic of the Bonapartists chose to see this gesture as an indication of German favor and a convenient prelude either to the emperor's reentry into Paris or, at the least, to the establishment of a regency for the Prince Imperial. They did not wish Germany's direct intervention on Napoleon's behalf but hinted that the display of a "friendly attitude" would render "a great service" in the forthcoming by-elections to the Assembly.[24]

Germany was unprepared to offer any such assistance. Nearly a month before his open endorsement of the Thierist regime, Bismarck had already indicated as much to Favre and Pouyer-Quertier at Frankfurt. Although the immediate occasion of that endorsement was the controversy over the seating of the Orleanist princes, Bismarck's warning to avoid "any crisis which might have as consequence a renewed civil war" was an admonition to the Bonapartists as well. The by-elections in July seemed to demonstrate that the chancellor knew where to place his bets: only one secure seat was added to the imperial party.[25]

In the face of these setbacks the Bonapartist leaders were nonetheless convinced that a large reservoir of political loyalty remained in the peasantry and the petite bourgeoisie if only a party apparatus could be geared up to tap it. But the leadership itself was seriously divided. One faction was close to the Legitimists in political reaction, religious orthodoxy, and ideological intransigence; another, directed from his Paris headquarters by Eugène Rouher, was more representative of the liberal empire and more pragmatically oriented toward developing a broad party base; and a third, still less coherent, reflected the ostensibly socialistic and anticlerical notions which in earlier days had been encouraged by the emperor's more speculative moments.[26] These groups lacked, above all, a consensus in the formulation of policy. What was the surest path to an imperial restoration: the electoral process, a *coup de main*, or a national plebiscite? The first, to judge from the electoral returns, appeared unpromising; the second would require some way to overcome the irresolution of Napoleon himself, the unreliability of the French army, and the admonition by Bismarck; the third depended on the uncertain possibility that Thiers could somehow be forced or persuaded to risk the republic in one great test of popularity. Both German agents and French police tabulated these dissensions with care. They concluded separately that the Bonapartists in fact had no coherent strategy and little prospect of success short of a dramatic upset in France's entire political structure. Without a clear sense of direction, propagandists for the imperial cause were left to agitate at random in hopes of creating a general malaise and combating what the prefect of police in Paris simply described as "public indifference" to political change.[27]

The only contribution of Napoleon III to the Bonapartist campaign was the launching of several ineffectual attempts at international diplomacy. One contact was established to the Russian court by an interview with the sister of the tsar. This was sufficient to send telegrams back and forth across the continent of Europe for weeks, prompting Bismarck to inquire whether Alexander had been led to revise his earlier, thoroughly negative opinion of a Bonapartist restoration. The speculation was finally quashed by the foreign minister Gorchakov, who reassured Berlin that the tsarist government was "completely indifferent" to the identity of the French leadership, provided that peace and order were sustained. This sentiment accorded perfectly with Bismarck's own policy, once more restated in this context: "to refrain from any interference in the internal affairs of France so long as *our* interests and rights remain beyond question."[28] Again, one should note the disingenuous character of such a pronouncement. Apart from the considerable latitude left to the chancellor's discretion in defining Germany's "interests and rights," it was hypocritical to imply that all French parties could benefit equally from the impartiality of the great powers. The problem of the Bonapartists and the monarchists alike was to overcome the natural inertia of French public life in the wake of war. The apparent satisfaction of Germany and Russia with the status quo was bound to inhibit the opponents of

the Thierist republic, especially those, like Napoleon III, who attached the greatest importance to traditional diplomatic formalities
between monarchs and ministers.

A second contact was opened with Austria. Relieved of his
premiership in Vienna in early November 1871, Count Beust had
at once assumed his new duties as the Austrian ambassador to
England. At the first opportunity he responded to an invitation to
visit Chislehurst. There he found Louis Bonaparte to be "a mild
old gentleman" who spoke of the French mistakes in 1870 "as if
he himself had had little or nothing at all to do with them." The
former emperor was frank that he was nursing ambitions for an
imperial restoration in France and, on closer questioning, confided to Beust that "he still hoped personally to mount the throne
again." Lest there be some misunderstanding, Beust made a special
visit to Thiers in Versailles to assure the French president that his
conversations with Napoleon were no more than a diplomatic
courtesy. There is no reason to doubt Beust's version of the story,
which, in any event, remained without a sequel.[29]

We can equally well discount the political importance of Napoleon's other personal efforts to promote the idea of "a dowry."
The Bonapartist hope was that Germany would make an imperial
restoration acceptable to the French people by promising a reduction in reparations and the return of Metz. It would then be possible to pressure Thiers into holding a national plebiscite, which,
with German concessions in hand, the Bonapartists felt certain to
win. But this feeling was shared by virtually no one, least of all by
Bismarck himself, who simply reiterated that the surest way to
make Napoleon impossible was "to declare him the Prussian candidate."[30] These meager results notwithstanding, the Bonapartists
generally displayed confidence that their party was gaining momentum and that it was everywhere acquiring new support. Following a *mot d'ordre* from Rouher's headquarters in the rue de
l'Elysée, the Bonapartist press began to soften its previously harsh
tone toward Germany and to print disclosures by unnamed sources
about impending patronage from Berlin. Nothing could have been
more calculated to infuriate Thiers. He was adamant that France
could "never return to the government which finished its disastrous reign at Sedan." He was convinced that the stories being

spread about a shift in Bismarck's sympathies were totally untrue; for that the chancellor was too much the "profound politician." In Thiers's opinion, the chancellor "wants to be paid: that is his ambition. He knows that the Bonapartists would encounter a terrible resistance, that France in upheaval would no longer be able to pay; and he ardently wishes the maintenance of the present government which alone wants peace and alone can obtain credit. Of all that I have *certain proofs*. . . ."[31] Although his correspondence amply documented this claim, Thiers was still taking no chances. After learning that Napoleon III and the Prince Imperial were regularly appearing on horseback for maneuvers at a military academy near Chislehurst, as if they were in training, he had a police agent dispatched to survey the Pas-de-Calais for the "rather improbable" chance that a landing might be attempted there. The Paris police were also ordered to suspend briefly two of the three leading Bonapartist dailies as a retaliation for the "provocation and audacity" of the imperial press. When it came to throttling his opposition, Thiers was anything but squeamish.[32]

So far as one can tell, the claims of Bonapartist propaganda made little impression on the French public; and for the most part, according to police reports, they were received in Paris political circles with "absolute incredulity."[33] Yet the rumors about revived German interest in an imperial restoration were not altogether without substance, since, once again, a qualification must be registered concerning Harry von Arnim. We have earlier recorded the ambassador's chronic distrust of Thiers and his disillusionment with the Duc d'Aumale after the spring of 1872. Thiers's faltering health and declining prestige could produce, in Arnim's judgment, only one of two political results: either a Bonaparte or a Gambetta. Any other solution would soon be vitiated by radicalism that was sweeping the French countryside. Things had already developed to the point that "the peasants are more radical than the Parisians." That being the case, Arnim concluded, "we should not dismiss out of hand the connections sought with us by the Bonapartists," the only political faction in France not to inscribe revenge on its flag.[34]

It is unnecessary to retrace here Bismarck's rationale for rejecting this view and for repeating ad infinitum to Arnim that "our first task naturally remains as ever to support the present regime." One should note, however, that the ambassador's analysis was far from groundless and that his suggestion was not dissimilar to the logic of Bismarck's own remarks about "Tell's second arrow."[35] But logic counted for less in 1872 than the Bonapartists' embarrassing lack of success in parliamentary by-elections. In all, twenty-eight were held that year; the imperial party bothered to contest only seven and won but three. As the months passed, moreover, the likelihood that Napoleon would dare to mount an expedition across the English channel faded altogether. For that, Arnim conceded in November, "the proper moment seems already lost."[36]

In reality, much more was at fault than the emperor's timing. After 1870 the anticipated surge of popular enthusiasm for his person and his party never materialized. Without it he was powerless to persuade Bismarck or to dislodge Thiers. As a result, there was no sensible alternative to awaiting the end of the German occupation and the fall of the first president. Yet by the time those events occurred, he was dead. The news that Napoleon III had expired on a surgeon's table at Chislehurst on 9 January 1873 created less of a stir than one might suppose. Twenty-eight months had elapsed since Sedan, after all, and the constant bustle of politicians during the interim had produced little observable movement toward Bonapartism. Moreover, the Bonapartists themselves were eager to minimize the importance of the emperor's demise. One of their spokesmen, General Fleury, even professed to see an advantage for the party, since "the man of Sedan," who in his final months had become "old, sickly, and listless," would now be replaced by the young and politically uncompromised Prince Imperial. All the Bonapartists needed was time to regroup, Fleury claimed, and for this purpose it would be helpful if the German government found some pretext "to lengthen the occupation of the French provinces."[37] Obviously this suggestion was preposterous. Such a remark was symptomatic of the bewilderment within the imperial camp and betrayed a persistent Bonapartist fantasy that wavered between two delusions: the *appel au peuple* and the supplication to Bismarck.

So far as Germany was concerned, Napoleon's premature

death served much the same function as Chambord's prolonged life: it crippled one of the contenders for the succession to Thiers's consulate. The Germans were thereby relieved of any necessity of taking direct action in an effort to steer the course of French politics. If neither the monarchist nor the imperial cause was mortally wounded, both were sufficiently weakened by internal strife and public indifference to remove them as immediate alternatives to the Thierist republic.

The Thierists

Adolphe Thiers espoused republicanism for the simple reason that it was the only system under which he could be the first citizen of France. An Orleanist by tradition, he became a republican through ambition—that is, through the conviction shared by every politician worth his salt that his own leadership was vital to his constituency. Thiers was persuaded that he alone was fit to lead the French nation out of the wilderness of defeat; and for all the damaging criticism which has been heaped on his reputation, there is still reason to judge that Thiers's presumption was not altogether unjustified. As the war with Germany ended, France had only a limited number of political options. By steering a course between restoration and radicalism, Thiers made himself perhaps not as indispensable as he claimed but certainly more plausible than any of his opponents.

Yet the sincerity of Thiers's commitment to the republican cause was at the time, and has remained, a subject for conjecture. Because an analysis depends finally on the subconscious of a single person, the truth of the matter can perhaps never be established. But as that person necessarily had to deal with others, an objective pattern of political actions can be discerned. While choosing his first cabinet in February 1871, for example, Thiers pleaded with Jules Favre, Ernst Picard, and Jules Simon to join him, with the explanation that "in order to establish the republic, an administration is necessary in which some republicans are represented." Favre expressed the belief that Thiers was "very sincere in using this language with us," and his two colleagues evidently concurred.[38] In his subsequent conduct as the chief executive, during months of difficult negotiations with the conservatively dominated Assembly, Thiers reminded the deputies more than once that the pact of Bordeaux cut in both directions. On the morning after the proclamation of the Paris Commune, he warned them not to mistake his intentions: "We found the republic established as a fact of which we were not the authors; but I shall not destroy the form of government which I am now employing in order to reestablish order."[39]

Thereafter, in the face of constant and barely concealed speculations about the choice of his successor, Thiers stubbornly consolidated his position as president of the republic; and it was on this basis, as we have observed, that he received the endorsement from Bismarck without which the structure of French politics would have been even more fragile than it was. But as a republican president, Thiers had one critical and incurable weakness: he lacked a broad party base. His strength derived from the office of the presidency rather than from an extensive political organization. The Thierists were a faction rather than a party. With no secure majority in the Assembly, Thiers was therefore subject at any moment to a parliamentary defeat in Versailles which could destroy his claim to leadership. Had it not been for the intense public feeling that surrounded the overriding issue of territorial liberation, his tenure would likely have been cut short by men who had no other reason to sustain him in office and who resented his domineering manner. Throughout the summer of 1871, Berlin was alerted "from one day to the next to see M. Thiers eliminated." Only the disunity of his opponents, as well as the fear of a prolonged German occupation in the case of a coup d'état, appeared to keep him afloat. "The supremacy of any other party will have civil war as a consequence," Waldersee reported from Paris, adding that Germany would therefore need to support Thiers "with every means."[40] But what measures could actually be employed by a foreign power to influence the functioning of the French political system?

For the answer to that question, the vote on the Rivet law in August 1871 offered an exemplary test. The issue was sharpened to a point both by Thiers's desire to have a formal confirmation of his presidential authority for the next two years and by the mounting conservative criticism that he was insufficiently zealous in prosecuting the "revolutionary elements" which remained after the Commune. As the bishop of Orléans, Monsignor Dupanloup, charged: "After having saved us, M. Thiers is in the process of losing us." Ominously, the first casualty of the ensuing tussle was Jules Favre, already in difficulty because of a private scandal, who was replaced as foreign minister by the less controversial Charles de Rémusat. "And it is very possible," Waldersee cautioned Berlin, "that within a short time the position of the president is to be newly filled."[41]

Both the capabilities and the limitations of German technique in attempting to influence the outcome were illustrated before Thiers's political survival was certain. First of all, Thiers was once more personally reassured by the German emissary in Paris that he could claim the full support of the government in Berlin, which regarded the continuation of his regime as "a guarantee for the correct execution of the peace." Although Waldersee was apparently acting on his own initiative in this case, his prior instructions were clear; and they were confirmed a few days later by Bismarck after consultation with the Kaiser. William and the chancellor were prepared "to cooperate free of charge (*gratis mitwirken*)." Of course, this cooperation had to be within the bounds of German self-interest and on the assumption of reciprocity for large or small sacrifices made in the French behalf.[42] Bismarck meanwhile moved to open a press campaign in support of Thiers. He ordered that editorials be written in semiofficial German newspapers of the loss of confidence toward France which would result if the president's position were shaken. The press was instructed to warn that the prospect of renewed political struggles among the French parties was bound to leave Germany "dubious and reserved in all questions affecting the evacuation." Obviously this message was not intended solely for the German reading public, and care was taken to see that it was conveyed to the Quai d'Orsay. As a result, Waldersee soon was able to report that "Rémusat will use the hint about possible reinforcement of the occupation army to work on the opposition."[43]

The evidence thus confirms that the Germans performed the customary rituals of diplomacy, by means of official dispatches and the newspaper press, in a deliberate effort to maintain Thiers in the presidency. Yet there was further influence. Through a secret channel, the "hint" of which Waldersee spoke took the form of an outright threat. In a private letter to Bleichröder, Bismarck's close associate Robert von Keudell noted the disturbing reports that Thiers was "tottering" and requested the well-connected financier to leave his Parisian friends in no doubt "that we regard the situation as very serious; that a new regime which inspires less confidence than the present one would have the consequence of an immediate increase of the occupation troops; that if it should appear as though hostilities were intended there, we would consider it advisable to anticipate them by an attack from our side; in sum, that the thought of a resumption of war . . . is generally accepted here and everything is prepared for it."[44] Since it is inconceivable that Keudell, of all people, would have made such remarks without the chancellor's advice and consent, we must consider these admonitions as part of an orchestrated campaign of intimidation. Consequently, the pieties of Bismarck's formal policy of nonintervention in French affairs again approached sheer hypocrisy. However literally one might regard the menace of a preventive war, the deliberations of the French Assembly were in fact being conducted at the point of a German cannon. Instructions were sent to military headquarters at Compiègne for "the concentration of our troops in the direction of Paris." Not until passage of the Rivet Law was confirmed, on the last day of August, did Manteuffel order that these troop movements be suspended.[45]

To quantify the effect of German pressure is manifestly impossible. The margin of the Assembly's vote, 480 to 93, could suggest either that Thiers had actually been less in jeopardy than the Germans supposed or that their efforts were more than enough to sustain him. In any case, Berlin was openly gratified at the result, and both the Wilhelmstrasse and the German press joined in a round of self-congratulation. For his part, Thiers exulted to Pouyer-Quertier that "Bismarck, just as he wishes, will remain in the presence of the same persons whatever happens."[46] It appears that Thiers was coming to relish the role of a Gallic Faust to the Teutonic Mephisto.

From this time on, however, the German connection with the

Thierists gradually became clouded by the Arnim affair. Contrary to the conventional wisdom in Berlin, Arnim argued that the Rivet debate had not strengthened the president but only exposed his weakness and consolidated the opposition against him. Besides, the republican regime was not suited to offer Germany "the most guarantees"—a view, as we have seen, which Arnim doggedly maintained throughout the year 1872, despite Bismarck's repeated and explicit contradictions.[47] To weigh more precisely the importance of this dispute, it will be necessary to summarize briefly Arnim's critique of Thiers and then to evaluate the inroads he finally succeeded in making on Bismarck's French policy.

Thiers was old and vain. From these two indisputable facts, Arnim deduced that his presidency might be ended abruptly at any time by an act of nature or of politics. Thiers's outrageous tantrums in the Assembly, while still effective against a disunited opposition, had made him a "comic figure" and a favorite of every malicious caricaturist in Europe. Yet this impression of puerility, or senility, was belied by the serious danger which the Thierists posed for Germany; they were, Arnim charged, rebuilding a French army larger than that of their imperial predecessors and already scheming to create a Franco-Russian alliance. Even if Thiers's own professions of innocence and peaceful intent could be accepted as sincere, which was doubtful, his increasingly obvious dependence on the Gambettist radicals was bound, sooner or later, to place the levers of power in less responsible hands. Thierist France was becoming a nation in which "no one can know on Monday what will happen on Tuesday." By withdrawing support from the president and thereby destroying his aura of indispensability, Arnim concluded, Germany could prevent a "red revolution" in France and leave Thiers to choke on "his vanity, his restlessness, and his duplicity."[48]

Two elements in Arnim's version of French politics were particularly disturbing for Bismarck, since both were corroborated by other sources whom he trusted. The first was Thiers's energetic supervision of the military reorganization. True, this was a convenience as well as a bother to the chancellor: a few inflated tales of French preparations for revenge were always useful when the time came for a vote on military appropriations in the Reichstag.

Although there was no question of an imminent attack by the French, Bismarck pointed out to William that "the notion of a *short* time is always relative" and that Germany's only real security was an unassailable military supremacy.[49] A report prepared by the general staff and delivered by General von Roon to Bismarck in the spring of 1872 confirmed that the French infantry was only beginning to rebuild and that both cavalry and artillery were still in complete disarray; yet the planning appeared "singularly calculated for the near future." During the balance of 1872 a conflict was therefore unlikely, but in 1873 France would be better prepared for "a second German war" than at any period before or after. In view of such an estimate, which he had to regard as authoritative, Bismarck could scarcely discount altogether Arnim's innuendoes that France might choose to resist militarily rather than to meet the final payments of reparations.[50]

The other troublesome aspect of Arnim's analysis was the fragility of Thiers's physical and political health. On this subject, Bismarck gathered extensive information through Bleichröder's private contacts in Paris. According to these reports, Thiers had a disease characterized by a decomposition of the blood, "which can become dangerous very suddenly." Hence, one would have to be prepared for "a sudden storm to break unexpectedly."[51] The president's political condition was not much better. During a trip to Paris in July 1872, Bleichröder wrote a confidential note to Bismarck in which he could "only confirm that the general sentiment is entirely against Thiers." The Assembly had swallowed his financial policies, the increased tariffs and indirect taxes, with great distress; and if an attempted French revenge could be ruled out for the time being, Germany must expect to encounter "an extremely hostile situation *after* Thiers." Since we know that Bismarck attributed a high degree of reliability to Bleichröder's assessments of French affairs, it is indubitable that he thereafter regarded the succession to the French presidency with considerable foreboding.[52]

By the autumn of 1872, then, Bismarck had no more reason to rely on Thiers's endurance than did Arnim. Yet the two men were more at odds than ever. Arnim wished, while the occupation was still in effect, to induce a brief period of upset from which might emerge a more stable regime and "a new evolution" in

France. "Nothing," he wrote, "is more likely again to weaken and to set back France ten years as a repetition of the Paris insurrections on a larger scale and a change of regime that occurs under our eyes and, to an extent, under our supervision." Thus, Arnim wanted not only to allow a change but to promote it, not only to permit widespread civil disorder in France but to provoke it—all in the expectation that Thiers's replacement, whoever that might be, would preside over a government more enduring and more accommodating to Germany than the current one.[53]

From similar misgivings about Thiers, Bismarck drew diametrically opposite conclusions. In the midst of financial transactions that assured billions to the German treasury, he saw no short-term advantage in a deliberate intervention to upset Thiers. Nor, in a longer run, would it serve German interests to encourage French stability. If France were actually to slide into radicalism, as Arnim projected, that would only create more dissension within the republic and frighten the rest of Europe. Although the future of "such an explosive nation as the French" remained uncertain, Germany would not "make conspiratorial use" of the political factions in France that were vying for the succession to the presidency.[54]

The resolution of this debate finally hinged on the mixed feelings of the Kaiser. Arnim's fault, so far as William was concerned, was not that he was wrong but that he presumed to rival Bismarck. On the margin of Arnim's dispatch in early October, quoted above, William had recorded that he was not in agreement with the ambassador's conclusions. But a month later, when Arnim expanded on the disadvantages for Germany of perpetuating "the Thierist dictatorship" and painted a more lurid picture of "the wild radicalism" that might result, William was distinctly more approving: "There is much substance in these arguments."[55] It was above all to prevent any further erosion of his own political status as the Kaiser's chief adviser that Bismarck began so harshly to condemn Arnim's reports from Paris as "fundamentally false and dangerous." Squarely confronted with the charge that the policies advocated by Arnim were "in absolute contradiction" to Germany's national interest, William could no longer equivocate. He therefore notified Bismarck that, "even though certain dangers might be attached to the consolidation of the Thierist republic," the chancellor's direction of political affairs had his approval.[56]

Thereafter, the Arnim affair degenerated into a personal vendetta which, in itself, is of little concern here. What must be underscored is that, by pressing his case against Arnim, Bismarck was at the same time awarding Germany's full and vigorous support to Thiers. Without documenting this effort in detail, one can quickly enumerate some of the forms it took: strongly affirmative messages to Thiers through the Manteuffel-Saint-Vallier contact in Nancy; a rare personal visit by the chancellor to Gontaut-Biron in Berlin; another press campaign in Germany to offset the "erroneous and unclear" rumors about a possible modification of policy toward France;[57] changes, even against Arnim's expressed wishes, of the ambassador's staff in Paris; curtailment of funds previously used by Arnim to employ secret agents and to maintain contacts in the French press corps; and harsh attacks mounted against Arnim and his political predilections. As we saw, the appropriate culmination of these measures came in mid-March 1873, when the final settlement of the reparations question was preempted entirely by Bismarck in Berlin, and Arnim was ostentatiously excluded from the negotiations.

In his postmortem of the reparations treaty, Bismarck was lucid and blunt. "The main thing for us," he wrote to Manteuffel, "was the rapid procurement of payments so long as Thiers is healthy and France solvent."[58] Such a statement suggests that the Reich was being operated much like a large business enterprise primarily concerned with securing its profits and convinced that the future would somehow take care of itself so long as the company stayed out of the red. Basic to this calculation was the view that the Thierists represented Germany's best available clients in France and that a clear option must therefore be exercised in their favor for as long as possible.

The Gambettists

The formative decade of the Third Republic began and ended with Léon Gambetta. The flair and forensic skill of this extraordinary personality made him a powerful political factor in a nation that adores both. Far better than the titular leaders of the other major factions—an exiled monarch, a disgraced emperor, an autocratic president—Gambetta embodied those qualities which the French admire in themselves and in others. Were it not so, the historian might be harder pressed to explain the steady accumulation of electoral support by the Gambettists, the most striking phenomenon of French politics in the 1870s.

From the beginning of his career, Gambetta's name was encrusted with both mythic and real attributes of heroic resistance to the Teutonic conqueror. The progress of the Gambettist faction thus benefited not only from what its leader was, an adroit politician, but also from what he symbolized, an unvanquishable defiance of Germany. No man had a more useful political image than Gambetta, garnished as it was by his famous flight from Paris in a balloon and by his intrepid military command in the months thereafter. This is the stuff of which genuine folk heroes are formed.[59]

If Gambetta's reputation was made by military resistance, however, it was paradoxically enhanced by his political neutrality during the Paris Commune. The excesses committed by both sides in the civil war left him untarnished. Because of the unconscionable brutality of the Versailles army, Thiers was irrevocably damned in the eyes of many republicans; whereas the communards were both condemned as extremists and mercilessly pursued by the government. Gambetta's opposition to the armistice with Germany and to the election of a royalist Assembly had meanwhile enabled him to withdraw with honor, leaving the first internecine conflicts of the republic to his political competitors. Since he did not reappear until after the establishment of the Thierist regime and the signing of the Frankfurt treaty, his election to the Assembly in July 1871 could easily be interpreted as a protest against both. Despite disclaimers that he intended to conduct himself in a spirit of loyal opposition, Gambetta was generally assumed to be, as Waldersee described him to Bismarck, a man driven by a "thirst for revenge."[60]

Yet Gambetta soon proved to be more astute and less irascible than supposed. After all, he faced both an Assembly heavily stacked against him and a regime which could surely count on the army and the police in any test of force. Initially the leftists were disunited in the parliament and disorganized in the provinces. Public indifference to further political change was a fact of life repeatedly confirmed by police investigations as well as electoral returns.[61] In the July by-elections, for example, the Gambettists were victorious in 22 of 121 contests, an encouraging omen perhaps but certainly no mandate for revenge or revolution. From his private correspondence we know that Gambetta possessed a clear sense of his limitations. He was constantly besieged with petitions from individuals and groups who urged him to lead a radical crusade for one cause or another, to rectify some personal or social injustice, to restore French grandeur or territory. A less political man might have responded impetuously. But Gambetta prepared instead for the long march.[62]

Whatever his tactics, Gambetta was obviously to be reckoned with sooner or later. For the Germans, therefore, the issue at first was not whether Gambetta constituted a danger to the Thierist regime but whether the radical threat in France was present or future. Since he was eager to sustain Thiers, Manteuffel tended to be an alarmist in his reports and advised Berlin that a renewed civil war in France would inevitably follow a Gambettist coup. In this emotion he was encouraged by Saint-Vallier, who, in turn, warned his own government of the loss in German confidence that would result from any sign of radical agitation.[63] Although he was unwilling to disavow Gambetta publicly, and thereby to forfeit some indispensable leftist support in the Assembly for his financial program, Thiers did denounce in private correspondence the "charlatans of patriotism" who were whetting the French appetite for revenge. This message, like many sent to Saint-Vallier, was addressed to Nancy but deliberately intended for Berlin. It was common practice, in fact, for Thiers to dictate long passages or entire letters carefully phrased for direct quotation by Manteuffel to Bismarck; and it was precisely in this manner that Thiers's electoral slogan of the "conservative republic" was often employed to reassure the Germans that Gambetta would be held in check.[64]

German agents concluded as early as July 1871, and subsequently reconfirmed, that Thiers and Gambetta had reached a politician's agreement: leftist cooperation with the government on the Assembly floor in return for relative freedom to campaign in the provinces. Various reports arrived in Berlin that Gambetta was receiving 200,000 francs a month from Thiers; that Gambetta was personally directing the radical leagues agitating for the recovery of Alsace and Lorraine; that he had been assured of support by the French freemasons; that he was actually dictating Thiers's foreign and financial policy; that he controlled the Prefecture of Police; and that among his potential collaborators were "the revolutionaries of the entire world," including "the chiefs of the International."[65] Little wonder that the Germans scanned Gambettist electoral gains with some attention. After a visit to Bad Ems in the summer of 1872, Manteuffel's adjutant, General von Tresckow, communicated the sense of concern among German military authorities to Saint-Vallier. The latter then placed the most drastic interpretation on this disclosure by telling Thiers flatly that if Gambetta seized power "the German army would intervene immediately under the pretext of obtaining securities and guaranties."[66]

Yet, at least until the autumn of 1872, Gambetta's public conduct afforded scant justification for such apprehension. True, he did launch frequent oratorical sorties into the provinces. But unlike those of popular tribunes of an earlier generation, his performances were openly supportive of the existing regime, and his rhetoric was anything but seditious. As the self-acknowledged "traveling salesman" of democracy, he regularly delivered a message that was neither intended nor construed as a threat to the stability of the republic. His performances were closely followed by German agents, who, while continuing to posit a revanchist motivation, credited him at least with toning down his former *politique de fou furieux*. If the popular drift toward republicanism persisted, they reasoned, Gambetta could well afford to bide his time until "the ripened fruit falls into his lap."[67]

So long as he continued to exercise restraint, then, Gambetta was an asset to the Thierist regime and consequently an acceptable risk for the Germans. But his reviving popularity inevitably served another function: that of providing French conservatives with the common enemy they needed to rally their divided ranks. One moment of bravado was enough. During a successful tour of the southeast in September 1872, Gambetta found that his confidence and elation were more than he could contain. Speaking in Grenoble, he celebrated the political advent of "a new generation" and predicted the imminent triumph of a "nouvelle couche sociale." Beyond that, he chided the French bourgeoisie for a failure to accept the reality that "the monarchy is finished."[68] The outraged response of French royalists took the form of renewed demands that Thiers disavow Gambetta and reconfirm the pact of Bordeaux. These coincided with Arnim's initial attempts to discredit Thiers with the argument that the president was "forging weapons against us—weapons that in all probability Gambetta will make use of unless we first intervene." The extent of the damage caused by the Grenoble speech was immediately assessed by Manteuffel, who hurried as usual to Saint-Vallier with reports of the "deplorable impression" in Berlin and an admonition that Thiers must react to dampen Gambetta's ardor. Although conclusive documentary evidence is lacking, it seems plausible that Gambetta's sudden decision to break off his trip was a response to a request from Thiers.[69]

Gambetta's behavior was better understood by no one than Thiers himself. Although he was angered by the increasingly strident tone of the radicals ("ils viennent de jeter le masque"), the president could cooly dissect Gambetta's fundamental dilemma. He needed to appear sufficiently radical to attract his leftist clientele and yet to act with enough moderation to present himself as a credible political alternative to the current government: hence the unduly impassioned oratory, which Thiers privately insisted was harmless.[70] Yet the pressure exercised both through the German embassy and by conservative factions of the Assembly—pressure to distance himself publicly from the radicals—was more than Thiers could indefinitely resist. In a parliamentary commission, so a German diplomatic agent reported, he was "very categorical" in denouncing the Grenoble speech as "bad, very bad." Nor was this to be simply a matter of combatting one phrase with another. Five military officers who had attended the Grenoble banquet were sentenced to two months' arrest and removed from their regiments.[71] According to Saint-Vallier, these actions succeeded in clearing the air and mollifying the Germans, although Gambetta still remained "le point noir." Predictably, a verbatim text of Thiers's personal assurances to Saint-Vallier that he had the situation in hand was soon filed in the Wilhelmstrasse. In effect, the Germans were being asked by Thiers to believe that Gambetta, until he himself adopted the conservative republic, had "no chance" of succeeding to the presidency. "Never," Thiers added for good measure, "has order been more complete in France than it is today."[72]

But the by-elections of late October 1872 delivered their own verdict. In six of seven departments the monarchist candidates were trounced; and though the government claimed the republican gains as support for the status quo, Berlin was more accurately informed by German agents in France that the victory was in reality Gambetta's. Thiers admitted as much in a letter to General Le Flô, archly referring to universal suffrage as "that great and serious difficulty for which time will perhaps furnish us a remedy." It was already apparent what specific measures Thiers had in mind: an electoral reform (replacing the *scrutin de liste* with a *scrutin d'arrondissement*) and the formation of a Senate to offset potential radicalization in the Chamber of Deputies. These were intended to check Gambetta, to placate the French conservatives, and to mitigate criticism from Germany. We know that none of the three objectives was finally to be realized. For his part, as Wesdehlen reported to Berlin, Gambetta was disinclined to offer much resistance to procedural changes, since "he knows that the future is his." Nor was the promise of such reforms adequate to dissuade Thiers's royalist opponents from conspiring to turn him out. Led by the Duc de Broglie, a conservative cabal began to form as soon as the Assembly reconvened in early November.[73]

The German response to these complications, once again, cannot be entirely explained apart from the Arnim affair. The ambassador's charges against Thiers reached their most abrasive and denunciatory point during the month of November. In support of his assertion that France was "marching to radicalism, to revolution, to the Commune," Arnim claimed to have reliable information that Thiers had struck a bargain with the Gambettists. He even disclosed the identity of the secret liaison between Thiers and Gambetta, a journalist named Genesco, and insisted that the interruption of Gambetta's propaganda tour had been arranged through that channel. Arnim also claimed that Thiers's vulnerability to a united conservative opposition had prompted Gambetta, "the future president of the republic," to organize a shadow cabinet in preparation for a seizure of power at the first opportunity. Gambetta had thereby placed himself in a position either to gain control of the government in all but title or actually to force Thiers's abdication in his favor. By the end of the month, when the president survived a vote of confidence in the Assembly by only thirty-nine votes, Arnim felt justified in writing Thiers off altogether: "From now on his policy will be essentially determined by the radical Left." In that case, he concluded, a serious crisis would soon ensue.[74]

The repercussions in Berlin were predictable. At Manteuffel's urgent request, Bismarck reiterated in the most categorical terms his exclusive preference for the Thierist republic: "We would deplore the triumph of whatever party, monarchist or otherwise." He instructed Manteuffel to persist in cooperating with Thiers, assuring him not only that this policy was his own but that "it is sanctioned by His Majesty the Kaiser." In actuality, William's susceptibility to Arnim's line of argument was the primary reason for Bismarck's hesitation to dismiss the ambassador at once. By his failure to be more decisive when there could no longer be the slightest doubt of Arnim's insubordination, the chancellor was by default allowing the notion to circulate freely in German military circles that Thiers had become, as Arnim castigated him, "the protégé of wild radicalism."[75] This course had two perceptible results: in Germany Bismarck was confronted with the most dangerous internal challenge to his authority since the altercation with Moltke during the war of 1870; and in France direct German influence on the political development was temporarily divided and diffused.

The contest between Bismarck and Arnim thus continued through the winter. Despite pointed reprimands from the chancellor, Arnim's reports were hardly less ominous than before. To be sure, the predicted crisis did not occur as soon as he projected, but he remained convinced that Thiers was being hopelessly squeezed between monarchists and Gambettists. For the most part, Bismarck remained on the defensive, spending an inordinate amount of time marking Arnim's dispatches with question marks and queries, denying the rumor spread by Arnim of "direct relations between Gambetta and the Berlin government," and displaying to French diplomats his unflagging sympathies for the conservative republic. If he were not a religious man, the chancellor facetiously told Gontaut-Biron, he would gladly watch the Gambettists come to power, since the resulting anarchy would be a salutary lesson for Europe. "But I am a Christian, and I ardently desire that order reign in France."[76]

If Bismarck could have had his way, presumably, Thiers would have retained the French presidency in perpetuity. But there were corrosive political forces at work that no man could control. Neither the plotting of monarchists and Bonapartists nor the agitation of Gambettists would be forever stayed by the glowering disapproval of a German chancellor, however firm his military and economic grip on the French nation. By the beginning of 1873, therefore, the Thierist republic was in deep trouble.

MacMahon

The possibility that Thiers might be succeeded to the presidency by Marshal MacMahon had been a matter of speculation since the days of the Paris Commune. As a career officer and colonial administrator, MacMahon had served every French regime from the July monarchy to the Third Republic with technical competence and political equanimity. Since his wounds at Sedan had left him *hors de combat*, he escaped any major liability for the debacle and yet recovered soon enough to assume command of the army of Versailles. His appointment to that post by Thiers was dictated by MacMahon's rank, availability, and relatively faultless record; it was not the result of a long or close relationship between the two men. Nor did their partnership prove to be harmonious. During the final siege, Thiers's overbearing pretentions to Napoleonic competence in military affairs provoked a sharp altercation between them at MacMahon's headquarters on Mont Valérien. Rumors of this quarrel quickly spread; and as the dissatisfaction of conservative leaders with Thiers mounted, political overtures to the marshal were soon forthcoming. Nothing came of this rift at the time, however, both because the feelers were expressly rebuffed by MacMahon himself and because among conservatives some doubts persisted about his aptitude for public office. The resulting impasse was, as Count Waldersee observed, "a certain guarantee for the Thierist regime."[77]

From these circumstances emerged a convenient division of labor: MacMahon was thereafter acknowledged as the first soldier of the republic, while Thiers remained the preeminent politician. Hence it was appropriate as well as symbolic when the marshal led the famous military review at Longchamps in June 1871 and received at its conclusion the president's embrace. At that moment the two men were, or wished to appear, partners rather than rivals. For more than a year thereafter, MacMahon's name all but disappeared from the list of political contenders. The person most frequently touted by German agents as the presidential successor was the Duc d'Aumale, since both Chambord and Napoleon III were considered disqualified. The president of the Assembly, Jules Grévy, was also regarded as a potential replacement for Thiers, but only as a transitional figure who would later bow out in Gambetta's favor. Otherwise there were only a few military men, whose political attributes were either unknown or undesirable, career officers such as Changarnier, Ladmirault, Chanzy, and Faideherbe. But these could not hope to rival MacMahon's prestige within the army, nor were they as acceptable to all conservative factions in the Assembly. Still, so long as the marshal ruled himself out and Thiers remained unshaken, a political draft was unlikely to develop. Before the autumn of 1872, therefore, nothing more substantial had materialized than vagrant rumors and sighs of regret.[78]

The machinery of succession was not set in motion until the opening session of the Assembly in November 1872, when Thiers bluntly announced that "the republic exists."[79] Such a pronunciamento was scarcely a surprise in itself, since Thiers's tricolors had been showing for some time. But his open display of arrogance stiffened the resolve of those who were planning to unload the president anyway, and it provided them with a quotable excuse to do so. If Thiers proposed to bar the door to monarchy—thereby rescinding his earlier pledge at Bordeaux—then someone had to be found to hold it ajar. And MacMahon, willing or not, was an obviously desirable candidate for the conservative factions who could agree on little else. Among those to make this elementary calculation was Harry von Arnim. The German ambassador foresaw that Thiers would once again threaten his resignation, as he had on several previous occasions, with the difference that the Assembly would this time be likely to accept it. If so, the probable outcome was a military triumvirate of MacMahon, Changarnier, and Ladmirault that would provide a convenient front for the eventuality of "MacMahon's dictatorship." Before the end of November, Arnim judged that a showdown between Thiers and the conservative majority was unavoidable, and he felt certain enough of the political drift to inform Berlin that "the election of MacMahon as Thiers's successor seems assured." Such were the prognostications that prompted Bismarck's redoubled efforts to dramatize Germany's backing for the Thierist republic.[80]

The current was actually flowing less swiftly than Arnim supposed. Instead of forcing an immediate confrontation, Thiers's opponents voted to establish a special parliamentary committee to make a formal investigation into the exercise of "public power." While this Commission of Thirty deliberated on the formal issues—the delimitation of presidential prerogatives, the drafting of electoral reform, and the creation of a Senate—Thiers was allowed to continue negotiations for the final evacuation of German troops. Above all else, this delicate bargaining with Germany explains the willingness of conservative leaders to temporize. The Paris Bourse was meanwhile left to fluctuate daily according to the latest conjectures about the possibility of a durable compromise between Thiers and the Thirty.[81]

Two episodes served to keep MacMahon's unannounced candidacy alive. One was the brief revival and then apparently total collapse of the fusionist campaign. In this instance the prime mover was the energetic bishop of Orléans, who attempted for one last time to deal directly with the Comte de Chambord. Dupanloup's initiative was quickly reinterred, however, after the publication of a letter from Chambord in February 1873, which retracted nothing from the principles stated in his disastrous manifesto two years earlier. Still left with two flags, fusionism remained without a standard-bearer.[82] The other event to affect the marshal's chances in early 1873 was the unanticipated death of Napoleon III. Released suddenly from their first allegiance, many Bonapartists were thereafter free to turn to the most attractive alternative. Perhaps unwittingly, MacMahon encouraged them to do so by attending a solemn mass for the deceased emperor at Sainte Clotilde in Paris. Naturally, his activity was closely watched by police agents and, of course, reported in the Bonapartist press with a tone of hushed reverence. The political implications could escape no one.[83]

The major difficulty seemed to be the marshal himself. Nearly all the evidence available in the public record suggests that MacMahon was void of political ambition, that he considered himself unfit for the presidency, and that he never consciously sought the office. As far as it goes, this version is essentially correct, and it has been duly canonized by authoritative historians. Yet it should not be overlooked that MacMahon was above all a military officer and that he had certain technical reasons for wishing to see Thiers dismissed. Since the summer of 1872 he had sat across from the president at closed sessions of the Conseil Supérieur de la Guerre and had doggedly opposed him on such central issues of military reform as mobilization procedures, the regional reserve system, and the structure of command. By January 1873 a deadlock had developed in military planning, which Thiers decided to break by taking his case directly to the Assembly, falsely claiming that he had already obtained unanimity in the CSG. Of MacMahon's resulting hostility toward Thiers the documents leave no doubt; and this feeling offers the most plausible explanation of his eventual willingness to become the instrument of those conservative leaders whose motivations were more strictly political.[84]

Thiers's final undoing was the widely publicized by-election in Paris between Charles de Rémusat and the mayor of Lyon, Désiré Barodet. Both were reluctant candidates, pressed to serve as stand-ins, respectively, for Thiers and Gambetta. Privately Rémusat expressed "a deep personal repugnance and grave doubts" about the assignment "imposed as a duty" by the president. Everyone knew that Thiers was hanging by his political teeth after embarrassing restrictions were placed on his parliamentary activity by a law passed in the Assembly in mid-March. Although the president was able to offset somewhat the impression of this rebuff by announcing the evacuation treaty with Germany, he needed to maintain some political initiative. Thiers therefore urged his foreign minister to plunge into the electoral venture, as Rémusat privately confessed, with "an exaggerated confidence in its success." The truth was that the conclusion of negotiations with Germany had made Thiers more rather than less vulnerable, because his foes no longer needed to procrastinate.[85]

Barodet had misgivings of a different sort. In the first place, he did not consider himself the appropriate person to represent the radical cause in the nation's capital; and he offered to step aside if the veteran leftist Alexandre Ledru-Rollin wished to run instead. Beyond that, he insisted that his candidacy must be regarded strictly as a protest against the conservative majority in the Assembly and *not* against the Thierist government, for whom it should constitute only a *"respectful warning."* But Gambetta was less fastidious and far more ambitious: he was eager to prove that Paris was still a radical stronghold and that no one could effectively rule there without his consent. Once Ledru-Rollin declined, Barodet acceded to Gambetta's wishes: "I am able to consign myself entirely to your excellent suggestions."[86]

The most generous interpretation of Gambetta's part in this affair would be that he was guilty of a severe miscalculation. Once Barodet was publicly endorsed by the Gambettists, his campaign against Rémusat was bound to become a direct challenge to Thiers, one which the president could no longer avoid. During a reception at the Elysée palace, on the eve of the balloting, Thiers made a brave show of confidence: "I have the country behind me, but the Assembly before me." The electoral count demonstrated otherwise. Barodet defeated Rémusat by forty-five thousand votes and far outdistanced a rightist candidate, the former military attaché in Berlin, Colonel Stoffel. In the shorthand of parliamentary factions, this meant that the Left had humiliated the Left Center and, by doing so, had validated the Right's accusation that the Thierist regime was impotent to contain radicalism. Thereafter, the question was not whether but to whom the presidency would revolve.[87]

Enough has been said to verify two conclusions: that the selection of Marshal MacMahon as the republic's second chief of state was not entirely impromptu; and that the course of events leading to that selection was primarily determined by French internal affairs and only tangentially influenced by Germany. Granted, the general context was such that no rational political decision could be reached without first calculating the German response. But in the face of republican electoral gains in both Paris and the provinces, rationality counted for less with the conservatives than survival. However reluctant MacMahon may have been, the Duc de Broglie and his colleagues turned to the marshal as their champion with a growing sense of desperation.

Even some of Thiers's erstwhile supporters shared the same urgency. The former minister of finance, Ernst Picard, warned that "the social question" had been resuscitated by Barodet's sweep, arousing the spirit of the Commune in the working quarters of Paris. Meanwhile, the director of the Banque de France stressed that the chronic political instability was also constricting France's economic recovery: capitalists were reluctant to invest and the Paris Bourse was unsettled by the evidence that "the conservative republic as well as the monarchy has been rejected by the revolutionary republic." Minister of the Interior Goulard also confided his personal apprehensions to Arnim, saying that neither the Thierist regime nor the Assembly was any longer capable of preventing "the gradual slide into a Gambettist or an even redder republic"; only the army remained reliable, and MacMahon was therefore the last resort.[88]

To Arnim's obvious hint that Germany should now indicate support for a military triumvirate, even if it were only a temporary expedient prior to a restoration, Bismarck retorted that it was "not *our* task to prevent the internal disintegration of France." Upon receiving Arnim's prediction that, if unchecked, the spread of radicalism in France would soon infest Germany and the rest of Europe, Bismarck scrawled in his bold hand: "To the contrary." The chancellor was unmoved despite Manteuffel's confirmation that a political crisis was imminent. In reality there was little more that Bismarck could have done. All his efforts to fortify Thiers and to intimidate his opponents had been insufficient to offset the gyroscopic momentum of French politics.[89]

As the climax approached, German influence suffered from two important limitations. One was the advanced stage of military disengagement from France: too much time had elapsed, too many troops were already withdrawn, too many indemnities had been allocated or expended for the threat of renewed hostilities to be entirely credible. Frenchmen no longer seriously disputed the terms which Thiers had accepted in 1871 and had negotiated since then. It remained only for the French nation to honor them; and for that purpose MacMahon, the most honorable of men, would do quite as well as Thiers. The other disability was the unresolved conflict within the German leadership. The four men whose opinion counted most lacked any consensus. Manteuffel was hostile to Arnim and resolutely loyal to Thiers. Arnim took the Paris by-election as proof that Thiers was finished, that his own diagnosis was vindicated, and that Germany's best prospect was to accept MacMachon as the surrogate for an Orleanist pretender. If less sanguine than Manteuffel about Thiers, Bismarck was determined to overrule Arnim by preserving the French president as long as feasible, presumably until after the completion of the reparations payments. William was personally loyal to his chancellor but listed politically toward Arnim: "To strengthen France may not be *our* task," the Kaiser wrote, "but neither can consolidation of the republic or encouragement of anarchy be *our* task."[90] These views tended to cancel one another. Consequently, for the first time since Sedan, the German grasp on France was noticeably weakened; and this fact must be counted among the explanations of MacMahon's quick succession to the presidency.

The immediate circumstances of Thiers's defeat and enforced resignation on 24 May do not require a detailed recounting. During the early part of the month William and Bismarck had been on a state visit in St. Petersburg, permitting the European press to draw an obvious contrast between the solidarity of the three continental empires and the isolation of republican France. Their absence left Arnim more than usual to his own devices, the precise nature of which has never been altogether clarified. His contacts in the political underworld in Paris were too extensive for him to have been totally unaware of what was happening. Yet his reports failed to convey any note of alarm. Even a few hours before the Assembly's vote of no confidence, he still professed to believe that Thiers would survive. When discreet inquiries from Broglie's headquarters were made of him concerning the possibility of a MacMahon-Aumale combination as an alternative, he recited the official litany of German support for Thiers; but he also indicated that Aumale's name might "at first" cause certain reservations in Berlin. In retrospect, only one interpretation of this remark is admissible: the ambassador was obliquely suggesting that Germany would have no initial objection to MacMahon as president and, moreover, that his government might even be willing thereafter to accept an Orleanist pretender. If the charge of Arnim's outright collusion with French monarchists cannot be conclusively documented, he was nevertheless demonstrably lax in conveying Bismarck's wishes to those who conspired against Thiers.[91]

In more than one regard, the events of 24 May marked an important rupture in the political history of the Third Republic. Had he been left to preside over the nation, Thiers would undoubtedly have impressed his personal stamp on every aspect of public life. With his compulsive manner and his astonishing energy, the first president was accustomed to modifying the fine print of every legislative act and dealing with the most remote details of administration. He seldom left letters unanswered, police reports and diplomatic dispatches unattended, or ministers in doubt about his intentions. In all this activity he was incomparably more dynamic than his successor. MacMahon's habitual lethargy in such matters was already legendary; and it is fair to say that many of the marshal's supporters welcomed a change for precisely that reason. Some historians have in fact concluded that the weakness of the French presidency might be attributed to MacMahon's performance in that office.[92] Yet the preceding analysis should demonstrate the dubiousness of framing the political development of France after 1870 in terms of a "presidential synthesis." From the outset Thiers's position rested on a temporary nexus of military defeat, foreign occupation, economic disruption, financial stringency, political impasse, and public apprehension. The overriding fact was not the dynamism of the president but the paralysis of the nation. After all, it was the conservative majority in the French Assembly which tolerated Thiers, not vice versa. Long before his actual resignation, Thiers was driven onto the defensive, his presidential powers legally and politically curtailed by forces over which he had no effective control. In a longer perspective, one is more struck by continuity than change in 1873. The party structure and the political possibilities remained much as before. The same contenders were left in place, each still dislocated and frustrated in a public process which as yet lacked firm contours.

Chapter 4

The Constitutional Compromise

The Limitations of Diplomacy

Although the precariousness of Thiers's presidency was everywhere taken for granted, the news of his sudden fall caught the German government by surprise. Less than twenty-four hours before the Assembly's vote of no confidence, Harry von Arnim had insouciantly reported from Paris that the Thiers regime was likely to retain a majority of forty votes. That the German ambassador remained in the capital, without even bothering to follow the debates in Versailles, was in itself indicative. Whether Arnim was simply misinformed or—as Bismarck later charged—guilty of dereliction, we cannot be certain. He failed, in any case, to alert Berlin to the possibility of an imminent crisis until the early morning hours of 24 May; and even then he was unable to confirm rumors of Thiers's impending resignation. Not until that afternoon did he wire that "in all probability Marshal MacMahon will take over the regime." Arnim's message that France had a new president, with the Duc de Broglie as his premier, was first received in Berlin at dawn of the next day, hours after press releases had been issued directly from Versailles.[1]

The earliest reaction came from the Kaiser. In a brief handwritten note William asked Bismarck to instruct Arnim to remain at his post, "since the bomb has exploded in Versailles." This message was relayed to the Paris embassy at once, but in an edited version that omitted any mention of an explosion and alluded only to "transpired events." Nor did Bismarck mention to Arnim William's personal observation that "MacMahon's appointment is at least reassuring." The chancellor had other ideas; and his orders were simply for Arnim to withhold any comment to the French pending further instructions from Berlin.[2]

A fortnight of elaborate diplomatic maneuvering ensued that involved all the major courts of Europe. A common view of this affair, which the editors of the *Grosse Politik* did nothing to dispel, has been that Bismarck emerged from the negotiations with a united front among the eastern European powers and an agreement, in keeping with the nascent spirit of the Three Emperors' League, that set a common policy toward France.[3] A full review of the documentation, however, reveals that the basis for such a policy was not in fact achieved. Instead, the chancellor suffered a quiet but nonetheless damaging setback. When properly understood, this episode not only provides an important clue to Bismarck's formal diplomacy in the 1870s; it also helps to gauge the diminishing extent of Germany's direct influence on France's internal development during the MacMahon presidency.

Two hypotheses were possible: either that the French republic was analogous to the American, thus allowing the presidential succession to be regarded strictly as a matter of France's domestic politics; or that the French regime should be considered a provisional creation of international treaty, thereby requiring any change in the presidency to be approved by the other European states. In the first case the new government of France would need only to notify the other powers of its existence. But in the second the French executive would have to seek a new exchange of ambassadorial credentials or, in other words, request formal diplomatic recognition. When distilled to its essence, the question was this: notification or accreditation?

Much to Bismarck's irritation, the English ostentatiously supported the former option. The suggestion of Britain's ambassador in Paris, Lord Lyons, that an exchange of letters among the European embassies would suffice, was rejected by the chancellor as "absolutely inadmissible." Rather, Bismarck set in motion his own campaign to gain support for the alternative policy, fully recognizing that he needed "above all complete cooperation with Russia, if possible also with Austria." Although he explicitly claimed that his actions were taken "without intention of influencing France's internal affairs," the implications were too patent to ignore. If Bismarck's view prevailed, after all, Germany would in effect maintain a veto over any future candidate to the French presidency.[4]

The linchpin was in St. Petersburg. If the tsar and his foreign minister Gorchakov could be persuaded to collaborate, it was unlikely that the Austrians would risk being out of step. Bismarck was therefore distressed to learn that the Russian ambassador to France, his old friend Count Orlov, was urging his superiors to concur with London. To counter this advice, the chancellor advanced the argument—which he conveniently ascribed to Kaiser William—that failure of the eastern powers to assert their diplomatic prerogatives would be tantamount of de facto recognition of the French republic. And this, in turn, implied "a general recognition of the principle of popular sovereignty," something that could scarcely be considered compatible with the interests of the European monarchies. A more frank appeal to reactionary instincts would have been difficult to conceive.[5]

At best Bismarck's efforts met, even initially, with only a qualified success. He was informed from the Russian capital that Gortschakov was "united with us on the question of principle"; but he soon learned that Orlov's instructions were merely to delay until formal "notification" of MacMahon's election had been verified. He was further disturbed by word that Vienna was doing likewise: temporarily suspending diplomatic contacts but not insisting on new credentials. On 28 May the chancellor consequently took his first steps in retreat by writing to Arnim: "I place more value on an identical posture of the three powers than on the question of accreditation."[6]

The French meanwhile proceeded with the process of notification. First, Broglie advised both Arnim and the Bavarian envoy in Paris, Rudhart, of MacMahon's accession and of his own designation to the Quai d'Orsay. Then he sent a long dispatch to Gontaut-Biron, asking him to convey the intentions of the new French government to pursue "a policy resolutely conservative, that is, pacific abroad and moderate at home." The French ambassador in Berlin thereupon dictated a letter to Bismarck which, so far as Versailles was concerned, served to restore full diplomatic contacts. MacMahon had also drafted letters to the various monarchs, but these were clearly regarded as a courtesy, in the sense of notification, rather than as a request for new diplomatic accreditation.[7]

Bismarck was not yet prepared to capitulate. If Gorchakov and MacMahon continued to disregard the question of credentials, he conceded, Germany would not persist. But the rulers of both France and Russia must then acknowledge a logical corollary that would, presumably, thereafter guide German policy: to dismiss the question of accreditation was "synonymous with mutual recognition of the republic as definitive, without regard to its current leadership." Bismarck's thrust was not unduly subtle, and the French ambassador immediately felt the point of it. The chancellor was serving notice that he would henceforth consider a monarchist restoration in France to be precluded. This was, to be sure, not precisely what MacMahon and Broglie had in mind. Obviously somewhat embarrassed, Gontaut-Biron all but promised that his government would do as Bismarck wished provided there were no delay in the resumption of official relations.[8]

By the beginning of June, then, Bismarck seemed to have regained the initiative. The French were beginning to buckle under his pressure, and both St. Petersburg and Vienna—so he claimed in a memorandum to Manteuffel—were prepared to join Berlin in requiring accreditation. At the same time, Bismarck made no secret of his dissatisfaction with MacMahon's effortless displacement of Thiers: "Without doubt our political situation has been worsened by the change." Although this statement may be taken at face value, it was also another volley in the chancellor's relentless campaign to disgrace Arnim, whom he held responsible for the entire affair and against whom he secretly began to gather incriminating evidence.[9]

Bismarck's confidence proved to be a mixture of bluff and wishful thinking. Arnim telegraphed from Paris that Orlov had received instructions to resume diplomatic contacts with the new French regime at once; if Germany failed to act accordingly, the united front would be broken. Bismarck responded that Orlov's orders were doubtless a result of the agreement between St. Petersburg and Berlin and that Arnim should continue to temporize, since nothing altered the fact "that we and Russia are doing the same thing, even though not simultaneously." The reality was that Germany was now left isolated. The English, Russian, Austrian, and Ottoman ambassadors had already made formal visits to Mac-Mahon, Arnim reported, and German reluctance was bound to be interpreted as a gesture of malevolence. The marshal had, in fact, already urged Orlov to persuade Arnim to seek an audience in Versailles. Although neither a presentation of diplomatic credentials nor an exchange of letters between MacMahon and William had been completed by 3 June, Bismarck finally relented by instructing Arnim to pay MacMahon the requested visit. It was another retreat.[10]

All these events occurred noiselessly. They apparently involved nothing more than the rustling of some diplomatic dispatches over a matter of principle, since there was at no time any question of annulling MacMahon's election to the French presidency. Yet the significance of the outcome should not be underestimated. In more than one regard the presidential crisis of May 1873 set the tone of Franco-German relations for years to come. Played out on the eve of the final German evacuation of French territory, it betrayed a limitation of Bismarck's brusque and often brutal domination of French statesmen. By no means did this affair automatically terminate Germany's direct influence in French internal affairs; but it revealed the relative ineffectuality of traditional diplomatic weapons to enforce German hegemony. Most importantly, it demonstrated that the Three Emperors' League would be something less than a carte blanche for Bismarck's imperious designs in the west. If the French republic was not yet *bündnisfähig* in the eyes of the other powers, neither was it to be left in the abjectly helpless condition of the previous three years.

These changes did not go entirely unnoticed at the time. Appropriately enough, the first to signal the collapse of Bismarck's diplomatic initiative was the Bavarian emissary to Austria, Count von Bray-Steinburg. Completely throttled by Bismarck during the negotiations leading to the treaty of Frankfurt in May 1871, Bray had resigned as Bavarian premier and retired into virtual exile in Vienna. Now he was able to report from there, not without a certain delight, of Bismarck's reversal. Like everyone else, he had at first supposed that the three eastern monarchies would act in accord. "But this assumption has proved to be erroneous." Arriving in Vienna in the midst of the crisis, Gorchakov had surprised the Austrians by agreeing with the view that "the certification of ambassadors and ministers takes place with the *French republic* and not with the current president." It was consequently expected of the Berlin cabinet, Bray wrote on 4 June, "that it will comply with the conception of the other two regimes. To make this easier, it is suggested here that no new credentials be prepared, but that the old ones should be confirmed." The cooperation of Russia and Austria as well as the disruption of the Berlin-Petersburg axis, he concluded, must be regarded as "something new and unusual in the politics of recent times."[11]

This version of the story was unquestionably overwrought. We are not confronted here with one of the great diplomatic revolutions of modern history; and the results, after all, were largely negative: the curtailment of Bismarck's arbitrary control over French affairs and the apparent disharmony of Germany with the other powers in regard to the Third Republic. Two decades would pass before these became of fundamental significance for the realignment of the European pentarchy. In a shorter run, moreover, the positive importance of MacMahon's succession and the ensuing diplomatic standoff was strictly psychological. After May of 1873 the French had a keen sense—which was not entirely justified, let it be added—of being once again masters in their own house. Broglie expressed that feeling well in summing up the preceding weeks. From the outset, he observed, French leaders had not considered that the presidential substitution implied the necessity for new diplomatic accreditation. True, they had found it opportune to modify their stance to accommodate "certain powers" who so desired. Yet "our opinion has basically not changed."[12] So far as one can judge, this evaluation was accurate; and it had a ring more of independence than of defiance. The German grip on France was far from broken in 1873. But it was perceptibly relaxed.

The Presidential Septennate

More than one general explanation has been offered for Germany's exigent treatment of France during the formative years of the Third Republic. The most traditional is biographic, an approach which acknowledges the virtuosity of Bismarck's foreign policy and stresses the complexity of his personal relationships with William, Moltke, and other members of the imperial coterie.[13] The chancellor, in this version, was a man driven to maintain German hegemony in Europe and to guard his own preeminence as William's adviser. He therefore sought at the same time to isolate France and to eliminate his most dangerous rival, Harry von Arnim. Both of these objectives dictated his initial hostility toward the new regime of Marshal MacMahon. Far from agreeing that MacMahon's election was reassuring, Bismarck regarded the marshal as the front for a "philojesuitic" conspiracy with monarchist inclinations and revanchist ambitions. France would henceforth be stronger, more militaristic, and increasingly desirable to others as an eventual partner in some anti-German coalition—an undigested morsel certain to arouse Bismarck's *cauchemar des alliances*. That Arnim failed to counteract this threat and neglected to lend firm support to Thiers had disqualified the ambassador as a competent agent of Germany's imperial policy. For these reasons, in Bismarck's estimation, Arnim had to be publicly exposed as an insubordinate in order that the Kaiser and the German public be brought to a keener appreciation of political reality.[14]

A second interpretation underscores the primacy of Germany's internal affairs. By 1873 it was already apparent that the national unification was in some respects misbegotten. An autocratic ruling clique found both its economy and its polity in difficulty: the integument of postwar financial speculation was already bursting and the Kulturkampf was beginning to deepen the inherent faults of an imperfect federalist constitution. What the Prussian crown had imposed by arms, within and abroad, would now need to be defended by overwhelming military prowess. Domestic tranquility, as well as European security, thus depended on the unassailable position of Germany's imperial dynasty. In this perspective Bismarck's foreign policy can be seen, above all, as a calculated response to internal tensions. Heavy military expenditures in a time of economic dislocation needed to be justified, and religious persecution had to be made plausible. For such purposes the specter of French revenge, shrouded in clerical black, was more than convenient.[15]

Although they differ importantly in style and emphasis, both of these analyses have a certain validity; nor are they mutually exclusive. But each minimizes the importance of France's internal development and fails to account adequately for the German response to objective circumstances that were essentially French in origin. The presidential crisis of 24 May had created a fluid situation with which the Germans were obliged to deal on its own terms. Specifically, the conservative factions which ousted Thiers had coalesced solely around their mutual opposition to him; thereafter, lacking any clear consensus on a pretender, they seemed to share only "a close association with the Roman Catholic Church."[16] The clericalism of MacMahon, his ministers, and the majority of the French Assembly was more than a figment of Bismarck's fevered imagination or just a useful scarecrow of German politics. It was also the umbilical cord that nourished conservative hopes of a monarchical restoration in France. To damage it would be to deprive French royalism of sustenance and to allow the republic a respite of troubled but uninterrupted growth.

In the initial decade after 1870, French clericalist agitation—or what could be interpreted as such—was simply irrepressible. Probably not since the twelfth century had France been the scene of so many religious pilgrimages. This was the great age of Lourdes, the Assumptionists, and the Sacred Heart. It would be absurd to posit a political motive as the sole explanation of these phenomena. Yet necessarily they were not without political implications when conservative members of the Assembly began to appear in numbers among the pilgrims. German observers were understandably quick to assume an identification between religion and revenge, a deliberate inversion of the Kulturkampf in order to unite "confessional and national feelings" in France. Suspicion was followed by the accusation that an entire campaign of religiosity was being orchestrated by the Broglie cabinet as the overture to a restoration. Explicit denials by French officials and assurances that their only concern was to sustain a nonsectarian "ordre moral" were received in Berlin with skepticism and some derision.[17]

There was good reason. By August 1873 fusionism was prospering once again. The clandestine but soon well-publicized visit to Frohsdorf of the Comte de Paris was only the most sensational of many indications of renewed fusionist activity. Of course, a full century later we have evidence that the monarchist deadlock actually remained unbroken.[18] But at the time that conclusion was less obvious. Rumors were cheap: that a compromise had been reached in the flag controversy; that Metz might be returned to France as part of an international settlement; that arrangements for a restoration were to be made under Russian auspices. Berlin was reliably informed that the Orleanist princes had acknowledged Chambord as the "*sole* royal pretender," and a contemporary German analysis of potential votes in the French Assembly confirmed fears that a prearranged fusionist program had a serious prospect of success:[19]

Extrême droite	40	Centre gauche Périer	35
Droite	80	Centre gauche Say	60
Centre droit fusion	150	Centre gauche Ricard	50
Centre droit pur	60	Gauche modérée	100
Flottants entre les		Extrême gauche	83
deux centres	30	Minority	328
Centre gauche Target	20		
Appel au peuple	30		
Majority	410		

Such an alignment of parliamentary factions was hypothetical but altogether conceivable. The Germans could not be certain, and Bismarck was consequently left to bemoan "the stupefying influence of women, priests, and parliamentary groups." Admittedly, there was something grotesque about a supremely rational diplomatist attempting to reckon with MacMahon's wife, Chambord's father confessor, and the "flottants entre les deux centres."[20]

Despite the apparent willingness of the Orleanists to humor Chambord, there were hints that a fusionist reconciliation was still unattained. The Legitimist press, notably Louis Veuillot's

L'Univers, continued to demand a public act of obeisance from the Assembly before Chambord's arrival as Henri V. Meanwhile, Broglie's own newspapers did not cease to reiterate that Paris was well worth a tricolor and to suggest that, until there was total agreement on the flag, the French people would need to be patient and to accept "a more modest provisional solution." Because the Frohsdorf visit seemed to rule out the immediate possibility of an Orleanist regency, the only implication was a continuation of Mac-Mahon's presidency. Yet the Legitimists were conceding nothing; instead, they were organizing in the provinces their own electoral committees, from which the Orleanists were rigorously excluded. According to the German military attaché, the French army was all the while standing by, unwilling to initiate a monarchist seizure of power but prepared to accept it as an accomplished fact. If the Germans were somehow to influence the outcome, the moment had arrived.[21]

For once, Bismarck found it unnecessary to create a justification for Germany's direct intervention in French affairs; the bishop of Nancy provided it for him. Perhaps another incident would have served the purpose quite as well, but this one was certainly ideal. The French even provided free publicity when the *Semaine religieuse de la Lorraine* printed a copy of the bishop's pastoral letter in which he instructed that public prayers be offered for the recovery of Metz and Strasbourg. The chancellor reacted at once, lodging an official complaint with Broglie in Versailles and having Gontaut-Biron reprimanded at the Wilhelmstrasse. Verbal apologies and contrite explanations that the bishop had acted on his own behalf were deemed unacceptable.[22] Bismarck insisted on a public disavowal by the French government. This was, of course, to touch Broglie at his most vulnerable point. The French premier attempted to counter with the charge that the German press was guilty of deliberate provocation. His protestations were swept aside, however, even though evidence then unknown to him proves that he was absolutely correct: Bismarck gave secret instructions that an editorial barrage be opened and that it be renewed periodically in the weeks ahead.[23]

Although they require no detailed enumeration, there were other signs that Bismarck intended to oppose "the odd combination of religion and revenge" which, as Arnim was advised to admonish Broglie, was unsettling all of Europe.[24] Three may be cited. First, on the diplomatic front, arrangements for the state visit in Berlin of King Victor Emmanuel advertised the isolation of France and the dubious prospects for an anti-German alliance with Italy.[25] Second, a confidential request from the Duc d'Aumale to visit Metz was both publicized and rejected by Bismarck, who used the incident to issue private and public remonstrances against the "hostile attitude" of the Orleanist princes toward Germany.[26] Finally, the chancellor resorted once more to casting dark hints of impending warfare. To William he compared the current circumstances with the period prior to the Crimean war twenty years before, when the great powers aimlessly allowed drifting events to carry them into an unwanted conflict—it was therefore Germany's duty to act, not simply to react. This was to state, in other words, the rationale of his French policy: to intercede whenever necessary and wherever possible in order to thwart the political extremes or, conversely, to preserve a moderate republic.[27]

That the Broglie government was worried and felt constrained by the German menace is demonstrable. This concern, together with the inherent discord of fusionism, kept the monarchist cause swaying in doubt. The autumn of 1873 witnessed the penultimate attempt of French conservatives to construct a united front; but this was basically an effort to circumvent Chambord, not to persuade him. The conservative plan, accurately reported to Berlin by Arnim on several occasions, was to draft a constitution based on the principles of monarchy, ministerial responsibility, religious freedom, and the tricolor. This would be offered to Chambord, who would presumably refuse it, thus opening the way for an Orleanist regency to be ratified by the Assembly. Optimism for this strategy was running high in Versailles by early October 1873, when Bismarck decided to take active countermeasures against it.[28]

The issue was decided before the end of the month; and the best explanation, after all, is that the divided French monarchists simply could not muster the necessary votes. The margin was thin but decisive. After carefully counting heads in Versailles, Jules Simon estimated that the antifusionists would prevail, 365 to 363, assuming that the Bonapartists would join with the republican opposition. A majority of two, as he observed to Thiers, was "not very brilliant," but it would suffice to defeat monarchism. If the Bonapartists should abstain, the republicans would just do likewise; and since a quorum of 370 was necessary—"a number which our adversaries will never attain"—the fusionists were bound to fall short of victory.[29] After two long conferences with Thiers, Arnim relayed this opinion to Berlin; and one of Bleichröder's most trusted agents reached the same conclusion: "I do not yet see a majority for Henri V." At the same time the fusionists themselves hesitated over their calculations, reluctant to bring the matter to a head until success was a "mathematical certainty."[30]

Still, one disturbing possibility remained: a sudden turnabout in Frohsdorf. Should this occur, every prognostication could be confounded and France might, within a few hours, become a monarchy. It was the extreme fragility of the republic under these circumstances which explains the strain, apprehension, and self-deception so evident at the time. Of this confusion the most frequently cited example was the Chesnelong mission to Salzburg on 14 October to meet with the Comte de Chambord. Somehow the sanguine leader of the monarchist delegation managed to gloss over Chambord's explicit affirmation that he would "never accept the tricolor."[31] Upon his return to Paris Chesnelong therefore continued to preach the fusionist gospel and many—among them Arnim—believed. According to the German ambassador, the fusionists anticipated a majority of fifty in the Assembly; and an additional factor had to be added: MacMahon's reported refusal to accept an extension of his presidency for several more years. For Arnim this combination meant nothing less than "a decisive signal in favor of the immediate installation of the monarchy."[32]

Such were the most recent dispatches from Paris at the moment of Bismarck's departure for Vienna on a voyage of reconnaissance. Because we know that the timing was not coincidental, it will not suffice merely to place this trip in the general context of diplomatic arrangements for the Three Emperors' League. In reality, the chancellor's purpose was more precise. He went to Vienna in order to investigate the chances for a restoration in France and, in an ostentatious way, to discourage it. He confronted the Austrians with reports that the Dual Monarchy was actively abetting the fusionist cause in France, a charge which the foreign minister, Count Andrassy, categorically denied. Bismarck nonetheless took the occasion to deliver a sermon: he warned "that the king of France would foment action abroad as a distraction from internal difficulties" and that the course of such action would be dictated "by his clerical views and obligations." In short, the return of Chambord from Austria to France was sure to increase the danger of another European war. Whatever the total impact of this message in Vienna, Bismarck left with assurances from Emperor Franz Joseph that a monarchist France would be unable to count on Austrian support.[33]

While Frohsdorf maintained absolute silence, the political activity in Paris and Versailles was intense. The prospects of a restoration seemed to rise and fall by the hour. As late as 30 October, Arnim wired that "all sides" regarded a monarchist majority of nine to twelve votes as secure, since it was "rather certain" that the Bonapartist deputies had been instructed "to vote for the king." But the issue had in fact already been decided otherwise. On the following day a letter arrived from Chambord, dated on 27 October, which delivered the crushing epithet of fusionism: "My person is nothing, my principle is everything." The monarchist disarray was complete. "Under these circumstances," Arnim told Berlin, "the Duc de Broglie considers the monarchy of the Comte de Chambord as definitively eliminated. The question what will happen now defies all calculation."[34] Actually, of course, it was quite obvious what the consequences would be. Since fusionism had collapsed, the French conservatives would necessarily fall in behind MacMahon. There was nowhere else to turn. We need not retrace the steps by which the passage of the marshal's presidential septennate on 20 November was arranged nor repeat the anecdotes of Chambord's pathetic sojourn to Versailles in one final vain effort to raise the white flag over France. These already belong to the accepted canon of French history.[35]

The critical question to raise here concerns the importance of German influence in determining the outcome. Although the answer cannot be exact, certain useful generalizations do emerge. It is clear, first of all, that the Germans were amply if not always accurately informed about France. They displayed, as the French chargé in Berlin observed, "a rather malevolent curiosity about our internal affairs."[36] Even though Arnim's reliability was suspect, he did have excellent contacts among French conservatives, and his dispatches could always be checked against those of other agents. It is equally apparent that French leaders were quite aware of being monitored and that they were extraordinarily sensitive to German criticism. The constant prodding of the German press, notably when the French government was accused of being an instrument of a militant ultramontane conspiracy, was both disturbing to Broglie and divisive among the monarchist factions striving for agreement. The evidence is irrefutable that Bismarck personally directed this hostile press campaign and that he deliberately inflated the bishop of Nancy's imprudence into a potential casus belli. Once the danger of a restoration had abated, the chancellor instructed that the German press henceforth discuss the bishop's pastoral letter "coolly and without bitterness." This was a clever form of manipulation which Bismarck had long practiced and which he continued to use expertly against the French.[37]

The impact of Germany's simultaneous diplomatic maneuvers is particularly difficult to measure. A French agent in Berlin described the "intense satisfaction" there over the fusionist collapse and the self-congratulation regarding Bismarck's successful mission to Vienna: "The Comte de Chambord, informed that he would not in any event be able to count on an Austrian alliance, preferred to abdicate with dignity. . . rather than pursue for a long time the monarchist cause, the practical result of which had been placed in question."[38] Although such an interpretation is not altogether implausible, neither is it literally verifiable. Apart from the impossibility of penetrating Chambord's inscrutable psyche, one must take into account the tendency of French informants to ascribe all manner of misfortune to the demonic power of the German chancellor. The most appropriate conclusion is surely not to suppose that Bismarck single-handedly blocked the restoration of monarchy in France. It is rather to suggest that the German influence was still a crucial component of French public life, apart from which the formative phase of the Third Republic would not be totally comprehensible.

The Techniques of Intimidation

Not in every instance can it be demonstrated that German intervention in French affairs was intended to achieve a specific result. As one of his biographers has put it, Bismarck was one who always preferred to wear a "reversible overcoat," to pursue several purposes at once and to hold open as many options as possible.[39] So it was with France: the chancellor might act to secure his general foreign policy (the Three Emperors' League, cooperation with the Italian monarchy); to meet internal political needs (a favorable party coalition in the Reichstag, the passage of a military appropriation); to prevail in a personal rivalry within the imperial entourage (against Moltke during the war of 1870, against Arnim thereafter); or to induce a direct reaction in France (combating ultramontane tendencies, discouraging increases in the French military budget). Bismarck's actions must ordinarily be evaluated in terms of some combination of these goals rather than as the single-minded pursuit of any one of them. The French republic was therefore often a primary objective, but sometimes only a pretext. We have already observed that Bismarck himself was perfectly aware of this distinction and, with his customary blend of candor and cynicism, referred to such episodes of deliberately manufactured alarm in France as a "cold shower." Whether or not a specific motive was in view, a sudden dousing of the French might at least serve to chill their ardor for revenge and to dampen any initiative for change.

A characteristic incident of this sort occurred in the winter months of 1873–74. It merits investigation not as an aggregation of factual details, revealing though they were, but as a paradigm of the emerging pattern of German manipulation and French apprehension. Once more the ostensible issue was ultramontanism, by now virtually a code word for persistent German suspicions that MacMahon and his "entire royalist staff" were continuing to brood over some dark plot. It is worth noting that more than one provocation might ordinarily be claimed by the Germans at a given time; their task was to select the affair best suited to exacerbate "the bad conscience" of the French.[40] To be effective as an instrument of intimidation, an accusation had to begin with a demonstrable French offense and had to prove acutely embarrassing to French officials once it was bruited in the press.

By these criteria, for example, an incident involving the Rothschild family seemed initially promising but was finally discarded by Bismarck as too tangential. This episode began with an ostentatious snub of Harry von Arnim by the Baroness de Rothschild at a formal dinner party; and it later reached a point at which the chancellor dictated a threat to withdraw the German ambassador and thereby create a rupture of diplomatic relations.[41] As usual the French were put through their paces: their verbal apologies were deemed "insufficient," and a written statement was demanded by the Germans. The German press renewed its familiar harping on the theme of France's unreconstructed and dangerous germanophobia, while both diplomatic and secret agents kept the telegraph busy with urgent dispatches. Had there not been some larger purpose, namely, that of keeping the French government constantly on edge, it would seem astounding that so much time and trouble was expended on such a trifle. In the end the only perceptible result was one more black mark in Bismarck's already bulging dossier of grievances against Arnim. A penitential visit by the Baron de Rothschild to the German embassy was hardly noticed, since by then the matter was eclipsed by the more fundamental question of French clericalism.[42]

Earlier, the German press campaign attacking the bishop of Nancy had been deliberately tamped down by Bismarck once the defeat of fusionism seemed assured. The resumption of editorial broadsides against France just before Christmas of 1873 coincided precisely with Bismarck's visit to Berlin from his estate at Varzin. This time the chancellor was exercised by a series of pastoral letters released by several other French bishops, the common theme of which was the reciprocity of Catholic revival and French patriotism. In customary fashion this theme was promptly given the most sinister implication by the Germans: the letters were dramatized as evidence of Vatican support for French preparations of "war against a neighboring state." When first confronted with this charge the Duc Decazes, the new foreign minister, simply claimed to be inadequately apprised of the content of the letters—a claim that drew from Bismarck a cutting rejoinder about the "worthless" judgment of "a statesman so poorly oriented."[43] By the beginning of January the cold water had been turned on full blast: Decazes was notified that Germany expected the French bishops to be prosecuted in court. "The increasing agitation of the episcopate" would have to be met by direct legal action of the French government, Decazes was told; otherwise, *very grave* complications" would ensue.[44]

How were the French to react? Decazes's private correspondence reveals that he was extremely distressed by the German threats, but he nonetheless scoffed at Bismarck's professed fears of French revanchist intentions ("Quelle triste et odieuse plaisantrie!"). In reality, Decazes held no illusions about France's military power; and, as he ruefully commented, "Our neighbors know the truth as well as, perhaps better than we." Hence, he concluded, the chancellor must have his own reasons, probably stemming from Germany's internal difficulties, for the rudeness toward France. The only sane way to respond to Bismarck's wrath, Decazes reasoned, was "to remove every pretext, every justification, every excuse for his ill intentions." The more calm and controlled the French demeanor, the more likely Bismarck would appear "crazed and intemperate." In this "moral war" imposed on France by Germany, Decazes would therefore deploy his most effective defense: "my courtesy, my imperturbable courtesy."[45]

Ever since the mediation of the German embassy in Paris had been all but nullified by the Arnim affair, the only useful diplomatic conduit between the two nations was the French ambassador in Berlin, the Vicomte de Gontaut-Biron, a close personal friend of Decazes. As a matter of course, Gontaut visited the Wilhelmstrasse daily. There he was none too subtly instructed that Germany's policy toward France was "to prevent the fusion of confessional and national element hostile to us [as well as] the consolidation of French governmental powers in a clerical direction."[46] Yet he had, as he admitted to Decazes, initially underestimated the intensity of German irritation, until the day in mid-January when Bismarck granted Gontaut one of those infrequent interviews that signaled a matter of more than routine concern. Although the chancellor retained his composure throughout, his language (as Gontaut recorded it) was menacing. If the present developments in France continued, Bismarck said, German security would be placed in jeopardy, and "we will be obliged to make war on you." Otherwise, France would gradually become a nation dominated by religious fanaticism and would "inevitably be launched into a war against us." Even though such an eventuality might not be imminent, it would clearly serve Germany's interest "to fight in two years, in a year, rather than to wait until you have completed your preparations." Despite a few concluding remarks about Germany's desire to maintain the peace, Bismarck left Gontaut with the distinct impression that he expected France to take some decisive legal action at once in order to halt the advance of clericalism.[47]

Two things were uncertain. First, what was the German motive? The Rothschild incident had evaporated; and to Gontaut the issue of the pastoral letters seemed already well on the way to a resolution. He could only offer Decazes a pair of speculations, both based on the premise that Bismarck was acting for reasons of domestic policy. Either he literally intended to scare up support in the forthcoming Reichstag elections, or he was building a case for increases in the German military budget. In the margin of Gontaut's private letter Decazes noted a third explanation of Bismarck's conduct: "He wants to associate us with the crusade against Catholicism." None of these conjectures was, of course, incompatible with the others; but whichever weighed most heavily for the moment, the two men could agree, Bismarck's intervention had undoubtedly placed France "in a very delicate position."[48]

The second question followed: what should be the French response? How could they placate German demands without mortgaging their own interests? Two legal recourses were available to Decazes, neither of them very satisfactory. One would require the bishops to stand trial in lower courts, under an 1819 law, on a charge of acting publicly in a manner injurious to the French state. But the validity of such jurisprudence, drafted decades ago by the Restoration monarchy, was dubious; and the willingness of local juries to convict a distinguished member of the episcopate was quite problematical. The other option was for the republic itself to bring a suit of libel (*appel comme d'abus*) against the bishops, a process which would disgrace the government in French public opinion, outrage and alienate the Vatican, and involve France as

Germany's accomplice in the Kulturkampf. No wonder Decazes hesitated and began to look for another exit.[49]

A convenient solution was found with remarkable ease. Ever since the frustration of the fusionist campaign, the Broglie cabinet had been under persistent attack from Louis Veuillot's extreme ultramontane newspaper, *L'Univers*, which accused the French government of betraying the cause of Catholic monarchy. Nor were Veuillot's editorials any more reticent in assaulting Bismarck and the Kaiser as persecutors of the Church. It is not surprising to discover that on at least one previous occasion, in the first week of 1874, the possibility of silencing Veuillot had been raised in a discussion between Arnim and Broglie. But at that time neither felt able to proceed: Broglie was fearful of losing conservative support in the Assembly, and Arnim had received a telegram from Bismarck advising him that it would "not be useful to make advertisement for *L'Univers*" by disclosing that its suppression was "a German requirement."[50] Yet once the chancellor delivered his ultimatum to Gontaut, the pressure was thereby intensified for the French to make some unspecified but dramatic gesture of appeasement—and for that purpose Veuillot now afforded a suitable foil. In the early hours of 19 January, Decazes wrote out an urgent personal note to Broglie: "This very night I beg you, without losing an instant, to send General Ladmirault an order to suspend *L'Univers* in the morning." Otherwise, Decazes warned, he would resign at once. Any delay might produce a serious crisis. "The opportunity is unique [and] might be decisive in Berlin. . . . In the name of heaven, do not hesitate."[51] Broglie complied. The government's action was then further reinforced by Decazes's vigorous denunciation of Veuillot before the Assembly and by a stern admonition to the French episcopate that inflammatory pastoral letters would not be tolerated in the future.[52]

The two-month suspension of *L'Univers* was a small price for the French regime to pay, especially since it temporarily rid Broglie of his most aggravating conservative critic. So far as Germany was concerned, moreover, the effect seemed eminently satisfactory. The German press fell silent again once Bismarck made it known that he wanted the entire affair "to be allowed now to rest." When the subject was politely raised at a dinner party in

Berlin, according to one French agent, the chancellor passed it off lightly with the remark that he merely wanted "to throw some cold water on the head of *messieurs les français.*"[53]

We have too often witnessed similar episodes not to draw some general conclusions. First among them is that German officials were accustomed to repeating hints of preventive war against France. This was a calculated tone of menace, more or less serious as Bismarck dictated, rather than a rash moment of excitement. The accumulated evidence simply does not support those generous interpreters of Bismarck who contend that the notion of a preemptive strike was entirely abhorrent to the chancellor. To be sure, Bismarck was perfectly orthodox in his conception of warfare as an extension of diplomacy. But to maintain military supremacy over France was for him a vital necessity; and to fight was therefore a viable option. No doubt he preferred to bully the French, to rely on his own agents and press lords rather than to summon generals and weapons which were beyond his complete control. Nevertheless, both before and after the termination of the German occupation, the efficacy of the "cold shower" depended on the credibility of force.[54]

Furthermore, in Paris and Versailles the threat of German aggression was altogether believable. "Everyone trembled before a new war," one German agent summed up, and a sense of relief was apparent in France once the incident was closed. The French were fortunate to have found in Decazes a shrewd and capable counterpart to Bismarck; yet his real strength derived precisely from a frank recognition of French inferiority and vulnerability. It was his willingness to place survival before pride that made Decazes the true successor of Thiers. Like the first president, Decazes comprehended the fragility of the ruling consensus in France and therefore admitted the necessity of a compliant attitude toward Germany. This attitude must figure importantly among the explanations of why many French conservatives were prepared to accept, and indeed to advocate, the adoption of a republican constitution.[55] In order to endure the slings and arrows of outrageous German demands, they were finally willing to tolerate the slow institutional evolution of a conservative republic.

The Wallon Amendment

The constitution of the Third Republic was the result of anxiety rather than of foresight. Its framers were looking backward, not forward, deeply worried about the many months of political and economic dislocation since the recent war. They were also, in further retrospect, apprehensive about the troubling precedent of plebiscitary autocracy which had prevailed in France during the two decades before 1870. A profound fear of those sibling offsprings of the Great Revolution—radicalism and Bonapartism— was thus the propelling motive behind the republican charter of 1875, much as it had been behind the monarchist charter of 1814. Two additional factors combined to create a sense of urgency. One, as we have emphasized, was the intimidating presence of imperial Germany. The other was a growing realization, within the French government and without, that the Assembly elected to restore peace three years before had become superannuated. If the conservative majority still intact by 1874 was not to squander its advantage altogether, it must soon act or else suffer the debilitating consequences of immobility and impotence.

This circumstance was not appreciably altered by the phase of quiet euphoria that followed the suspension of *L'Univers.* The welcome calm could not possibly endure, as Decazes explained in private to his friends, and hence "Albert and I" were determined to use the respite to obtain a new electoral law and to create a second parliamentary chamber as a conservative bulwark in the future.[56] This explicit reference to Broglie was significant, since it indicated that, failing a positive resolution in favor of monarchy, a defensive phalanx of conservative forces might yet be mustered behind MacMahon's presidential septennate: better to draft a republican constitution than be forced later to accept one. Only thus, Decazes was convinced, would it henceforth be possible for France "to live and let live."[57]

This tactic was not without its complications. Broglie's order to muzzle Veuillot's journal had, as he feared, cost him a segment of Legitimist support; and for a politician whose meager personal popularity was already a liability, this was backing that he could ill afford to forfeit. Broglie's premiership was consequently in jeopardy, and the warning flags were run out again. Would it be yet another cabinet squabble or, this time, a real coup d'état?[58] In the midst of this uncertainty Decazes emerged as the pivotal figure both in French politics and in German calculations. It was he who was best positioned to attract support across the party spectrum for the constitutional project; and it was also he who had demonstrated an unrivaled capacity to deal successfully with Berlin. Like Thiers before him, Decazes was acceptable. He was, moreover, determined to end France's internal instability by establishing a government that was both "tricolor and authoritarian"—in other words, by solidifying the conservative republic.[59]

When the Broglie cabinet did finally collapse in the middle of May 1874, it was hardly the shattering event some had anticipated. Decazes himself had been among the most nervous, fearing that "the slightest crisis will lead us to catastrophe."[60] But, for a circumstantial reason, MacMahon moved with unaccustomed alacrity to resolve the matter. As it happened, Broglie's fall coincided exactly with the arrival of Chlodwig zu Hohenlohe as Harry von Arnim's replacement in Paris. When the French Assembly failed to provide a new premier at once, MacMahon took the problem in hand, writing out the new list of cabinet members himself and explaining: "I must have a minister within twenty-four hours to receive the German ambassador." The choice thus fell without incident on a *ministère de trève* headed by General de Cissey and Decazes. This brief glimpse into the presidential chambers suggests how the German presence might specifically affect the rhythm of French politics as well as its general tenor.[61]

Although he was a Roman Catholic, the brother of a Cardinal, and a former prime minister of Bavaria, Hohenlohe had long cultivated his reputation as a faithful exponent of Bismarckian policy. His appearance in the French capital marked the beginning of a reliable ambassadorial tenure which proved beneficial to all concerned. It began well enough with an elegant presidential reception at the Elysée palace, an occasion which drew a rather sullen crowd of onlooking Parisians. If some hostile faces were in evidence, as Friedrich von Holstein remarked, at least there were no demonstrations: "no dead cats or rotten apples, not even whistles." But the real significance of the formality between Mac-

Mahon and Hohenlohe did not go unnoticed in the French press, which accurately reported that the new ambassador presented his credentials neither to the nation nor to the president but to "the French republic."[62]

The essential question nonetheless remained as before: what kind of a republic? Hohenlohe's assignment, in effect, was to derive the most plausible answer. To do so he had to feel his way carefully through the labyrinth of French political factions, the eventual alignment of which would determine the outcome. Without stalking him step by step, we may fairly approximate his general perception of the situation by a series of propositions:

1. The eclipse of fusionism revealed the futility of a rightest coalition and required the reorientation of the Right Center in the Assembly toward a compromise with the Left Center. The intended objective was a new centrist block which would sustain MacMahon's septennate until the marshal could be quietly replaced in the presidency by the Duc d'Aumale, who was considered to be the most political of the Orleanist pretenders.

2. The chances of *la république aumalienne* were scant, however, because its success could only be assured by a permanent rift on the parliamentary Left. All indications were that the leftist factions were unlikely to part company, certainly not if doing so would mean only a boost for the Orleanists. A secure centrist coalition was therefore improbable.

3. The principal benefactors of an impasse in the Assembly would be the Bonapartists. The by-elections of 1874 had already provided evidence of their recuperating strength, and sooner or later it would become apparent that Bonapartism was "the only form of monarchy which has a prospect of success in France."[63]

4. Ineluctably, as a consequence, the French were bound to experience a polarization of political forces. The decade would not end before an open contest was joined between monarchism and republicanism—that is, finally, between Bonapartists and Gambettists.

5. Meanwhile, the status quo would probably be maintained by the passage of electoral and constitutional legislation. Many conservatives would support this legislation in order to shore up their eroding position in the parliament; and many republicans

were prepared to acquiesce in it because they were sufficiently confident that popular opinion would sweep them to power once the first Assembly was dissolved.[64]

In most regards Hohenlohe's analysis was both accurate and prescient. It also accorded with Bismarck's view that Germany's role should be to perpetuate discord in France, whether by abrupt intrusion or by ostensible indifference. For the time being the latter tactic appeared more appropriate, particularly as Hohenlohe found himself frequently solicited by leaders from the various French factions, each of whom felt that German patronage "could be of use in the achievement of their objectives."[65] Germany's abstention under these circumstances was a conscious policy, a passive reinforcement of the prevailing inertia in France. Another "cold shower," or at least a more active participation in French affairs, would be useful only in the event that the political impasse was broken and some motion began in a direction unfavorable to Germany. Until such time, the Germans could afford to treat France with benign neglect.

Such was the case in the summer of 1874 when the anticipated reform proposals first reached the floor of the Assembly. Debate centered on a motion by Casimir-Périer that "the government of the republic shall be composed to two chambers and a president." As Hohenlohe summarized it, the adoption of this principle would be tantamount to an admission that a monarchy was impossible, a provisional regime harmful, and a republic therefore necessary.[66] That Casimir-Périer was the son of a former Orleanist minister under the July monarchy made his defection to Thierist republicanism particularly painful to the conservatives; and led by Broglie they managed to stir enough resentment to defeat the motion. The Assembly thereupon voted to adjourn, a maneuver that merely suspended the constitutional issue until the autumn, because only outright dissolution—demanded in vain by the Gambettists —would have forced new parliamentary elections. For several months the fate of the French political system was consequently left in abeyance.[67]

During this interim the German preference for Decazes was dictated partly, but not primarily, by the foreign minister's pliability in matters diplomatic. Documentary evidence of two of the international incidents of the time—the French recognition of the Spanish republic and the removal from Italian waters of the *Oré-noque*, a French vessel heretofore left at the disposal of the papacy —confirms that in both instances Decazes was submitted to direct German pressure. But his personal exasperation about Bismarck's "brutal provocations" was tempered by a determination to afford Germany not the slightest public pretext for accusations of French revanchism. The German press, at the chancellor's instigation, nevertheless printed such charges; and the publication of previously classified dispatches during the concurrent trial of Harry von Arnim further exposed the German intent to manipulate and isolate the republic. Yet Decazes's policy remained one of appeasement. The Germans therefore had little reason on diplomatic grounds to wish his removal from the Quai d'Orsay.[68]

No less crucial was Decazes's growing importance in French domestic affairs. Secret German reports predicted that a moment of political crisis would occur in January 1875, soon after the reconvening of the Assembly in Versailles. The government would demand immediate adoption of a constitutional draft; but if a favorable majority were not obtained for it, the result would be what Decazes privately called a "petit coup d'état." MacMahon would prorogue the Assembly at once, hold a plebiscite, and attempt to govern with the support of the army, the police, and the bureaucracy. During this extraparliamentary hiatus, Decazes conjectured, the Bonapartists and the radicals would be quashed, opening the way for some form of Orleanist control by 1880, when the marshal's septennate was due to lapse. Admittedly, this bold plan had one deficiency: it might fail. In the event that Mac-Mahon proved unable to gain a plebiscitary mandate, he would be forced to resign and France would be plunged into a state of anarchy.[69]

By the end of 1874 such a prediction was not fatuous. Certainly the German government regarded the extreme alternatives —the inauguration of a military junta or else a complete breakdown of political authority in France—with the utmost seriousness. Essential to avoiding them, so it seemed in Berlin, was the success of Decazes's constitutional project. Thereupon, the familiar signs of renewed German activity began to appear: agents were dispatched, coded messages were exchanged, the press was alerted, and the chancellor himself took command in Berlin—despite his shopworn disclaimer that no foreign power was in a position "to influence directly the outcome."[70]

German prognostications were close to the mark. On 7 January 1875, Hohenlohe wired that the French cabinet had resigned. The ambassador's confidential discussions with several French leaders, among them Decazes and Thiers, convinced him that MacMahon himself lacked the courage to attempt a coup; but the marshal was meanwhile consulting with the one man who might try, the Duc de Broglie.[71] When a fortnight passed without any apparent resolution, Hohenlohe telegraphed that the replacement of Decazes by Broglie was increasingly probable. The response from Berlin was prompt and unequivocal: Bismarck instructed Hohenlohe to inform the French that "the Duc Decazes, through his accommodating, capable, and successful conduct of affairs, is far more welcome to us than the Duc de Broglie and inspires greater confidence in good relations." At the time of Thiers's deposition from the presidency, the German preference for him had been somewhat obfuscated by Arnim's vacillation. But now Hohenlohe delivered the chancellor's message to Decazes in the most categorical terms: "What we want is that you remain in office." Still, a certain public discretion was required, lest German involvement prove to be a liability for Decazes. "Speak with the marshal," he advised Hohenlohe, "but otherwise with no one." The ambassador agreed and on the following day, 23 January, he confronted MacMahon with Bismarck's message of support for Decazes. The marshal responded at once, "I will keep him."[72]

The extent to which MacMahon's resolve was actually stiffened by German insistence cannot be precisely determined. We can never know how the president might have reacted had Bismarck supported Broglie with the same vigor. It is striking, however, that the foregoing sequence of encounters coincided exactly with the first indications that a resolution of the constitutional crisis was imminent. The elimination of Broglie's candidacy was a prelude to the dissolution of a conservative front. The reintroduction of the Casimir-Périer motion—five days after MacMahon's pledge to Hohenlohe—was defeated in the Assembly, it is true, but this time the margin was thin; and the slippage of another dozen votes would make the difference. On 29 January a new amendment was brought to the floor by Henri Wallon: "The president of the republic is elected by an absolute majority of the votes of the Senate and the Chamber of Deputies united in a National Assembly. He is named for seven years; he is reeligible."[73] In this version emphasis was placed on the presidential septennate, but the effect of establishing a distinctively republican constitution was nonetheless explicit. The narrow victory of the Wallon amendment and the passage, by more substantial majorities, of further constitutional legislation in the month of February have often been narrated in the political histories of the Third Republic. These accounts need only be supplemented by Hohenlohe's cryptic understatement to Bismarck: "For Germany this development is not unfavorable."[74]

At the time it would scarcely have occurred to any politically alert Frenchman to regard the new constitution as the foundation of a durable form of government. No one expected it to last. Most conservatives resigned themselves to the settlement out of despair over the fumbling attempts to find an alternative. The combination of internecine feuding, public indifference, and German disapproval had been enough to thwart the monarchist cause and to induce its supporters to accept a provisional solution. Only two possibilities of a restoration, both of them still distant in 1875, remained: either a total collapse of the system would create circumstances favorable for a Bonapartist coup; or a solidification of MacMahon's septennate would permit the Orleanists to effect a transition to the *république aumalienne*. By creating an upper house and establishing an electoral procedure (*scrutin d'arrondissement*) supposedly favorable to local notables, the constitution at least seemed to afford a breathing spell for conservative ambitions. But obviously this was considerably less than a solid political victory for the French Right.

Neither was the Left ideally served. The Gambettists and, beyond them, the radical fringe were still far from realizing their first and fondest expectations. In reality they, too, were temporizing in the hope that an order better suited to their liking would eventually emerge. As of 1875 they had not yet appreciably budged their

social superiors from political power; and by accepting the constitution they recognized that it was premature to proclaim "the end
of the notables." For the Left, then, the constitutional settlement
meant important concessions, including the implicit admission
that a legal restoration of the monarchy was still possible.[75]

If France was henceforth officially republican in name, in
many regards it still remained conservative in substance. The result of the standoff in 1875 has often been described as a republic
without republicans. Yet it would be more precise to say that
France had become a Thierist republic without Thierists. Among
the various conceptions of France's ruling system, it was that of
Thiers which most nearly corresponded to the reality—except, of
course, for the absence of his personal leadership, a flaw that he
hoped to rectify in the near future. It is consequently fair to conclude that, from the day of Thiers's resignation in May 1873 to
the adoption of the constitution nearly two years later, French
politicians had been engaged in an elaborate parliamentary game,
the object of which was to discover some definition of their nation other than that of the first president. Having failed to do so,
they reluctantly conceded that France was indeed a conservative
republic.

One of the easy clichés of French political history, suggested
by Thiers himself, is that the French thereby adopted the form of
government which divided them the least. This deserves to be
regarded as a clever word of self-congratulation rather than as a
serious analysis of the constitution. The settlement of 1875 was a
compromise only in a negative sense. It was the result of a fundamental disagreement which had not been resolved and which was
sure to provoke further conflict. The constitution was no water-
shed, no great divide, no end or beginning of an era, but only the
perpetuation of a bitter combat. Few recognized this fact more
clearly, or took more satisfaction in it, than the Germans. "The
confusion in France," Hohenlohe predicted, "is still far from being
at an end."[76] This was both to register the German view of the
French republic and to reveal the principal motive behind the
adroit exercise of German influence since the summer of 1873.
The truth was, as seen from Berlin, that the French had actually
retained the form of government that divided them the most.

Chapter 5

The Deadlock

The Effects of Economic Interdependence

The utility of the traditional dating of political history has increasingly been brought into question. It is no longer feasible to speak uncritically about "the age of Bismarck" or even to take for granted that the war of 1870 was of epoch-making importance. In part, this chronological reassessment is only a matter of an altered emphasis: the revolution of 1848, for example, may be characterized not primarily as a wave of unsuccessful political insurrections (a turning point that failed to turn was A. J. P. Taylor's famous bon mot for it) but rather as the culmination of an era of socioeconomic dislocation and the prelude to a long phase of industrial growth. For most of Europe, moreover, the economic spurt after 1848 ended not in 1870 but in 1873, a date now adopted by some historians as the beginning of a so-called Great Depression. Some specialists in German history prefer to emphasize the years 1878–79 as marking the refounding of the Kaiserreich, including the ratification of protectionism, the termination of the Kulturkampf, the introduction of antisocialist legislation, the collapse of National Liberalism, the realignment of Bismarck's ruling coalition in the Reichstag, and the conclusion of a diplomatic alliance with Austria-Hungary.[1]

No matter which of these three criteria is considered paramount—the war, the onset of depression, or the reorientation of German policy—they all point to the critical importance of the 1870s. That much we may assume. But our problem is both more precise and less obvious: how did this historic mutation affect the relationship between France and Germany? In general terms, of course, the answer is simply that France was reduced to a European power of second rank, whereas by the end of the century the German nation emerged as demographically, industrially, and militarily superior. Yet this explanation conceals as much as it reveals, and it provides only a very blunt instrument of analysis for that formative period when the nascent French republic was overshadowed by a newly united German Reich.

More promising as a beginning is the hypothesis of "long swings" in economic development. According to this theory, in support of which a mass of statistical data has been assembled, Europe experienced a phase of sustained growth from 1849 to 1873, followed by a fitful depression until about 1896, whereupon a remarkably vigorous expansion once more resumed.[2] Despite the plausibility of such a pattern for Europe in general and for Germany in particular, the explicative value of these "Kondratieffs" has not gone unchallenged. This criticism has ordinarily taken one of two forms: the advocates of the theory have claimed too much for it, as if *everything* that occurred in a given phase could be explained in relation to economic growth, or they have misrepresented the *entire* character of the nineteenth-century economy, by implying that deflation was an exception rather than the rule.[3] Both of these objections have a certain cosmic quality. One charges the proponents of long swings with the fallacy of post hoc, ergo propter hoc; the other draws a basically different picture of the century by stressing the steady decline in prices (while allowing for exceptional inflationary bursts in the 1850s and early 1870s) over the eight decades before 1896. After reviewing the controversy, we may conclude that there is *something* to the notion of Kondratieffs, although they provide us with less certainty about economic trends and political consequences than several writers have supposed.[4]

Here we must adopt an altogether different stance, because, when one departs from the realm of theoretical exposition and inquires about the utility of Kondratieffs for understanding Franco-German history in the 1870s, two problems immediately arise. The first pertains to Germany alone. To employ the suggested model of long economic trends is to accept a division of the latter half of the nineteenth century, from 1849 to 1914, into three distinct phases. But this procedure overlooks, or at least underestimates, the extraordinary character of the years 1870 to 1873. The economic statistics for that period are in fact quite untypical of the general pattern of Germany's rate of growth. Adding them to the two decades before the Franco-Prussian War creates a distortion, since the growth rate was neither so rapid before 1870 nor so slack after 1873 as such a configuration purports to demonstrate. Each of the long swings was in reality a series of short swings, of which 1870–73 was far and away the most violent. By emphasizing the uniqueness of the brief and dramatic postwar boom of financial speculation, private investment, and joint-stock mergers—and by isolating those statistics from the periods both anterior and posterior—we gain a substantially different and more accurate impression of Germany's real growth rate. Specifically, the contrast between the "Industrial Revolution" (1849–73) and the "Great Depression" (1873–96) becomes far less striking when these periods are measured by typical performance and when the extraordinary statistical boost of 1870–73 is not arbitrarily awarded to the former.[5]

The second problem centers on France. Among the major nations of western and central Europe, the French economic development accorded least well with the overall European pattern. This fact has long been recognized and often ascribed to a national "stagnation": France is said to have had either no industrial revolution or, at best, one which was muffled by a deficiency of demand and high costs of production.[6] This is naturally a complex issue in its own right. There are, after all, no fixed criteria of stagnation engraved in stone. All sectors of the French economy did not suffer an identical fate, and some actually thrived. It is only in comparison to Germany that the weakness of the French performance after 1870 becomes fully apparent. Such a discrepancy cannot be analyzed by referring exclusively to a long-term model. The fairly rapid French economic expansion of the 1850s, as we have earlier witnessed, was already beginning to wane by the late 1860s. The immediate effect of the war of 1870 and of the subsequent reparations settlement was to slow further the French impetus by soaking up government capital, discouraging private venture, and temporarily reducing financial circulation to a trickle. Thus the economic imbalance between France and Germany from the war's end until 1873 could scarcely have been more marked. While one nation was extricating itself painfully from the financial wreckage of military defeat, the other enjoyed the most exhilarating speculative bonanza in its history. Neither case can be satisfactorily explained as merely the culminating moment in a general European phase of economic growth. It remains to be established, moreover, that the French and German growth patterns later in the decade were also not parallel, nor were they identical in the 1880s.[7]

Yet, even if we discard a theory of long swings as being in this instance of too little utility for our purposes, doing so need not imply an excessive preoccupation with short-term fluctuations. A longer view is still necessary in order to place the Franco-German economic relationship in proper perspective. We may begin with the unassailable proposition that after 1870 the overall production of both nations grew, but at different rates (see table 3).[8] Under closer scrutiny, the exceedingly raw numbers of GNP may appear in several different lights. For instance, another set of statistics (table 4)—at once deceptive and revealing—establishes the relative value of manufactured products of the two nations. At first glance, Germany seems to have lagged behind France until the turn of the century, but as the abstract numbers of industrial output measure only the national level of achievement relative to each other in 1913, it is solely the *rate* of development that is thereby indicated. Knowing that the actual German level was nearly twice that of the French by the beginning of the Great War, we can gain

Table 3 | *Annual Average Growth of Product, 1870–1913 (in percentages)*

Country	Total	Per Capita	Per Man-Hour
France	1.6	1.4	1.8
Germany	2.9	1.7	2.1

Source: J. D. Gould, *Economic Growth in History*, p. 22.

Table 4 / Indexes of Industrial Production, 1870–1913 (1913 = 100)

Year	France	Germany	Year	France	Germany
1870	40.0	19	1892	63.6	42
1871	41.3	21	1893	61.5	43
1872	45.8	24	1894	62.7	45
1873	43.8	26	1895	59.5	49
1874	46.5	27	1896	64.4	50
1875	47.1	27	1897	66.7	53
1876	47.7	28	1898	68.6	56
1877	46.5	27	1899	71.7	58
1878	47.4	28	1900	67.9	61
1879	46.0	27	1901	67.7	59
1880	49.4	26	1902	66.3	60
1881	54.1	27	1903	70.8	65
1882	55.3	27	1904	66.9	68
1883	54.5	29	1905	74.6	70
1884	52.5	30	1906	76.1	73
1885	52.0	31	1907	79.3	79
1886	52.9	31	1908	77.8	78
1887	53.7	33	1909	83.1	81
1888	55.6	35	1910	81.1	86
1889	58.4	39	1911	88.8	91
1890	57.3	40	1912	102.3	97
1891	60.3	41	1913	100.0	100

Source: B. R. Mitchell, *European Historical Statistics, 1750–1970*, pp. 355–56.

some sense of the rapidity and magnitude of Germany's growth over the long span of years since the war of 1870.

A few other observations are worth making. Germany began much further back than France, both relatively and absolutely. National unification and the annexation of Alsace-Lorraine were something of a stimulus, but they did not at first remarkably alter the distance between the two countries, because of France's brief postwar recovery. In the late 1870s both economies hesitated, the 1879 level of industrial production being nearly identical with that of 1874. Then, after 1880, Germany began to move steadily upward; whereas French industry, following a brief spurt at the time of the Freycinet plan (1879–81), began to sputter once again. Hence, France's 1882 level of production was not reattained until 1888. By 1890 both France and Germany still had miles to run before reaching their 1913 rates of performance. This observation should not disguise the fact that the incomparably greater amplitude of the German effort outstripped the French in virtually every regard.[9]

No matter how many variables are considered, and no matter which set of statistics one chooses to emphasize, the result is always the same: in the latter part of the nineteenth century, France performed well below the level of other industrial nations. The contrast with Germany makes that fact all the more compelling. Even by the most flattering criterion, the per capita rate of production, France fell percentage by percentage to the rear (see table 5). Despite some unavoidable irregularities in the procedure of computation, the available data demonstrate how the alarming fall of the French demographic rate was paralleled by a drop in the level of economic growth. Consequently, the much lower popu-

Table 5 | Net National Product: Decennial Rates of Growth

Country	Total Product (%)	Population (%)	Product per Capita (%)
France (1901–1910 prices)			
1831–1840 to 1861–1870	26.3	3.9	21.6
1861–1870 to 1891–1900	15.7	1.9	13.5
Germany (1913 prices)			
1850–1860 to 1910–1913	29.2	11.1	16.3

Source: Kuznets, *Economic Growth*, pp. 10–11.

lation coefficient notwithstanding, France's lead in per capita production was lost.[10]

Apart from this slow demographic growth, which placed some limitation on demand and served to that extent as a cause in itself, the general factors contributing to France's retardation have often been enumerated: poor distribution of income and of wealth, high foreign investment in proportion to capital investment in domestic industry, inadequate and noncontiguous fuel resources, persistent deflation in the agricultural sector, expensive transportation, immobilization of private capital in government securities, heavy expenditures for bureaucratic and military personnel, unduly high consumption of food and spirits, inadequate entrepreneurial fervor reflected in the longevity of family enterprises, and so on.[11] To this list must be added France's special relationship to Germany. We shall attempt to establish, as we proceed, that this relationship was not only a standard of measurement or a symptom but also an intrinsic factor in France's mediocre economic performance after 1870.[12]

So much for the general context within which short-term fluctuations occurred. We should bear in mind that government officials charged with formulating economic policy at the time had scant evidence of long-term developments. Such current data as they possessed were usually gathered bimonthly from the arrondissements of Paris by the Prefecture of Police or presented more sporadically in analyses of national trends prepared by the Chamber of Commerce. These indicated that small-scale industry and commerce had been most harshly struck by the recent war. Above all, tiny shops and boutiques were expiring, a fact ascribed to the extraordinarily rapid and economically unsound proliferation of them in the 1860s. Bankruptcies were frequent just after 1870 and continued into 1873, when, in the month of March alone, 170 small Paris firms went out of business. But during that spring, French economic prospects began to brighten, and the Prefecture of Police could predict a "slight amelioration." It appeared that French industry had suffered less than commerce; if anything, the immediate problem was a danger of overproduction in a domestic market still short of liquid capital.[13]

The response of French businessmen to the new tariff treaties imposed by the Thiers regime was at first mixed. Some had been already hurt by the free-trade agreements of the early 1860s; they therefore favored a system of protection and indeed demanded government subsidies. But those who held a secure niche in the home market were mostly indifferent to the tariff issue; and a few, especially in the luxury trades, remained hopeful of a revival in foreign trade and objected to protectionism in any form.[14] In sum, by 1873 pessimism was not the universal mood in French business circles. Despite the huge reparations to Germany, the payment of war indemnities within France, and the insufficient harvest of that autumn, indications were that France had survived the worst and was beginning to revive. Even the most grudging of German critics had to concede, all in all, that the postwar French economy had displayed "a most extraordinary solidity."[15]

The same could not be said of Germany. Concern about overheating of the economy and excessive speculation was already bruited in 1872. The first dramatic indication of serious difficulty appeared in May 1873 in the wake of bank failures and a plunging stock market in Vienna. When he sought a professional evaluation of the situation several weeks later, Bismarck was advised by Gerson von Bleichröder that the *Wiener Krach* could not fail to have repercussions in Germany—especially as the boom in property values there had been too rapid since the war, and some economic retrenchment was in any event probable. Still, Bleichröder was optimistic that the German stock market would recover by the late autumn of 1873 and, presumably, the economy would be thriving again in the following winter.[16] Such did not prove to be the case. Just as France was apparently emerging from the postwar doldrums, Germany was beginning to slip into a protracted economic crisis. With his eye on Germany's major commercial outlets, the French consul in Hamburg pointed out the obvious: that every nation on the continent would soon be touched and that a simultaneous slump in Britain and the United States would inevitably contribute to "a public catastrophe in Germany." This judgment was corroborated by the Quai d'Orsay's man in Frankfurt, Charles de Hell, who kept a steady watch on the German banking world. His detailed reports showed that the 1873 harvest was inadequate, the financial situation was deteriorating, and both commerce and industry were malfunctioning under "very unfavorable conditions" of economic contraction.[17]

These developments dictated a number of important consequences for the French republic. First among them was a reinforcement of the political status quo. This took place not merely because Bismarck wished it or because of some urgent diplomatic dispatches exchanged between embassies, but because France was part of an interlocking supranational market economy of which Germany was the closest and now most vulnerable member. The German financial crisis could not persist without sending a tremor through the Paris Bourse and raising the fear in France of disastrous ramifications. At one extreme, French Legitimism was by 1874 a lost cause; whereas at the other, the instigation of a "radical red democracy" (as one of Bleichröder's agents in Paris termed it) was certain to provoke a sudden collapse of the stock market.[18] From the standpoint of the French business community, it followed that the most feasible option was a conservative republic. This choice was not without its own difficulties: French commerce was still lagging, the tariff issue was unresolved, the huge public debt remained, and increased parliamentary opposition against indirect taxation made a balanced budget virtually impossible. Yet the perils of change were far more frightening; and the natural reflex of French business in the face of Germany's deepening financial troubles was to sit tight.[19]

Secondly and more specifically, there was a generally dampening effect on French investment capital. A sustained economic recovery was inconceivable unless huge sums were forthcoming from the private sector. But the alarming news from Germany made investors disinclined to take a risk. A useful barometer of such trepidation was the postwar attempt to resuscitate the Crédit Mobilier. After its failure and disbandment in 1868, the Crédit Mobilier had remained defunct until November 1871, when it was refounded under the presidency of Baron de Haussmann, who claimed to dispose over an available capital base of 80 million francs (compared to the prewar listing of 120 million). The records show that the bulk of Haussmann's investments were initially placed abroad: in Egyptian bonds, Spanish and Ottoman loans, Rumanian railways, transatlantic cables, and the like—all of which met little opposition. Indeed, the only serious criticism which Haussmann received at a shareholders' gathering after the first full year of operation was "that the Society has immobilized a part of its capital in industrial affairs," a charge Haussmann was quick to counter by boasting that his efforts had earned a net profit of nearly 5 million francs in 1872.[20] Yet during the summer of 1874 the Crédit Mobilier was already in difficulty, something that Haussmann could blame only on a combination of political instability in France and financial crisis abroad, "first in Germany, then in America."[21] When matters further worsened and Haussmann was forced to concede that no dividends could be paid for 1874, he was unceremoniously deposed. He responded with some bitterness ("Vous avez, messieurs, table rase"), contending that no investment policy, however wise, could have succeeded under the given political and economic conditions.[22] Even allowing for a measure of self-justification in such a view, it was certainly true that by 1875 private French capital had ample reason to be cautious.

A third consequence was as yet only anticipated but was already the subject of some speculation: a return to protectionism. In his own way, it may be recalled, Thiers had earlier supported those who argued that France had been hurt more than helped by the free-trade legislation of the 1860s. Yet the new tariffs of his administration were selective; and, so far as Germany was concerned, their effect was limited by the most-favored-nation clause of the Frankfurt treaty. The German policy, in turn, was designed to impose duties only as a retaliatory measure in order to maintain equilibrium within the existing framework.[23] By the spring of 1875, however, the effects of Germany's inability to snap out of economic lethargy were manifested in increasingly strident criticism of the Berlin government's laissez faire. French consular agents regularly reported these signs of discontent, especially evident among industrialists from Westphalia and the Ruhr, and described the growing agitation for tariff barriers against French and British manufactured goods.[24] They were less well informed about the intense debate within the German government, where the free-trade faction, still guided by Bismarck's chief economic adviser, Rudolf von Delbrück, battled with the protectionist critics. Among the latter was Bleichröder, who pounded the chancellor with contrary advice: "Our commercial policy must be changed if Germany's industry is not to collapse altogether." Bismarck was susceptible to this view, particularly as he was angered by editorials in the Parisian press that contrasted French recovery with German decline. "In reality," Bleichröder comforted the chancellor, "it is virtually impossible in European finance that a state such as Germany should be suffering while the neighboring countries prosper. I foresee setbacks in France as well as England."[25]

In at least one respect this remark was unquestionably correct: whatever the eventual outcome of the protectionist debate in Berlin, developments there were certain to have a significant impact in France. The two economies were too closely connected for the result to have been otherwise. It will be our task to document more fully this interdependence in the specific context of the late 1870s, in order to ascertain how France's economic performance was later affected. As for Germany, the year 1875 ended as badly as it had begun. "The stagnation is general," Charles de Hell wrote from Frankfurt; "no one dreams of beginning a new enterprise."[26] Any remaining optimism on the Paris Bourse correspondingly began to fade. Despite the growing availability of investment capital, Charles de Rothschild informed Bleichröder, the number of transactions there was becoming "very insignificant."[27]

Naturally, the historian might find in these circumstances evidence to confirm a theory of long-term economic cycles. A phase of expansion had just been exhausted, it could be argued, and France was beginning to feel the first effects of a general downward trend. But there may perhaps be an unintended fatalism in such a view; and there is certainly an inadequate appreciation of the factors that disturbed France's economic growth immediately after 1870: the military disruptions, the indemnities, the political dissensions, the social problems, the commercial restrictions, and the psychological malaise—all of them aspects of the relationship with Germany. To insist that these were effects rather than causes of an economic pattern is analogous to asserting that the writings of Voltaire, Diderot, and Rousseau were products of the Enlightenment. A heuristic principle is useful only if it does not lead us to distort or to idealize the reality which it purports to describe.

The War Hoax of 1875

Few incidents in modern history have received notoriety so much out of proportion to their actual importance as the alleged "war scare" that agitated Europe in the spring of 1875. Past generations of historians have labored mightily, with more or less success, to untangle the snarl of diplomatic and journalistic complications that surrounded the affair—only to conclude with virtual unanimity that a genuine threat to peace never really existed. Undeniably, nevertheless, a great deal of public emotion was generated at the time; and it is evident that this feeling was to contribute in an important if unintended manner to the solidification of a republican mentality in France.[28]

Here it must be sufficient to establish the rhythm of events rather than to attempt a detailed narration of them. The first thing to note is that the beginning of the alert should be dated not from the final week of February (as the editors of the *Grosse Politik* have misled many commentators into believing) but from the last day of January, when Bismarck first received confidential information that the French government had ordered a printing of 600 million francs in 20-franc bills. Understandably concerned about the possible implications, the chancellor at once inquired of Hohenlohe whether the French intention might be to create an instant war chest. To this the ambassador felt he could "definitely assure" that in France "no sane person, especially none of the present rulers," thought it possible to challenge Germany militarily; all the more so, he added, since the French lacked any diplomatic alliance. Yet the news, by Bismarck's own account, made a "substantial impression" within his inner circle of advisers. Although he recognized that "strong political and military grounds argue against the assumption that France soon intends to make war against us," the chancellor nonetheless instructed Hohenlohe to remain on the alert and to observe strict silence. Meanwhile, in Berlin, the pertinent documents were classified as top secret and placed in a special file.[29] It was in this context that news of French importation of horses from eastern Europe assumed some importance. The shipment of about nine thousand steeds by rail from Trieste via Italy into southern France had already been reported by the German consul in Nice in January and reconfirmed by him in more detail on 12 February. Not until a fortnight later did Bismarck notify Hohenlohe that he intended to impose an embargo on the exportation of German horses to France, explaining that the French purchases represented "an armament notoriously directed against us." But the chancellor still did not contend that a conflict was imminent; his stated objective was merely to retard the French military reorganization "in case we have to mobilize in about three years."[30]

To accord with this brief recapitulation of the origins of the affair certain conclusions are required. We may dismiss from the outset any notion that the embargo was ordered in a moment of panic or that it was intended to induce a sense of crisis. Nor was its motive primarily political. The reasons for so believing can be precisely defined: the French army was simply unprepared for a military campaign; the composition of the French Assembly was frozen until the next parliamentary elections, still in the indefinite future; the character of the conservative republic was not immediately threatened; and in Decazes the Germans had just the man they wanted at the Quai d'Orsay. Thus the original German purpose could only have been to preserve the status quo, not to upset it. The imposition of the embargo was not a hasty reflex. It was one more sign of Bismarck's displeasure with the speed of French recovery, a reminder to the French of German superiority, and an expression of the determination to maintain it—all of which was particularly appropriate on the eve of the forthcoming debate in Versailles of a military reform bill that was to establish the structure of the French army.

The evidence leaves no doubt that these signals were well understood by civilian officials on both sides. In particular, Decazes remained his imperturbable self, lamenting to Hohenlohe that Bismarck had acted on "false information" and displaying documents to prove that no French orders had in fact been placed for German horses during several previous months. Hohenlohe did not choose to contest the matter with Decazes in private; but his subsequent commentary on this encounter was revealing of the close rapport between the two men and of the climate that continued to prevail between their nations: "At this opportunity, as on previous occasions, I was able to confirm that the French regime—and not Decazes alone—treats the relations of Germany to France with a certain anxiety, and that every symptom of German dissatisfaction with France makes a deep impression here."[31] Decazes had perfectly well comprehended Bismarck's message, in short, and he was responding in an appropriate manner. There was some subtlety in this which depended on an established nexus of personal relationships among well-bred Europeans. The specifics were not really at issue and gross threats were hardly required. The knowing hint, the deliberate gesture, and the unguarded aside were enough.

Within the military it was a different story. Stationed in Paris was the extraordinarily competent German military attaché Major von Bülow, a man of great technical expertise but in no sense Hohenlohe's alter ego. He did not maintain close contacts within the French general staff, nor did he serve as a channel of communication; it was his duty to observe French military affairs and to report them to Berlin.[32] Even when they were superbly informed, consequently, German military leaders lacked a readily available and trustworthy means of consultation with their French counterparts. Moreover, many of the highest German officers—starting with Moltke—had long harbored misgivings about leaving what they regarded as military matters in civilian hands. In both the wars of 1866 and 1870 this had been a major source of dispute within Prussia's ruling caste. Now the episode in 1875 proved to be a third such instance. So far as the general staff was concerned, the French military reorganization was extremely ominous, and polite diplomatic signals were not sufficient. A memorandum circulated by Moltke and the minister of war, General von Kameke, contended that the new cadre reform betrayed "beyond a doubt" the French intention of creating a numerical superiority over Germany for their standing army. The question was thus posed: how could a more urgent and forceful indication of German disapproval be communicated to the French?[33]

Such was the situation at the beginning of April, fully two months after the secret tip to Bismarck about French bank notes and five weeks after the embargo. The French press was quiet and Friedrich von Holstein confirmed from Paris that the French government gave "*absolutely* no indication" of stirring trouble. What few rumors of impending crisis were circulating, he wrote, could probably be traced to financial rivalry between the banking houses of Rothschild and Pereire, in which the former sought to depress the Bourse by fomenting stories of Germany's aggressive intentions.[34] This absence of any immediate provocation and the meandering pace of events suggest that publication of alarmist articles in the *Kölnische Zeitung* and the Berlin *Post* was a deliberate effort, emanating from the German military, to supersede the all too gentlemanly procedures of diplomacy and to administer a more direct and far sterner warning to the French high command.

Countless man-hours of historical research have been expended on a single question: was Bismarck personally responsible for the publication of the newspaper editorials that provoked so much emotion in the spring of 1875? Two observations are in order. By now, first of all, it is surely apparent that the ultimate truth will never be established unless some amazing new revelation is forthcoming from an as yet undetected source. Secondly, the actual importance of irrefutably establishing the chancellor's guilt or innocence has been exaggerated. If Bismarck was not directly to blame—and the circumstantial evidence suggests that he was not—neither can he be entirely exculpated. More than anyone he had contributed to the ambience of intimidation that prevailed between an almighty Germany and a subdued France. Even granted that Bismarck was ordinarily a cautious man, it is hardly uncommon in times of stress for zealous associates, acting on general instructions, to exceed the limits of what their chief might literally have wished. This was probably one such occurrence. All in all, therefore, Bismarck merited little sympathy for the disconcerting results.[35]

Despite the intense public reaction in France, Decazes responded in private with remarkable equanimity. He interpreted the alarm as just another of "the many symptoms of discontent" in Germany. True, there were scattered reports of German troop movements, but no official recriminations had come from Berlin and his relations with Hohenlohe had never been closer. If Germany really wanted to attack France, Bismarck had no need to create an artificial crisis ("une querelle d'Allemand") before presenting Europe with a military fait accompli.[36] At the same time, Hohenlohe, who was obviously caught off guard and was altogether mystified, begged Berlin to explain "the actual context." Bismarck's reply that the editorials were "also surprising to me" may be taken as disingenuous or not; the operative fact remains that he did not totally disavow them, insisting instead that the French military preparations were indeed "disturbing." His only official action was to have a somewhat guarded rectification inserted in the official press.[37]

Thereupon complications ensued which have often been described as a "second phase" of the affair and ordinarily attributed to a clever intrigue by the Duc Decazes.[38] This is a half-truth at best and requires, just as Hohenlohe requested, a clarification of the actual context. Decazes's opportunity was created not by indiscretions of the newspaper press but by the patently exaggerated accusations and threats that continued to originate in official Berlin. A principal source of these was unquestionably the German general staff. Moltke's views on the advantages of preventive war had already been expressed on at least one previous occasion, in 1867; and in 1873 he reiterated them to a shocked British ambassador, Odo Russell.[39] On a visit to Berlin Hohenlohe now heard the same theory advanced by other "highly placed military personnel," prominent among them General von Kameke. Hohenlohe himself was not untouched: "I cannot deny this idea [has] a certain justification," he wrote to Bismarck, although he found reason to doubt that the French could be induced, given the "convalescent" state of their army, to accept a military challenge.[40] But the most ardent proponent of a preemptive strike was one of Bismarck's own subalterns, Joseph Maria von Radowitz, who drafted a confidential memorandum that was sent to the German embassies in London and Petersburg: "There can be no doubt that the preparations which the French regime is undertaking, in order to place its army as soon as possible in combat condition, far exceed the requirements of a peaceful policy and the material resources of the country." It was also Radowitz who expounded the preventive war thesis to the French ambassador in Berlin, fully aware that his remarks would be reported at once to Paris and from there spread to the other European capitals. In a passage later expurgated from the published version of his diary, Hohenlohe recorded a private conversation in which Radowitz showed himself "entirely for war" and expressed the opinion that "we should subdue France completely by starting a war next year and not wait until France is ready."[41]

In view of these facts, it makes far more sense to describe the reaction of Decazes as defensive than to portray it as a ruse cleverly calculated to exploit a fleeting moment of tension. The French had consistently backed away from a confrontation; and they displayed, as Hohenlohe conceded, "more consternation than bellicosity."[42] Both Decazes and Thiers personally sought out the German ambassador to offer assurances that France could not and would not be drawn into a senseless conflict, and Gontaut-Biron carried the same message directly to Berlin from Paris. As a gesture of appeasement, Decazes canceled a projected state loan of 800 million francs and soon let it be known that the French military budget for 1876 would be reduced by 35 million.[43] Yet Berlin persisted in casting suspicion on Decazes: now for the first time the German ambassador in Petersburg was informed of the 600 million francs in new bills printed by the French government (more than three months earlier!); moreover, he was told that "this extraordinary measure can only be regarded as preparation for the eventuality of war."[44]

Again, the rhythm of events provides a clue to their significance. This was early May, a month after the newspaper alert. During the intervening weeks, Decazes had remained impassive in the face of what seemed to him a series of German provocations. Not a diplomatic counteroffensive but the lack of one was troublesome for the Germans. If the charges from Berlin lacked credibility, they were bound to elicit sympathy for the French—hence the belated revelation of the alleged French war threat, knowledge of which Bismarck had carefully guarded since January, as ostensibly fresh proof of France's aggressive intentions. Not until 5 May was Decazes himself first confronted with this matter by Hohenlohe and told that Germany therefore had every reason to regard the French military preparations as "threatening." That conversation followed within hours the message to Petersburg, cited above. Notably, it preceded by a day the publication of a controversial article in the London *Times* which placed blame for the protracted alarm on Germany.[45] This tight sequence demonstrates that the Germans were deliberately escalating the affair rather than allowing it to abate; and it establishes that Decazes, even if he directly inspired the *Times* editorial, was responding to rather than initiating the latest development. In sum, a search of personal papers and classified German documents does not sustain the charge that an unprovoked intrigue by Decazes was primarily responsible for inaugurating a "second phase." Instead, it was the sustained thrust of German intimidation since the beginning of the year which he finally sought to parry.

The rest is familiar from published documents and diplomatic histories: the British government's offer of mediation; the noticeable coolness of the Russians to protestations of German innocence; the widely expressed irritation, even by the Kaiser, with the blustering of the "incorrigible" German press.[46] Bismarck's subsequent explanations were lame and unconvincing. He claimed that the English reaction was "completely incomprehensible," since a peaceful resolution of the controversy had been secure "for weeks and months." He made elaborate efforts to reassure Petersburg and Vienna. And in characteristic fashion he elaborated his favorite theory of conspiracy: that a wave of germanophobia had been created by Catholic priests, scheming women, unreliable diplomats (especially Gontaut, whom he wanted dismissed at once), and an alliance of the clerical-French-Polish press, which in all European and other countries and languages systematically supports this unrest."[47] After reviewing the details, we have little justification to accept these sweeping innuendoes as an appropriate description of what actually occurred. The diplomatic events of 1875 revealed nothing more than the continuing French sensitivity to German demagogy.

The Politics of Polarization

The enduring political configuration of the Third Republic was slow to emerge. It would be mistaken to assume that the deadlock of the early and mid-1870s was identical with the political structure of the "stalemate society" after 1878.[48] As we shall subsequently consider, the French republic was refounded at the end of the decade, and the second version had relatively little in common with its forebear. This fundamental realignment was of course a result of the definitive victory of a republican consensus. But there is no reason to be satisfied with such a bland summary or to stop short of a more precise characterization of the transition in progress.

The Thierist republic could be fairly described in political terms as a narrow and fragile centrist regime constantly endangered on its flanks by powerful conservative and radical factions. The government was obliged to oscillate between these two poles; and, as the decade advanced and both factions more stridently asserted their claims, an erosion of the entire system became discernible. The French polity can thus be framed in much the same image as Trotsky's famous analysis of "dual power" in revolutionary Russia: a process of polarization that finally had to be resolved in one sense or the other.[49] But an important qualification needs to be added: neither pole was monolithic, for three general reasons. First, each of the factions was in reality a swarm of contending interests. Conservatism continued to be torn by the rivalry among Legitimists, Orleanists, and Bonapartists; and likewise the presumption of the Gambettists to represent French radicalism was never uncontested by others on the Left. Second, the ideological issues were always ambiguous. At no time were clear alternatives simultaneously posed between monarchism and republicanism, clericalism and secularism, or capitalism and socialism. Third, the perennial French tradition of multipartism was simply ineradicable. It would be fatuous to suppose, even as the polarization became increasingly pronounced, that France stood on the verge of a two-party system and that a great opportunity was somehow lost to anglicize French politics. If the desire for simplicity and symmetry has often been an intellectual virtue esteemed by the French, in their public life it is an impulse they have usually resisted to the last.[50]

Yet, after all, the number of available options was finite. After previously establishing the five political alternatives of the immediate postwar period, we may now extend that analysis by briefly reconsidering each in turn. In so doing the specific objective must be twofold: both to evaluate the impact of polarization on those bidding for power in France and to appraise the German response as the entire process approached a critical stage.

The *monarchists* had not fared well since Thiers's fall and the inauguration of MacMahon's septennate. Not only had Chambord's feckless rejection of the tricolor eliminated the Legitimists from contention, it had also foreclosed a sturdy alliance with the Orleanists. The concept of fusionism had suddenly disappeared from the political lexicon. Instead, there was much talk and some evidence of an informal parliamentary entente between Orleanists and moderate republicans in opposition to the Bonapartists. The Legitimists, in any event, were cut adrift. If any hope remained for the monarchist cause, it would initially have to come under the guise of a *république aumalienne*. In his capacity as the commander of a French army corps, Aumale kept himself available, although his only conspicuous action in 1875 was to suspend a provincial newspaper for printing remarks injurious to the German Kaiser. This was a small gesture, to be sure, but it continued the standard practice by serious political aspirants of making their conciliatory disposition toward Germany known to Berlin and to the French public. Yet Aumale and his family still lacked a substantial base of popular support; and it required no shrewd analyst to conclude, as did President MacMahon, that "the Orleanists do not have the country for them."[51]

The consequences were fairly predictable. Political activity for the Orleanists generally consisted of defining more closely their differences with the Legitimists—a rather useless exercise, the German chargé in Paris remarked, since "this divorce has long ago been consummated." Meanwhile, there continued the attrition of Orleanist politicians who drifted or defected toward the Left Center, that is, who accommodated themselves to the conservative republic. The longer this process continued, the more credible became the Bonapartist claim to lead the parliamentary Right. The Orleanist princes were thereby placed in the impossible situation of being able neither to dominate the existing government nor to alter its form. Their support was slowly ground away as the political wheels turned, and the elections of Senate and Chamber in early 1876 left the faction that bore their name in growing disarray.[52]

The *Bonapartists* could only benefit from the monarchists' loss. Predictions of the imperial party's demise after the death of Napoleon III had been premature. In fact, the signs of Orleanist-republican cooperation in the Assembly could be interpreted as one response to a Bonapartist resurgence. "The conservative party in the country," Hohenlohe concluded as early as the spring of 1875, "is to a great extent Bonapartist." He remained convinced that the ultimate contest in France would pit the Bonapartists against the republicans, on the grounds that the only constitutional confrontation that the French people were capable of understanding was the one between conservatism and republicanism, of which the respective champions would prove to be an imperial pretender and Léon Gambetta. The formidability of the Bonapartist challenge was confirmed by the government's undisguised attempt to inhibit the party's political activity and newspaper press. Despite that discouragement, the Bonapartist leadership persisted in the confidence that the *appel au peuple* would become irresistible and that the movement would soon arouse that popular enthusiasm which the monarchists had failed to stir.[53]

An attempt to gain German patronage, or at least approval, was also undertaken by the Bonapartists. In this case the intermediary was the Abbé Cadoret, who, after exploratory talks in England with Empress Eugénie and Prince Lucien Bonaparte, sought out the German ambassador to revive interest in the imperial alternative. This approach was not totally without success, especially when conciliatory editorials miraculously began to appear in the Bonapartist press. Bismarck was sufficiently impressed to have Hohenlohe instructed that Germany had "no reason to reject or discourage this faction," since "on the whole Bonapartism would still constitute the least fanatical form of government in France, in the political as well as the religious sphere."[54] Yet two major obstacles blocked the way. One was accumulating evidence that the Vatican, after abandoning Chambord as a lost cause and coming to regard the Bonapartists as the most likely proponents of conservatism, was quietly preparing the French clergy for a political realignment; if so, nothing was more likely to undercut German cooperation than the suspicion of an ultramontane plot. The other problem was statistical: the electoral returns for the new French parliament simply did not confirm Bonapartist expectations. The notion that a national plebiscite would sweep the party into office at the first propitious moment was thus exposed as an illusion, raising in turn an awkward question about what route the Bonapartists could possibly pursue to power.[55]

The *Thierists* had also suffered an eclipse in 1873 and 1874, but it was only temporary and not total. Never a political party, the Thierist cause was still a force to be reckoned with. If the others should default for one reason or another and MacMahon was somehow forced from office before the expiration of his term, the conservative republic might yet again coalesce around the almost mythical personality of its first president. Since his resignation, Thiers had consorted with those centrist politicians who clustered daily in the anterooms of Versailles and the salons of Paris. Everyone regarded him as highly influential, without being quite certain of the nature or purpose of his influence. He was known to maintain close contacts with the German embassy, even though the subject of these consultations was always a mystery. In short, the old man's political clout was potential rather than actual. With his customary immodesty Thiers shared in the thrill of anticipation, savoring thoughts of his comeback and "considering himself more and more as the only decisive personality."[56]

In at least three regards such ambition was something more than personal vanity. Major political decisions could not be made without considering Thiers's position and possible action. One of the reasons for the Buffet cabinet's opposition to the *scrutin de liste*, for instance, was a fear that Thiers might be too successful as a candidate in national elections and severely embarrass his successor. "The struggle over the two forms of suffrage," Hohenlohe stated with some exaggeration, "is thus strictly speaking a struggle between MacMahon and Thiers."[57] Moreover, although he lacked the secure underpinnings of a national party structure, Thiers did have able parliamentary lieutenants—skillful and well-placed men, such as Jules Simon and Léon Say—who kept their patron informed, conveyed his wishes, cultivated his mystique. Finally, the

Thierists held the inestimable advantage of an opening to the Left. The widely publicized insults once traded by Thiers and Gambetta were years in the past; and the likelihood that they might form a political tandem represented one of the most significant consequences of polarization.[58]

The *Gambettists* maintained the sort of confidence displayed by disciplined long-distance runners who purposely remain a few strides off the pace and await the proper moment to sweep by opponents still toiling in front. Their gains, both political and psychological, seemed relentless. The selection in 1875 of a new Commission of Thirty, the steering committee of the Chamber, was a clear victory for the Left which Hohenlohe described as a "first decisive step toward destruction of the majority."[59] Gambetta's personal acquisition that year of the chairmanship of the parliamentary budget committee also afforded him an enormous leverage that he was to apply with increasing effect. His policy remained one of patiently cultivating a new majority of moderate republicanism. Even his opposition to the adoption of a *scrutin d'arrondissement* was largely pro forma, so confident did he feel that the parliament would eventually consolidate his victory, whatever the procedure of election might be. For Gambetta's adoption of this methodical strategy, one of Bleichröder's agents, on a tour of the provinces, offered an explanation: the French peasantry wanted "*peace at any price.*" To them the willingness of the moderate republicans to bide their time was very reassuring; whereas the more strenuous efforts of the monarchists and Bonapartists, especially during the international complications of 1875, seemed to portend unnecessary trouble and further risk. The mood of the country was political apathy and a profound distrust of adventure.[60]

There were other reasons for Gambetta's caution. Since he deliberately sought to attract support among the centrists—and therefore refused to support full amnesty for the exiled communards of 1871—he had to weather severe criticism from within the radical ranks. Nor could he count on the unqualified loyalty of the Thierists, correctly recognizing in Jules Simon a personal rival as well as a political ally. The umbrage of the largely Orleanist cabinet also placed him under some constraint; technically, France was still under martial law, which meant that he could be abruptly prosecuted for any public activity interpreted by the regime as seditious. By 1876 the Gambettist grip on the Chamber was consequently strong but not unbreakable. Although Gambetta was clearly in ascent, being the single French politician who had most profited from polarization, he was not yet in command.[61]

MacMahon was not in an enviable position. A presidential republic was never a realistic possibility after 1873. The marshal had been chosen precisely because, unlike Thiers, he represented no threat to parliamentary supremacy and the party system. He was supposed to be above politics, which actually meant that he was more often a nervous bystander than an active participant. On the evening before the decision in favor of a *scrutin d'arrondissement*, Hohenlohe found the president fretting and uncertain about the outcome; and later MacMahon was relieved that no decision or action would be expected of him. His own diffidence reflected the inertia of the nation, reinforced it, and depended on it.[62]

But the reality was that republicanism was "growing over Marshal MacMahon's head."[63] His original supporters had boosted him to the presidency to hold the republicans in check, not to preside over the dissolution of conservatism; and now they expected him to take their side. His only attempt to do so on the eve of the parliamentary elections in 1876 was politically ineffectual but personally revealing. He solemnly urged Frenchmen to support his "conservative and truly liberal policy," which he defined as "defense of the social order, respect of law, devotion to country, beyond the sentiments, aspirations, and obligations of party." If this seemed somewhat elusive and apolitical, his concluding exhortation was less so: that the people join him in discouraging those who might menace national security through "the propagation of antisocial doctrines and revolutionary programs." When the balloting nevertheless brought heavy republican gains, MacMahon's dilemma became disturbingly clear. Either he would need to move leftward with the electorate or else he would have to participate in a conservative reaction. The middle, in either event, could no longer hold.[64]

So long as this metamorphosis of French politics was slow and inconclusive, the Germans had little reason to abandon their malevolent neutrality. Throughout the adoption of constitutional legislation and the period of elections, Berlin had remained silent, neither advising nor consenting, complacent in the belief that "in any case the next Chamber will be republican."[65] Evidence of direct German intervention can be established with certainty in only one instance: assisting the Duc Decazes to win a seat in the eighth arrondissement of Paris. Distressed with the composition of the Senate, from which he was excluded, and threatened by stout opposition from a Bonapartist candidate for the Chamber, the foreign minister appeared to be on the brink of enforced retirement. Hohenlohe was already informed of this possibility and of the fact that Decazes had once offered his resignation to MacMahon, and then reluctantly withdrawn it.[66] The German ambassador was thus receptive to a confidential hint that Decazes's chances of survival would be significantly improved should Germany publicly agree to end the infamous horse embargo several days before the election. When Bismarck concurred and the embargo was lifted in time, Hohenlohe was hopeful that, through "the efforts I am making with Thiers and others with Gambetta," the favorable publicity would assist Decazes to victory. How many French voters were actually persuaded by these maneuvers cannot, of course, be measured. The evident assumption is nonetheless noteworthy that a signal of German approval was considered politically advantageous for Decazes, who did manage to win. But it remained an isolated incident, an attempt to maintain the French foreign minister rather than to alter or impede the general political drift of the Third Republic.[67]

Such a conclusion accords both with the public record and with the extant private correspondence of the period. Against it can be set only some contemporary speculation from French sources of dubious reliability. When the translation of a speech by Gambetta was reproduced in the official *Reichsanzeiger*, for example, Gontaut-Biron took it as evidence of "an accord of ideas, perhaps of tactics, between the chancellor and the [French] radicals." The ambassador also expressed his conviction that Bismarck was maintaining "established relations" with Thiers. Some French conservatives even charged that German money had been secretly passed to aid republican candidates in the electoral campaign. But it is difficult to see in these unsubstantiated accusations more than a cluster of sour grapes.[68]

Only one symptom of polarization elicited a strong German response. Some weeks after the republican landslide Hohenlohe was informed of a newly formulated program of the Bonapartists: "Maintenance of the principle of the *appel au peuple*; firm defense of the Catholic Church and of the interests of the landholders and the army; unreserved support of the marshal; war to the end against the Orleanists and republicans." Drafted by Rouher and approved by the Bonapartist crown prince, so Hohenlohe reported, this strategy was based on the premises that "within a certain time the natural development of things must lead to revolution" and that the conservatives could then seek "to gain power through a *coup de main*." Bismarck retorted at once with coded instructions sent to the major German embassies: the Bonapartist platform represented "an extreme pessimism" and revealed "a very dangerous game" which could only produce "a danger for the European system." To acquiesce in this eventuality was an unacceptable risk for Germany. By contrast, "the maintenance of the present constitutional form and the peaceful evolution of the country by legal means would offer Europe far greater guarantees." If there were to be a future test of political strength in France, in other words, Germany would not hesitate to take a side.[69]

The Signs of Erosion

What France was witnessing in 1876, let there be no mistake, was the slow dissolution of a whole public ethos. Although the political arrangement of the time was of course a unique improvisation of the postwar era, it was also in some sense a reversion to the conventions and practices of the July monarchy. That Thiers had been the last of the Orleanist ministers in 1848 was not entirely coincidental, and one might say that his efforts were intended to revive the political system that had been temporarily displaced by Louis Bonaparte. The crucial difference at first was Thiers's own idiosyncratic brand of leadership, so dynamic and so different from that of Louis Philippe. But for this deviation had been substituted the surrogate monarchy of Marshal MacMahon, appropriately controlled by an Orleanist cabinet. Thus the improvised republic of 1870 had brought a renewal, not a revolution.

The foundations of this structure were now being permanently eroded. Not since the months immediately preceding the insurrection of February 1848—the Paris Commune excepted—had there been such widespread extraparliamentary activity in France. And the reasons were much the same: a perception that the true interests of many Frenchmen were simply not being represented in the regular political process and a complaint that those who ruled were unable to cope with the nation's problems. The eloquent words of Alexis de Tocqueville to the final Orleanist Assembly were no less appropriate in the 1870s than when they had been spoken three decades before:

> Do you not see that there are gradually forming in their breasts opinions and ideas which are destined not only to upset this or that law, ministry, or even form of government, but society itself until it totters upon the foundations on which it rests today? Do you not hear them repeating increasingly that all that is above them is incapable and unworthy of governing them; that the present distribution of goods throughout the world is unjust; that property rests on a foundation which is not an equitable foundation? And do you not realize that when such opinions take root, when they spread in an almost universal manner, when they sink deeply into the masses, they are bound to bring with them sooner or later, I know not when nor how, a most formidable revolution?[70]

Once again popular protest was taking the form of political banquets. Despite police surveillance and the continuing restrictions of martial law, these semiprivate gatherings flourished everywhere in France. The thrust of the new banquet movement was patently anticlerical. The one thing that all banqueters could agree upon, however divergent their views might otherwise be, was a condemnation of ultramontanism. Political conservatism was assumed to be a euphemism for clerical influence, the front for Vatican interference, the cover for a Jesuit plot, the mask of ignorance and obscurantism. Although somewhat muted in the popular press because of censorship, such rhetoric was commonplace at the banquets. Police records show the true extent of this campaign and its harshness. Months before Gambetta cast his famous gauntlet challenging the Church to a duel, the banquet orators had coined the phrases of contention: "Notre ennemi, c'est le cléricalisme"; "le clergé est notre ennemi à tous"; and so on. Under the surface of official decorum a French Kulturkampf was already beginning.[71]

Otherwise the popular protest was far from speaking in chorus. No one was subjected to more severe criticism, in fact, than Gambetta himself. Particularly vulnerable because of his rejection of a blanket amnesty for the communards, he was under constant pressure to cut a less conciliatory figure in the Chamber and in public appearances. Detractors attempted repeatedly to call him to account at banquets organized in Paris for that announced purpose; and his refusals to appear provoked various charges that he was a toady to the bourgeoisie, an agent of Bismarck, and a political opportunist.[72] After a motion of no confidence was adopted by a large majority at a banquet in his own district of Belleville, Gambetta finally consented to a public defense of his position. Before a massive gathering estimated by the police at nine thousand, he conceded nothing to his critics, and he again renounced the amnesty bill, describing the Commune as the unfortunate convulsion of a deceived populace. As he apparently intended, these statements "clearly separated him from the intransigents" and thereby assured that the label of opportunism would henceforth be, for better or worse, identified with his name.[73]

The indiscipline and sheer variety of protest movements indicated that French radicalism was suffering from the typical ailments of political adolescence. Everyone had a speech to make, a manifesto to publish, an axe to grind; and all wanted the platform at once. The cause with the most compelling and far-reaching significance was the effort to organize a labor congress to meet in the capital city in early October 1876. This undertaking proved to be divisive and somewhat disappointing for its participants; but at least, as the vigilant prefect of police had to concede, the congress represented a purposeful step toward its stated objective: a "federation of workers" that would link Paris and the provinces, industry and agriculture, France and the International.[74] Far less significant at the time, and destined to remain so for the balance of the century, were simultaneous efforts to found organizations of students and of women. Both produced their articulate advocates at banquets and labor rallies, yet neither was as yet able to establish a separate identity nor to attract a large following.[75]

An exception in the respect can be made for freemasonry. By its secretive nature the masonic movement was partially camouflaged in the public arena, but the police took care to follow its personalities and political activities. Both the Scottish and Oriental rites were highly active in France during the 1870s, and many of the later republic's important politicians first became masons at that time. A single lodge in Paris, La Clémente Amitié, could boast such names as Emile Littré, Jules Ferry, and Gambetta.[76] A masonic gathering, although unreported in the press, might therefore have a political significance at which the uninitiated could only guess, since the freemasons functioned as a kind of underground general staff for republicans and radicals of all stripes. As distinguished from the banquet movement in general, of which it was in effect an elegant relative, masonry was more precisely anti-Catholic than anticlerical. Its leadership tended to think in manichean terms well suited to a polarized political system. As one of them formulated the positivistic masonic philosophy at the inauguration of a new lodge in Belleville in August 1876: "There is no middle course; today one must be Catholic or freemason, a man of shadow or a man of light." Such a view, not at all untypical, was frankly impatient with past compromises and was symptomatic of the transition toward a new republican milieu.[77]

Grievances against the existing state of affairs were not exclusively ideological in nature. Wildcat strikes, especially in the metal and building trades in Paris, were an almost daily occurrence. Precise statistics were not kept and are difficult to establish, but the frequency of labor disputes was very alarming to government and business circles alike. Since the importance of syndicalism was still negligible and no regular channels of arbitration or collective bargaining existed, the workers usually found their employers better organized and more powerful. That they were nonetheless undeterred from striking testifies more clearly to material want than to political agitation. The most prominent workers' demand was invariably an increase in wages, often a pitifully small amount. Strikes sometimes dragged on for weeks because the patrons refused an increment of fifty centimes a day or 10 centimes an hour. The prefect of police, whose own office served on occasion as a place of confrontation for the two sides, followed these disputes carefully and observed "the most hostile [and] regrettable attitude" of the workers toward their patrons. Socialism was not yet the issue, a living wage was. Many workers remained indifferent to the syndicates for the paradoxical reason that they seemed to obtain so little results. But there was no other place to turn, and the future development of trade unionism, despite these inauspicious beginnings, was only a matter of time.[78]

Part cause and part effect, the strikes were only one aspect of the deepening trouble of the French economy. Measured by both morale and performance, 1875 had been an erratic year for industry and commerce, but the spring of 1876 augured well.[79] However, the seasonal slump of that summer was more drastic than before, and an anticipated improvement in the autumn was long in coming. In August and September Paris suffered a new epidemic of bankruptcies at a rate three times that of the previous year. Once again the small shops and boutiques were struck the hardest, and fortnightly police reports from the city's twenty arrondissements confirmed that "confidence is tending to diminish."[80] Despite the news that a world's fair was scheduled in the capital for 1878, presumably to be a boon for public works, this general pessimism was accompanied by an increasingly sluggish performance of the stock market. Daily fluctuations were usually related to news about foreign affairs. A rumor of widening conflict in the Middle East would sent stock notations down; then a reassuring announcement from Berlin that the war was likely to remain localized was sufficient to raise them again. But the underlying problems were more intractable: governmental instability, strikes and bankruptcies, languishing commercial relations with the depressed economies of central Europe, Belgium, and England. If there was no shortage of capital in the French marketplace, financiers remained justifiably hesitant to invest heavily at a time when they had economic as well as political reasons to fear an approaching crisis.[81]

To speak of a French cult of decadence at this juncture would doubtless be premature. There was some sense of futility, however, which was chronically aggravated by an awareness of the German presence. France invariably suffered from a comparison with the Reich, often made in the republic's early years, which implied that no matter how much the French exerted themselves to cope with their mounting difficulties, they would still fail to regain the rank of a major power.[82] This pervasive consciousness of collective inferiority was known to have an irrefutable basis in fact. Statistics released in the summer of 1876 showed that the French rate of population growth had slowed to barely one-third that of Germany. The number of marriages in France was actually declining: 352,754 in 1872; 321,238 in 1873; 303,113 in 1874. Substantially bolstered by the annexation of Alsace and Lorraine, Germany's population was meanwhile burgeoning. In strictly military terms the implications of this demographic gap were disturbing enough.[83] Beyond that, in a psychological sense, France's recuperative powers were inevitably placed in doubt. The nation seemed to be losing ground to Germany; and, if so, the rhetoric of revanchism was bound to have a hollow ring. This was indeed the case if we may judge from the decline of irredentist organizations in the latter half of the decade: for example, the Societé d'Alsace-Lorraine, whose number of adherents in Paris earlier reached fifteen thousand, had dwindled to only six hundred by 1876. For the moment, at least, real problems were crowding out vain hopes.[84]

In the midst of all these pressures and contending interests, the French government appeared powerless and at odds with itself. An ultramontane party of order was lining up against a republican party of movement. The possibility of a parliamentary impasse between the Senate and the Chamber was evident from a split vote on higher education. A debilitating struggle within the administration was likely to result from an attempted republican purge of prefects, mayors, and diplomats. When compromises could be reached they were regarded on both sides as impermanent and unsatisfactory; and it had become a strain to think of the president as an impartial arbiter of the national interest. A decisive confrontation was becoming unavoidable.

Chapter 6

The Test of Strength

"Salutary Fear" and the Crisis of Seize Mai

By the beginning of the year 1877 nearly ninety months had elapsed since the outbreak of the war of 1870. During all that time German supremacy had weighed on France as an immense burden. The pressure of that load was constant; and the weight was not to be measured solely in individual incidents of German interference in French public life. It was, rather, the cumulative effect that sapped the energy and confidence of the republic and left its leaders perpetually apprehensive about the next step. Even when there was little substance to them, the daily rumors of foreign intervention were sufficient to maintain the tension which every Frenchmen felt and which no political figure could deny. The French were afflicted, as one German boasted, with a "salutary fear" of Germany that could not fail to affect any contest for control of the Third Republic.[1]

The unresolved internal deadlock was characterized by two issues, each of which disclosed more deep-seated problems. The first of these was the amnesty question. We have already observed how the demand for a pardon of the communards divided Right from Left in the parliament and, moreover, why it also widened the rift between opportunist and intransigent republicans. Gambetta's refusal to champion an unconditional amnesty undoubtedly pleased more moderate elements whose support he sought, but at the same time it alienated the more radical segment of political opinion. At stake was the ability of Gambetta—who else could it be?—to rally all of the leftist elements to the republican cause once the moment of testing came. Hohenlohe's surmise that Gambetta's position had been at least temporarily shaken, and that he knew it, was accurate.[2] Hence the prospect of a major political upheaval, especially one for which he could not be directly blamed, was not unwelcome to Gambetta. In order to assemble the republican forces behind him, nothing could be more useful than an aggressive reactionary challenge. The time for that, however, had not yet arrived. On the first day of December 1876 a compromise bill proposing partial amnesty, approved in the Chamber by a slender margin, was rejected in the Senate. The deadlock continued.[3]

The second controversy centered on the budget. Among the formal topics of debate were such matters as funding of military chaplains, detachment of military personnel to public funerals, maintenance of a French embassy at the Vatican, and financial support of faculties at Catholic institutions of higher learning. The least common denominator, of course, was the future relationship of Church and State in France. Many republicans were impatient to bring this issue to a head; and they were openly dismayed by the Senate's attempt to restore appropriations curtailed by Gambetta's budget committee in the Chamber. In this instance the increasingly vocal anticlerical view was still not sustained, even though Gambetta did manage to retain his presidency of the committee. But everyone knew that the next year's budget would inevitably pose the same problems. Only the solutions might be different.[4]

At least these skirmishes were enough to bring down the Dufaure ministry and to oblige MacMahon to search for a new cabinet. The choice of premier fell on Jules Simon, a formidable man of the Left Center closely associated with Thiers. As the marshal privately admitted to Hohenlohe, the selection of a rightist under the circumstances was impossible, since it could only be a temporary measure prior to dismissing the parliament and thus, in his own words, to creating a "ministère de dissolution."[5] This was close to confessing that a full-scale crisis could not be averted—it could only be delayed—unless MacMahon and the conservatives were willing to acknowledge the republic as France's permanent form of government. For his part, Simon's oracular declaration that he was "profoundly republican and profoundly conservative" expressed two things: a reaffirmation of the basic formula of Thierist ideology and an intention to freeze the existing situation for as long as possible. Helpless to do otherwise, short of provoking a turmoil, MacMahon declared himself satisfied that a modus vivendi had been found and proudly introduced his new premier at an Elysée reception for diplomats and politicians. For several of the French republicans who attended, this was the first invitation to the presidential residence. Yet they could hardly overlook the fact that only two ministers in the previous cabinet had actually been replaced and were accordingly absent. In reality, it was still business as usual.[6]

Like the domestic scene, France's foreign affairs remained calm but chronically ominous. A conflict between Russia and the Ottoman Turks had been threatening to erupt for months and, as usual, the possible repercussions among the other powers were disturbing. It is little wonder that the French displayed some symptoms of paranoia. Decazes was convinced that Bismarck was pushing Russia to an aggression against Turkey; and in his private correspondence this assumption became generalized into a frequently repeated epithet about the chancellor's "evil designs."[7] Generally a worrier himself, Gontaut-Biron stoked the foreign minister's suspicions with accounts of recurrent hostility toward France in the German press. These were further magnified by the story, necessarily troubling after the alarm of 1875, that "certain German officers" were again contemplating "an imminent war against France." Moreover, there was an erratic and irrational quality to all of this, since Bismarck remained totally in seclusion. For the French he remained unapproachable and unfathomable. Gontaut found him "a sphinx" and "a living menace for all of Europe." Although the exact nature of that menace was never certain, it was nonetheless effective. As one French agent commented with grudging admiration: "If Bismarck's spies accurately inform him about the terror he inspires in us, he ought to be satisfied."[8]

The Germans were perfectly aware of the intimidating effect this situation produced in France, and they took care both to cultivate an appropriate image and to gauge its impact. Hohenlohe was certain that "the dominant, indeed the completely overriding feeling in France at the moment is the fear of becoming involved *prematurely* in a war with Germany." Any effort by the French regime to take a more active role abroad would therefore meet with instant popular disapproval. The restraint on domestic affairs was similar because, according to Hohenlohe, "it is very well known here that the German government prefers the republican form of state in France." The German ambassador even went so far as to claim, inversely, that an indication of support from Berlin for French conservatism would strengthen the dynastic factions and encourage them to bid for power. But one of Bismarck's inimitable black question marks penciled in the margin beside this comment expressed the chancellor's own skepticism. That the German presence weighed *against* sudden and erratic motion in French politics had become axiomatic; that it could effectively be brought to bear *for* a specific purpose or party was a corollary yet to be demonstrated.[9]

Frequent note has been taken of the attempts of various French political groups to solicit some sign of German patronage. With a decisive contest for leadership soon to be joined, such activity became more than a perfunctory ritual. Those most acutely discomforted by the lack of German approval in 1877 were the Bonapartists. They had the most to lose from total inertia and the most to gain from a dislocating crisis. But in making this position too evident, the imperial faction suffered a sharp reprimand in the German press. In keeping with the accepted *règles du jeu*, the Bonapartists then made a renewed effort to reassure Berlin that they contemplated no coup d'état and were content to await the termination of MacMahon's septennate in 1880. "In three years," Rouher boasted within easy earshot, "the entire country will enthusiastically demand Napoleon IV and a revision of the constitution." Essentially the same message was communicated to the German embassy from the party's young colonels, Clément Duvernois and Raoul Duval, who conceded that "the thought of seizing the regime by violent means must be abandoned as infeasible." Such statements, astutely leaked through reliable contacts, revealed something of the constant constraint placed on French politics by the "salutary fear" of Germany. It can be added, however, that this particular act of contrition had little effect. Bismarck again disclaimed any serious negotiations with the Bonapartists and still offered them no public indication of a willingness to sponsor or favor the imperialist cause. German support for the moderate republic thus remained intact; and "so long as a Jules Simon cabinet exists," Hohenlohe judged, "I believe the Bonapartist agitation can be considered ineffectual."[10]

The survival of the Simon ministry was placed in question in the spring of 1877 by the onset, at last, of the Russo-Turkish war. For more than a year the so-called Eastern crisis had been anticipated in France with foreboding—partially with an eye to French investments in Ottoman bonds, of course, but also because a conflict was bound to raise the level of tension throughout Europe and hence with Germany. French agents quickly confirmed that the effect was just as expected.[11] With an inhabitual flourish, Decazes exclaimed: "The die is cast and the great adventure is about to begin!" Despite Hohenlohe's customary disclaimers about Bismarck's "good intentions," the French foreign minister was apprehensive, as his private correspondence testified. Jules Simon was also worried and took the extraordinary step of forbidding all direct contact of French functionaries with their German counterparts: "I am quite preoccupied by what a maladroit subprefect might write at this moment."[12] Within a few days he also had reason to be concerned about what a malevolent field marshal might say: Moltke's sudden declaration that Germany would reinforce the garrison in Alsace-Lorraine caused a shudder throughout France. Once more German troops were massing to march onto what was, after all, still regarded as French soil. As a consequence, the kind of public alarm that had persisted in 1875 again gripped France in 1877 when the month of May began.[13]

Another source of anomie was the more strident tenor of French radicalism. We have examined the muted, sometimes clandestine character of radical opposition prior to this time. Insofar as this restraint was self-imposed, and not the direct result of state censorship and police surveillance, it had been based on the calculation that an unduly vociferous campaign to turn out the conservative rascals would only be frightening to the French public and therefore counterproductive at the polls. That premise was fundamental to Gambetta's tactic of moderation, which, despite radical criticism, he had successfully imposed on the Left. But the temptation to step out more boldly was always present, and a specific occasion was provided by the Lablond interpellation: a motion in the Chamber that required the cabinet to explain what steps were being taken to curb ultramontane agitation within France. Even a fairly astute defense of his policy by Jules Simon on 3 May was entirely overshadowed by the aroused rhetorical performance of Gambetta, who ended with the phrase every radical had been waiting to hear from him: "le cléricalisme? voilà l'ennemi!" This statement meant an end to ambiguity, a rejection of compromise, and a challenge to join in political combat. Suddenly vulnerable from both sides, Simon's position was quickly shattered. "The impression was powerful," Bismarck was informed, "and Gambetta has thereby made himself master of the situation."[14]

One need scarcely look further for the pressing reasons that led MacMahon to dismiss Jules Simon on 16 May and to recall as premier his old friend and private counselor Albert de Broglie. The alternatives were inescapable. Either the president would have to tolerate Gambetta's ascendency in the Chamber, permit a steady electoral drift to republicanism, and endure the excesses of a more unrestrained anticlericalism and anticonservatism; or else he could return to that group of men who had originally conspired to place him in office and with them attempt to reassert command of the nation in the name of "moral order." No politically informed person was in doubt as to the real significance of MacMahon's choice of Broglie. This was not just one more cabinet change or another episodic realignment of parliamentary coalitions. The character of the republic and perhaps its existence were being placed in jeopardy.

In general terms this development had long been expected and analyzed by the Germans. Only the timing of Simon's disappearance had been uncertain; and that came, as Hohenlohe admitted, with "astonishing rapidity."[15] The Germans had done nothing deliberately to provoke MacMahon's impulsive action, nor was there any reason why they should have interfered. A political impasse was crippling to France. To break it, one way or another, might produce a French nation more potent and less predictable. If the Germans had not created the French deadlock, their influence had often been exercised to maintain it—both positively, by encouraging the conservative republic, and negatively, by discouraging the aspirations of any single faction to mobilize the conservative cause. To a great extent, moreover, the prevailing climate of public apprehension in France was of Germany's making. "In recent days," Hohenlohe had written from Paris only forty-eight hours before Simon's resignation, "fears of a war with Germany have again gained the upper hand here."[16] Even when flimsy and fully unjustified, these rumors had recurred with such disconcerting regularity as to be a ubiquitous element of French public life. No political decision could be rendered, no electoral campaign conducted, no ideology articulated without taking the German menace into account.

Politics and Prefects

No less critical than the search for a durable form of government was the need for an efficient corps of administration. The two were closely related. Before 1789 the French monarchy had long attempted, with limited success, to develop a bureaucratic network to serve the interests of a central regime. That purpose was better implemented after Napoleon's creation of the modern prefectoral system in 1800. Like all Bonapartist innovations, however, this was hardly intended as an act of impartiality. To be a high functionary was to hold a political appointment. The notion that France was erratically governed but securely administered throughout the nineteenth century is therefore dubious. At the departmental level, at least, the two were virtually inseparable; and given the frequency of political upheaval before 1890, the profession of prefect was necessarily hazardous.[17]

At no other time in French history were there more administrative changes than in the 1870s. By the end of the Second Empire the prefectoral corps was firmly Bonapartist. A first drastic purge occurred during the war, when Gambetta ordered the wholesale introduction of republican functionaries in those territories outside German control. Most of these appointments did not survive the military defeat, but they did free Thiers to make new nominations on a piecemeal basis in 1871. Appearing almost daily in the *Journal officiel* over a period of months, his choices were cautious and frankly political: "I have given more than ten prefects to the Legitimists," he once complained, "and they are still not satisfied."[18] Nor were Thiers's other opponents. Within two days of his enforced resignation in May 1873, twenty-nine of the eighty-six prefects were replaced or relocated; and most of the rest were soon to follow. The spoils system thereby passed to Broglie and Buffet (since MacMahon took a personal interest only in military affairs), and they gradually substituted loyal conservatives as prefects, subprefects, secretary-generals, and legal aides. The effect of these personnel changes at departmental headquarters was to reinforce the political polarization: while by-elections were inching the nation toward republicanism, bureaucratic appointments were consistently contrary. Behind the constitutional formalities and parliamentary maneuvers of mid-decade, therefore, a less publicized struggle was already in progress to dominate the state apparatus.

One more turn came with the replacement of Broglie and Buffet by the Left Center cabinets of Dufaure and Jules Simon. This political shift away from the Right Center was soon translated by a new round of dismissals and appointments in prefectures throughout France. By early 1877 bureaucratic attrition was wearing away the foundations of MacMahon's presidency and with it the last hope of a conservative comeback. If favored by sympathetic administrators, republican candidates might achieve a decisive majority in parliamentary and municipal elections and then move to sweep the marshal from office. Such was the unnerving prospect with which Broglie and others confronted MacMahon just before the dismissal of Jules Simon. In this perspective the crisis of *seize mai* was, above all, the excuse and the occasion for yet another administrative purge. Already, by 19 May, Broglie and his minister of the interior, Marie-François de Fourtou, had dismissed or displaced more than two-thirds of the entire prefectoral corps; and in the summer months no less than a thousand public officials were cashiered by the new regime. The electoral campaign of 1877 was thus to be contested while control of the administrative machinery was tightly grasped by opponents of the republic.[19]

Precisely how this advantage was exploited can be gathered from the papers of Fourtou's ministry. The first priority was accorded to selection and encouragement of official candidates. "The government has not only the right but the duty," Fourtou instructed his prefects, "to make known to the electorate those candidates who support and those candidates who oppose its policy." The voters were to be left in no uncertainty about who had the marshal's blessing. "Yet it is not sufficient to have designated the candidates; it is necessary to give them active, powerful, efficient cooperation." Any veneer of political neutrality was thereby stripped away, and in the end every conservative candidate received the personal endorsement of the president.[20] Special favors and finances were also distributed through the bureaucracy. Free train tickets for mayors and other officials were made available to lengthen the receiving lines during MacMahon's electoral tours. On such occasions prefects were asked to submit additional nominations for the Legion of Honor; and they were instructed to display large portraits of the marshal throughout their departments as well as to print and post his public declarations. Although the total allocations can only be guessed at, there is ample documentary evidence of extraordinary subsidies awarded to diligent prefects both through conservative electoral committees and directly from Fourtou's office.[21]

Along with the propaganda effort, the government conducted a simultaneous campaign of censorship. Whereas ministerial directives were always prominently displayed, the distribution of republican posters and newspaper press was hindered. The prefects were told to assure that "the acts of the government everywhere receive the greatest publicity." At the same time restrictive laws of 1830 and 1849 were invoked in order to require republicans to obtain an official stamp of authorization to distribute, display, or hawk printed matter. These measures resulted in a number of confiscations and fines which contrasted with the uninhibited flow of equally slanted government publications, such as the *Bulletin des Communes* edited in the Ministry of the Interior.[22] Hence, in practice, the political polarization was pushed to its limit by Fourtou's decree that "the journals are presently divided into two distinct categories: those that attack the government and those that defend it." The consequence was sometimes fairly ludicrous: witness the seizure of four editions of *Punch* which contained unflattering caricatures of President MacMahon. But it became less amusing when twenty-one criminal cases involving republican publications were referred to the Ministry of Justice for prosecution.[23]

Limitations were also placed on freedom of assembly, and restrictions were imposed on the political activities of local officials who were sympathetic to the republican cause. For these purposes the government cited an 1855 law that allowed mayors and municipal counselors private but not public expression of their preferences. That Fourtou and many of his prefectoral appointees had functioned in the bureaucratic ranks of the Second Empire reinforced the republican contention that the government was thereby reverting to an authoritarian past. Sensitive to this criticism and fearful that ugly incidents or outright suppression of electoral banquets might do harm to the conservative image, Fourtou was initially circumspect in applying what he himself called "the modes of repression." Some cafés and cabarets were closed, public reprimands issued, and the like. As the campaign progressed, however, the screw was slowly tightened; and by October 1,743 mayors had been dismissed and 3,271 legal suits filed. To be sure, these measures still fell considerably short of the blatant imposition of a dictatorship. But they were sufficient to reveal the ruthlessness of an embattled regime.[24]

Because we lack any reliable scientific measurement of public opinion in the nineteenth century, it is impossible to assess at regular intervals the effects of the cabinet's efforts to manipulate the electoral outcome. Yet a fairly distinct sequence of ebb and flow of the campaign was nonetheless discernible. The electoral period consisted of three successive phases: (1) the government's early initiative, (2) a republican resurgence, and (3) a confusion of countervailing tendencies following the death of Adolphe Thiers. Throughout, the strategy of both sides was dictated by one central concern: to establish which was the party of peace. We must ask, then, whose claims were more credible and for what reasons they appeared so.

From the outset, conservative propaganda stressed that the nation was being called upon to support the president's personal leadership. Only he could guarantee stability at home and abroad. This was the theme of political brochures that began to flood the countryside: "Le Maréchal devant l'opinion," "La politique du Maréchal," "La situation nouvelle," "Paix et travail," and so on. One of the most widely distributed and discussed of these was the first, of which at least four hundred thousand copies were printed.[25] It advanced as an explanation for *seize mai* that MacMahon had acted to guard against "the perils which the progress of radicalism created for public order and peace." Even though the constitution had awarded "a preponderent role" to the president, he was faced with a recalcitrant Chamber and an uncooperative prefectoral corps. "Thus we were heading toward a triumph of radicalism, toward the legal Commune. . . . " By his bold decision, however, the marshal had arrested this development, confounded the demagogues in France, and perhaps even averted "a disastrous war." All this he had done to fulfill his obligation to "conservative France," to the army which had shed its blood against the Commune, and "to Europe which is watching us." Now the French people must ratify his action or else be pulled into conflict and revolution fomented by the agents of "cosmopolitan Socialism." There could be no compromise, no middle way, and no abstention. Accordingly, in order to counteract the vast subversive network of radicalism, the government would "make use of all its rights."[26]

The government's strategy was to suspend the parliament temporarily until the administrative machinery was ready, then to have the Senate vote to prorogue the Chamber, and finally to fix an autumn date for new elections. Meantime, the republican factions were left to gather their forces. Although it was not yet apparent to the public, the heretofore informal alliance between Gambetta and Thiers was being solidified. While the one busied himself with preparations for a national campaign, the other assembled a republican brain trust.[27] Thiers and his friends were utterly confident that he would soon be returned to the Elysée; and the logical person to be his premier was his former nemesis, Gambetta. This prospect was also reflected in charges stated in the early conservative brochures and repeated throughout the campaign: whatever their methods, there was in reality no distinction to be made among republicans, radicals, and revolutionaries. In the conservative version, in other words, the electoral contest actually pitted MacMahon, the candidate of order and peace, against

Gambetta, the true leader of French radicalism and the harbinger of catastrophe.[28] This was the point of the first conservative thrust, and it initially seemed successful. By the final week of June, when the dissolution of the Chamber was confirmed and the electoral season was officially opened, Hohenlohe advised Berlin to expect some conservative gains. Even should the republicans manage to retain a majority, he estimated, they were still likely to see their margin reduced. If so, MacMahon might after all survive until 1880.[29]

Yet in the summer months the initiative passed to the republicans, a phenomenon attributable only in part to their own efforts. Deprived of any governmental assistance or financial aid, republican committees in the provinces were initially kept busy with organizational problems, the selection and publication of electoral lists, and the attempt to raise attendance at their political rallies. At the same time the conservative factions proved to be, as usual, their own worst enemies. Their most aggravating problem was the choice of candidates. Every decision by a prefect favoring one group drew immediate criticism from the others. Since Fourtou was a veteran Bonapartist, he was naturally suspected of exercising his authority to the detriment of Orleanists and Legitimists. But any personal intervention by Broglie to support a monarchist brought the opposite complaint.[30] This persistent factionalism was compounded by MacMahon's manifest inadequacy as a campaigner for conservatism. French observers and German agents concurred in evaluating the cool reaction of the populace to his visits in provincial capitals. Hohenlohe concluded that the president had been "somewhat discredited" by *seize mai* and by sponsoring a reactionary cabinet: "The marshal's temperate nature stands in a too glaring contrast with the aggressive statements put in his mouth by the ministers. . . . "[31] His backers were frankly worried. Informants within French financial circles, closely connected with the Rothschilds, reported by midsummer a growing concern that the official campaign was misfiring and that major transactions on the Paris Bourse were therefore being deliberately stalled by fearful investors. The entire conservative strategy was in trouble.[32]

By contrast, Gambetta was brimming with confidence. At a

rally in Lille during August he made his most expansive oration of the campaign, predicting that the republicans would further increase their number of deputies in the Chamber. In that event, MacMahon would be forced "to submit or to resign." Gleefully celebrated in the republican press, this remark offended the marshal deeply and brought a legal suit that ended, in effect, with Gambetta's conviction for *lèse majesté* and his vilification as a danger to law and order.[33] But for more than one reason, as we shall shortly consider, such a charge was simply not credible to a majority of the French electorate. As the summer passed, therefore, not only the strategy but the substance of conservative propaganda became dubious. Increasingly, Fourtou fretted about the possibility of a massive abstention among those who were insensitive to the alleged radical threat. He accordingly gave instructions to the prefects to impress upon the voters that "the debate is not, as one would have you believe, between the republic and the monarchy: it is between radicalism and the government of the republic presided by Marshal MacMahon."[34] Unless the latter conception were made to prevail, and unless Gambetta became equated in public opinion with a menace to domestic and international harmony, the conservatives would be hard pressed to defeat the republicans.

One of the more formidable impediments to conservative plausibility was the presence of Thiers on the republican ticket. Of all French politicians, he could least be accused either of softness toward radicalism within France or of adventurism abroad. As the executioner of the Paris Commune and the liberator of French territory, Thiers was difficult to gainsay for sheer respectability—a fact on which moderate republican propaganda capitalized by placing his photograph beside that of Gambetta on electoral posters. Yet in reality it was Gambetta who managed and dominated the republican campaign. His was the hand in Thiers's glove: he personally drafted letters to provincial committees which the former president had only to sign.[35] As Gambetta realized, just the appearance of Thiers's name on the republican masthead was invaluable in blunting the conservative rhetoric of alarm; and the daily insults to Thiers in the conservative press could do no serious damage to his record or reputation. He seemed alert and indefatigable. On the first day after a strenuous journey to Dieppe, Thiers appeared "strikingly fresh and spirited" during a visit to Hohenlohe, who remarked that "his age will be no hindrance for him to assume the presidency again."[36] But Thiers's private physicians knew better. His blood was rapidly decomposing. Decazes was informed of this and, aware that "Berlin desires his success," passed word on to Gontaut that "Thiers no longer exists either as an intelligence or as an influence. The sad old man is nothing but an unconscious instrument of the great conspiracy which flatters and exploits him." It was a harsh judgment, not totally inaccurate but scarcely fair as the epitaph of an octagenarian who chose to expend his final gasp in a political fight. On 3 September, a few hours before the republic's seventh anniversary, Thiers was dead.[37]

The consternation among republicans was apparent to everyone. Suddenly the conservative propaganda had acquired a new edge—despite Gambetta's prompt and supposedly reassuring announcement that Thiers's place would be taken by Jules Grévy. Whatever their personal sentiments for the deceased, MacMahon's political lieutenants could not suppress their satisfaction. Decazes was told in confidence that "the movement in favor of the conservative cause is immense."[38] But one must observe that such a statement reflected little more than the opinion of a few bureaucrats in Paris and that it contained some measure of wishful thinking. After all, a political polarization had been in progress for many months, a process that virtually precluded a dramatic turnabout. An important repercussion of Thiers's death was certain to be felt in the months ahead should the republican leadership actually face the problem of governing without him. But the facile assumption that the republican campaign was suddenly crippled lacked firm evidence.[39]

Despite a perceptible change of momentum because of Theirs's disappearance, then, one need not posit massive shifts of voter allegiance from one phase of the campaign to the next. What can be documented is an alteration of style. Especially characteristic of the closing weeks was the active entry of the Church into the conservative campaign. This was first signaled when, during an excursion to the southwest in September, MacMahon was greeted by Cardinal Donnet, archbishop of Bordeaux, as the "supreme hope" of the French people. Donnet went on to add in Biblical cadence: "Fear nothing, the hand of God is upon you . . . for you are of the race of those through whom the Lord can and will save Israel."[40] If such language was enigmatic, a pastoral letter from the bishop of Bourges was not: "Let us pray for the great cause of order to which the salvation of the country is attached! Let us pray for the conservative parties. . . . May the next elections give us an Assembly strong, united, conservative, Christian. . . ." The faithful were exhorted to celebrate a *triduum* in early October, with three hundred days of indulgence to be granted for each of the observances and a plenary indulgence for the final communion on election eve.[41] This was followed by other such pronouncements, notably from the bishops of Arras, Chambéry, and Limoges. Thereby, wrote the German chargé in Paris, the French clergy had "openly entered the political arena." Actually, the regime would probably have preferred a more discreet expression of support, he added, since an increased suspicion of clerical designs could only benefit the republicans. Political initiatives at the top, in short, were no guarantee of commensurate electoral results below.[42]

The aptness of that analysis was illustrated by a memorandum to the prefects in which Fourtou deplored spreading rumors that the regime was under clerical influence and therefore might be led "to compromise the maintenance of peace." Such patent distortions, he instructed, should be repressed and their perpetrators punished. The minister of justice also addressed similar advisories to all judges and law enforcement agencies.[43] And in more grandiloquent language an electoral manifesto by MacMahon reiterated the same message: "No, the republican constitution is not in danger. No, the government, respectful as it may be toward religion, does not obey clerical pretensions, and nothing could impel it toward a policy endangering the peace."[44]

There was a defensiveness about this rhetoric, a note of apology that was generally typical of the conservative mentality after 1870 but that was, above all, dictated by the specific circumstances of *seize mai*. For MacMahon and the Broglie cabinet, the election was essentially an attempt to retain something that was slipping away. The vicissitudes of the campaign, including the untimely demise of Thiers, could not realign the political tilt. In reality, the conservatives were at a disadvantage from the outset, despite the financial and administrative means at their disposal. Why was that so? The reasons were complex, of course, but one explanation bears more weight than the others. For all their efforts, the conservatives were unable to persuade the French people that they truly represented the party of peace. In that role they had swept to power in 1871 while Gambetta retreated into exile. But by 1877 the current of popular opinion was reversed, and it was the Gambettist republicans who had successfully created an image of themselves as the champions of internal and international conciliation. For that crucial advantage, it now remains to demonstrate, they owed much to Germany.

The German Connection

If ever a case can be made for Germany's direct influence on French affairs, it must be demonstrable at this juncture. We have dwelt sufficiently on the general ambiance of *seize mai* and taken an adequate sample—among political elites, on the stock exchange, in press and public—to posit a high degree of French susceptibility to German admonitions since 1870. We have also examined the themes and techniques of the conservative campaign and observed that a crucial metamorphosis had occurred during the republic's first decade: namely, that the identity of conservatism as a party of peace became blurred beyond recognition. Within France the factionalism of the Right had proved to be a particularly rancorous form of political suicide; and abroad nothing seemed to darken the eastern horizon so quickly as the prospect of a monarchist or Bonapartist restoration with clerical backing. Thus by 1877 it had become more plausible to equate the tranquility and security of the French nation with the triumph of republicanism.

In order to draw this analysis together, it is now necessary to establish that the Germans consciously and effectively intervened in France to assist a republican victory. The foregoing adverbs are chosen advisedly, since this argument requires both the documentation of German policy and some indication of its impact. Merely to prove that certain attitudes or inclinations existed in Berlin would not in itself suffice. We also need to trace the means by which these were implemented. In the end the extent of German influence may not be precisely quantifiable. Yet any necessary inexactitude of such science should not be too discouraging so long as the problem has been explicitly formulated, the groundwork adequately prepared, and the assumptions made clearly visible. With these conditions met, we may proceed in good conscience to the indispensable citation of chapter and verse.

In general terms, the consequences of *seize mai* had been anticipated by the German government months before the event. As early as February 1877, Hohenlohe was speculating about the possibility of a Broglie-Fourtou ministry, another prefectoral purge, and the eventuality of national elections.[45] Still, as we have witnessed, the German ambassador was flustered by Jules Simon's abrupt dismissal. On the afternoon of 16 May he spent more than an hour closeted with Decazes and yet emerged none the wiser for the encounter. The difficulty was that Decazes, long the Germans' best official contact, was out of sympathy with MacMahon's action and consequently out of favor. The French foreign minister at first hoped that the marshal might be content with a revamped Orleanist cabinet; but he suspected what was on MacMahon's mind, since he inquired of Hohenlohe what the German reaction would likely be to a Broglie-Fourtou combination. The curt response was, "Not favorable."[46]

It may be taken for granted, then, that the German displeasure with *seize mai* was common knowledge from the beginning. The initial press reaction in France reflected that fact. Hohenlohe noted "the expressed anxiety. . . that peace could be endangered." He at once began the conscientious performance of his ambassadorial duty to gather information on French internal affairs from newspapers, secret agents, personal contacts, and official visits. In addition to his long discussion with Decazes, he also conferred with Thiers, Prefect of Police Voisin, Broglie (whom he treated with "restrained politeness"), and MacMahon. These soundings enabled him to identify for Berlin the new slate of ministers, to outline in detail the Broglie cabinet's electoral strategy, and to present an informal appraisal of the motivation for the marshal's "sudden decision " to drop Simon. In Hohenlohe's judgment MacMahon had been moved neither by "far-reaching plans for a restoration of the monarchy" nor, in any immediate sense, by "ultramontane intrigues." He was simply fearful that Gambetta's political power would soon overshadow his own; and, personally pressed by his wife and by Broglie to assert his authority, he had decided to halt the radical drift before it was too late. In doing so the marshal was fully cognizant of the risks involved. Specifically, he and his close advisers "feared the impression that the creation of the new cabinet would make in Germany and Italy."[47]

These initial apprehensions cannot be traced to a precise cause and may simply be attributed to a residue of "salutary fear." Initial government reaction in Berlin was in fact restrained and correct, less overtly hostile than it had been at the time of the presidential crisis in 1873 or during the public alarm of 1875.[48] But in one conspicuous regard the circumstance was identical: Bismarck hurried back to the German capital to take personal charge of French affairs. The chancellor's frame of mind could be described, in a word, as skepticism. His marginalia on daily memoranda—always the most authentic evidence of his spontaneous thoughts—were utterly caustic about the "energetic assurances" offered by the French. The notion that a change in France's internal affairs would have no bearing on the conduct of foreign policy was, he indicated, just nonsense. On the back of one memo he scribbled in heavy black pencil: "A clerical France is altogether incapable of maintaining durable peaceful relations with Germany." This note was crossed out, but a few days thereafter the phrase was repeated in official instructions to Hohenlohe. And much the same version was meanwhile being printed, as if on cue, in the Berlin press. Even lacking absolute proof of a direct link in this instance, one may observe that the discrepancy between Bismarck's first reaction and the published indications of German policy was very slight indeed.[49]

Special mention should be made here of an analysis by Germany's military attaché in Paris, the recently promoted Lieutenant Colonel von Bülow. Sober and measured in judgment, he enjoyed the confidence of all those who customarily received his reports via the Wilhelmstrasse: the Kaiser, the chancellor, the war ministry, and the army's general staff. Throughout 1875, it may be recalled, Bülow had steadily held to the opinion that the French army was totally incapable of a military campaign and therefore posed no immediate threat to Germany. But now he was less categorical and advised Berlin that a "bloody conflict" was no longer "outside the realm of possibility"—in which case the Germans would do well to mind Gambetta's earlier statement: "La dissolution c'est la préface de la guerre."[50] Despite the evident modification of Bülow's opinion which this report represented, it still left the threat of French aggression hypothetical and distant. Yet to sharpen the point required only a slight ellipsis reminiscent of the abridged Ems dispatch of 1870. Exactly one week after the crisis had begun, the first general instructions were dispatched by special courier from Berlin to German embassies in the major European capitals. Therein the new French regime was severely chastised for instigating a chain of events that could only be terminated by "acts of force and a coup d'état." Because of this foolish risk and "the aggressive policy of the Vatican," Germany was placed in "greater danger than before"—hence Lieutenant Colonel von Bülow's closing citation of Gambetta's words: "La dissolution c'est la guerre [*sic*]."[51] Thus the German government adopted and deliberately propagated the view that *seize mai* had created a clear and present danger to European peace.

The German decision to intervene more decisively in the French elections fell in the final week of May. A long report filed by Hohenlohe disclosed that he had established a reliable contact with Gambetta through a former Alsatian named Hartmann. By means of this agent Gambetta was urging that the Germans offer unambiguous public support to the French republicans. The inducements were three: (1) his party would completely abandon any aspirations to revenge and the recovery of lost provinces by force, whereas "a military success" would be indispensable to the conservatives ("correct," Bismarck commented); (2) the republicans were prepared, once in power, to open "a thoroughgoing campaign" against ultramontanism; and (3) the possibility would then be created for Germany and France "to clasp hands." Before basing his political strategy on these assumptions, Gambetta desired assurances that they were shared by Germany. Replying on his own initiative, Hohenlohe felt able to quash the rumor that his government in any way approved of *seize mai* and to certify that "the German regime, as much as ever, regards the peaceful development of the republic in France as desirable." Germany would, moreover, "greet with joy" a stand against ultramontanism by the republic, something which should indeed ensure more cordial relations between the two nations. Still, as Hohenlohe had to remind Hartmann, a too obvious encouragement for the Gambettists "could only harm their cause if it appeared that they were allowing their policy to be guided by German inspiration."[52]

In other words, to approve or disapprove was one thing; to intercede effectively was another. German sentiments could no longer be in doubt. The problem, however, was to introduce them into the French electoral procedure without a counterproductive effect. Hohenlohe had a suggestion: "One thing must not be overlooked. The French populace presently fears nothing more than a war with Germany. If the republican party successfully convinces the country that a republican regime would secure peace, whereas a regime of the other parties would lead to war, then the nation will opt for the republican party despite the exertions of Monsieur de Fourtou and his prefects."[53] Henceforward this became the explicit theme of a propaganda campaign orchestrated in Berlin. Instructions to that effect were issued by Bismarck on 29 May through his son Herbert. Newspaper editorials and diplomatic agents were to make it known "that the republic in France would be for us the surest chance of peace; with any monarchist French regime we would be very quickly involved in war."[54]

The chancellor also took particular care to cultivate contacts with the Italian government through his envoy and old friend Robert von Keudell. Without committing Germany to any binding obligation, Bismarck wanted Keudell to stress the mutual danger for the two nations because of certain "volcanic elements" in France which "might seek an outlet in war." In making the German desire for a republican triumph clear to the Italians, and by restating that the conservative alternative would inevitably provoke armed conflict, Bismarck calculated "that this would be very promptly repeated in Paris via Rome."[55] Leaving little to the imagination, Bismarck had statistics planted in the press which demonstrated that France would be hopelessly outmatched in a conflict against the combined forces of Germany and Italy; and he specifically instructed that "this be drafted so that it is apparent that we would not leave Italy in the lurch."[56] Such telling details, though only a fraction of the available evidence, should be sufficient to remove any doubt as to the deliberate effort made by the Germans in the summer of 1877 to drag MacMahon and the French conservatives down to defeat. "The time has come," Herbert von Bismarck summarized the viewpoint of his father, "for us to influence the French elections as extensively and as forcefully as we are able in order to convince the French voter that he would be voting for war if he were to cast his ballot for the present French cabinet."[57]

Enough for German intentions; can an equally conclusive case be made that the political process in France was thereby significantly affected? It cannot, the answer must be, if one insists that acceptable proof can be sought only in the form of statistics. There is some numerical evidence worth our consideration, but it falls short of irrefutability and can be given no more weight than it deserves. Rather, we must patiently follow the general plan of this work, which is to begin with the impact of Germany on the French political elites and then to observe the concentric circles of influence as they developed less distinctly but nonetheless unmistakably.

At the highest level of government French officials were quite aware of the German strategy and were visibly sensitive to the charge that the conservative cause was merely a front for ultramontane ambitions. Reports of the virulent press campaign in Germany were conveyed through both diplomatic and private channels to French leaders,[58] who took great pains to deny close ties with the Vatican. In the presidential box at the Longchamps raceway, to cite a characteristic example, Hohenlohe was beset throughout one June afternoon with vigorous disavowals from MacMahon, Broglie, and Decazes: "All of the gentlemen exerted themselves to prove to me that the present cabinet had nothing to do with the ultramontane party and also that it would be entirely impossible to implement an ultramontane regime in France. . . ." Let it be added that Bismarck annotated Hohenlohe's account of this scene with a series of cynical remarks and passed off the French disclaimers as "shadowboxing." In the chancellor's view the Germans should continue to make no secret of their "worry and mistrust" regarding France and to advertise that "ultramontanism is war."[59] This sort of talk especially alarmed Decazes, who became convinced that both Bismarck and the German military command had already made a decision for war; they needed only to overcome the scruples of the Kaiser. As in 1875, Decazes was determined to do nothing "which might furnish our enemies the shadow of a reason or even a pretext" for mobilization.[60] But this was to mistake the entire character of *seize mai* and to think strictly in the classical terms of diplomacy. In fact, the Germans intended to establish that a conservative electoral victory would be reason and pretext enough for war, no matter what French statesmen might do. When William complained that Germany's opposition to the current French government was too explicit, Bismarck retorted behind his back that an expression of sympathy for Mac-Mahon by the Kaiser would be far more dangerous to peace than the German government's frank disapproval.[61]

There was a fine line between an indication of preference and outright interference, and the Germans were not always fastidious about overstepping it. When restraint was exercised, the reason was often tactical, as when Bismarck agreed to defer his demand for dismissal of the promonarchist French ambassador, Gontaut-Biron, whom he again accused of misleading William about the true state of affairs in France. But at the same time, in instructions kept secret from the Kaiser in order to avoid any "spirit of contradiction," Bismarck told Hohenlohe that the French electorate should again be cautioned that "the 363 [republican deputies] mean peace, the reactionary coalition war."[62] For propaganda purposes William's opinion was thus totally ignored; and the official, personal, and press contacts of the German embassy in Paris were utilized to elaborate Bismarck's French policy without equivocation. By midsummer Hohenlohe was persuaded that the effects were apparent and that the republican movement held a commanding lead. "What gives it an advantage," he assured the chancellor, "is the security of Your Excellency's support. That now has great importance in France. The French people still live under the impact of the German invasion and [they] want peace. Any policy of the regime that tends to threaten the peace will be condemned by the French nation."[63]

Germany's continuing diplomatic flirtation with Italy in 1877 was designed to maximize such fears and thereby "to exercise a practical influence on the elections."[64] After eliciting a private agreement from Italian officials on the desirability of maintaining a republican majority in the French Assembly, Robert von Keudell received instructions from Berlin to seek a public declaration "that a monarchical restoration in France could involve them in a war." Under repeated German prodding, the Quirinal complied.[65] The widely publicized Crispi mission to Berlin in September, barely a fortnight before the French elections, can only be described as a political stunt intended to impress the theme of Italo-German solidarity on the most remote peasant in France. If this accomplished nothing else, it shifted the burden of proof uncomfortably onto the Broglie-Fourtou regime, which was thereafter forced to stave off persistent stories that an anti-French military alliance had either been formed already or would be the first result of a conservative victory at the polls.[66]

While MacMahon's supporters reacted defensively, the republicans sought to turn the increasingly open German endorsement to their profit. Gambetta, with whom Hohenlohe for the first time began lengthy political consultations, was fully apprised of the German propaganda campaign in his behalf and attempted to put its main themes to good use. The charge of an ultramontane cabal was, of course, paramount. His own attack on "le gouvernement des prêtres, le ministère des curés" was, he assured Hohenlohe, an accurate reflection of a growing popular sentiment that the regime was helpless to counteract, since "the French peasant changes his mind only once every fifty years."[67] At the same time Gambetta's major press organ, *La République française*, ran daily summaries of German editorials and offered them as proof that an electoral setback for the French republicans might impel Germany and Italy "to seize the initiative in a conflict which no human force could any longer avoid."[68]

Despite the repressive efforts of Fourtou's prefects, it is certain that these menacing overtones and undertones were detectable throughout France. To be sure, this is far from asserting that the elections of 1877 were determined solely by threats emanating from Berlin. Monocausal explanation has no place here.[69] Political scientists have frequently analyzed the multitude of underlying social, economic, religious, and geographic factors which affected the electoral pattern of the Third Republic. Yet these are still insufficient to define French political life without taking into account the psychological moment induced by the lost war and the continuing apprehension about Germany. A public attitude marked by a desire for stability and a resistance to change was "a distinctive trait of French society in its entirety between 1870 and 1940."[70] It was the republican electoral strategy, deliberately aided by the Germans, to exacerbate those feelings of insecurity while calumniating MacMahon's regime as a band of adventurers. To judge from the obvious tension manifested in the course of the campaign, this propaganda had a considerable effect on French public opinion.[71]

But just how much is "considerable"? The only way to measure the impact of an issue on the French electorate would be to examine the outcome department by department and candidate by candidate. Although such evidence is by its nature scattered and still incomplete, an accumulating corpus of monographic investigations does tend to corroborate the foregoing generalizations. These local studies substantiate that, even in the areas furthest removed from Germany and often least inclined to republicanism, the character of the 1877 election was dominated by the issue of war or peace with Germany. Some examples should suffice to establish this conclusion.[72]

The department of Indre-et-Loire was situated just on the edge of military hostilities during the war of 1870. It retained a rural character, with about three-quarters of the population engaged in agriculture. After noting the strong elements of continuity—local traditions, socioeconomic conditions, the leisurely pace of life—one is left to account for the fact that the electorate there had returned three different verdicts in little more than a year: favoring the Bonapartists in May 1870, the monarchists in February 1871, and the republicans in July 1871. A careful look indicates that the population voted each time against any sudden upset and that they again did so in 1877: "One is forced to conclude that psychological factors played the determining role."[73] The republicans were finally more successful because they better exploited the public fear of crisis and change. It is notable how often the word "security" appeared in the electoral propaganda of both sides. In the final days of the campaign the conservative press sought to capitalize on this emotional issue: "It is a question of preserving France from the bloody and terrible trials which she has recently been condemned to endure."[74] But in this case it was the republicans who prevailed.

Further to the south, in the Tarn-et-Garonne, progovernment publications displayed much the same tenor. MacMahon was arrayed heroically as the national savior, while Gambetta was castigated as "the promoter of *guerre à outrance*" and as an "ally of the foreigner." The republican line was naturally to the contrary, portraying the marshal as an unwitting harbinger of war and revolution. We can be certain that such recriminations received wide circulation in a department that had four daily newspapers, two conservative and two republican, with a combined distribution of about five thousand: one for every fourteen voters, of whom eight or nine could read. This is not to count the dozens of public meetings and electoral rallies conducted by the candidates. Again, close investigation confirms that "in a most striking fashion . . . the essential argument employed in both camps was that of the consequences in foreign affairs."[75]

The same was true in the department of Gers. There the campaign was particularly heated by republican attempts to unseat a leading Bonapartist deputy, Paul de Cassagnac. Consequently the department was, as Cassagnac later complained to the Chamber of Deputies, "inundated with brochures." He took particular exception to an electoral almanac distributed by his opponents in more than ten thousand copies. It is worth quoting:

> Above all it is a question of knowing whether we shall be free to reap what we have sown; or if we shall be called, young and old, to rejoin our regiment to go to war; and if the foreigner, after having defeated our generals and crushed our armies as he did in 1870, will come to take over our wealth and to harvest in our stead the wheat and the wine that we have cultivated with such care. It depends on you, voters, to prevent [this] by choosing republican deputies who will conserve the peace by conserving the republic.[76]

Thereby placed on the defensive, Cassagnac felt constrained to counter the argument that conservatism meant war, as he did before a packed school auditorium at Eauze in late August 1877:

> You have peace and you will keep it because the Marshal wishes it. . . . That does not prevent your having been told, and you may perhaps be told again, that we conservatives want war. No, we do not want it! . . . I repeat, war is not to be feared so long as the Marshal is in power; and it would only be a threat on the day when, by a lamentable turn of events, the republicans might return to the head of the government from which we chased them on May 16.[77]

Particularly striking in this statement is the recurrent theme of antirepublican propaganda that the Gambettists, rather than their conservative opposition, were the true disturbers of national tranquility.

Next to Gers was the department of the Basses-Pyrénées, with its large Basque population. This had been the only province in southwestern France to vote republican in February 1871, when the central issue of the campaign, apart from the primordial religious question, had been termination of the war with Germany. But in the parliamentary elections of 1876 the Bonapartists made a comeback, and the six deputies from the department were equally divided between conservatives and republicans. In the tight contest of 1877 each side claimed to be the proprietor of order and charged the other with fomenting anarchy. The intensity and unsubtlety of republican scare tactics were patent in this attack on, respectively, a monarchist and a Bonapartist candidate: "Do you want to see Henri V in 1880 . . . , the government of priests, and to risk a war for the Pope with Italy? Then vote for de Luppé. Do you want the return of the Empire and fresh disasters, the definitive dismemberment and the total ruin of France? Then vote for d'Ariste."[78] In this instance we can clearly perceive how national propaganda themes were tailored for local constituencies. But the refrain of civil and foreign war remained essentially the same throughout. The recurrence of this theme could simply be ascribed to the still lingering humiliation of 1870. Yet the frequent reiteration of certain slogans in all parts of France also betrayed a conscious and coordinated effort by the republicans to make the most of their German support.

Nor were the conservatives to be outdone. As the campaign progressed, they increasingly fought fire with fire. Even in the Vendée, to choose the ultimate example of a monarchist stronghold, citizens were exhorted in the final hours to "remember what the Prussians think of our approaching elections: THE MORE RADICAL THE ELECTIONS, THE MORE SATISFIED PRINCE VON BISMARCK WILL BE."[79] Here the conservative riposte was obviously that a republican triumph might bring further revolutionary disorders within France and military invasion from abroad. In this rural and reactionary outpost such a resurrection of the Great Fear in order to discredit the republicans might still maintain some credibility. But across the nation a majority of French voters was otherwise persuaded.

The Collapse of Conservatism

The election of 1877 was not totally unambiguous. True, early returns gave the republicans a virtual sweep of Paris. But subsequent results from the provinces revealed a conservative steadfastness there that belied Gambetta's excessive optimism. Conservative incumbents lost in fewer than twenty races; and new conservative candidates managed to dislodge nearly sixty republicans. Yet, despite this net loss of almost forty seats, the republicans still emerged (while some districts remained in doubt) with a majority in the Chamber of more than a hundred. The bureaucratic management and huge expenditures of the regime had been to some effect; but they had failed to alter the essential fact of republican preponderance. The popular vote, here in round numbers, probably affords the truest sense of magnitude:

Registered voters	10,000,000	
Abstentions	2,000,000	
Ballots cast	8,000,000	
Republicans	4,350,000	(54%)
Conservatives	3,650,000	(46%)

These figures show that the conservatives were defeated, not routed. Had there been significantly fewer abstentions, or the shift of a few percentage points in their direction, the political deadlock of months past might well have been perpetuated.[80]

The important factor, as so often, was not margin but momentum. Having successfully withstood a challenge at some cost, the republicans were determined to exploit their residual advantage. Gambetta's *République française* ruled out a compromise and demanded that no concessions be granted to the minority. Any ruse or use of force to deprive the republicans of victory should be stoutly resisted. Nor, because of departmental elections (*conseils généraux* and *conseils d'arrondissement*) scheduled for 4 November, was there time to relax. And in fact the outcome of these contests soon brought heavy republican gains throughout France and further consolidated the verdict of October.[81]

In the face of republican implacability, the conservative options were reduced to only three: to mount a military coup d'état; to have MacMahon dissolve the new Chamber when it convened and then to risk everything on a national plebiscite; or to carry on by obstructing the republican Chamber at every turn with the powers of the president and the Senate. Although no longer in a realm of pure fantasy, as events soon proved, the first of these was the least likely. The utilization of force was compatible neither with MacMahon's character nor with his sense of duty; and the unqualified loyalty of the entire army to his person was far from assured. The second alternative would be less violent but was scarcely more promising. Decazes confessed his opinion to Hohenlohe that MacMahon would be fortunate to gather even three hundred thousand votes in a plebiscite; and if he failed in such an attempt, the harsh dilemma of "submit or resign" would be unavoidable. As for the third choice, there was little reason to believe that the Senate could long be held as an effective antirepublican bastion, particularly in view of the irascibility of the conservative factions. Given the Orleanists' inveterate distrust of Bonapartism and their desire to have Aumale succeed MacMahon to the presidency of the republic, a conservative majority would not be secure in the Senate even if the electoral balance held steady. The prospects were, in short, that MacMahon would remain isolated and embattled.[82]

Insofar as German efforts had long been expended to encourage just such a result, the renewed mood of self-congratulation in Berlin was appropriate. One person who did not share it, however, was the Kaiser. His predilection for MacMahon was undimmed, and he tended to read the French electoral returns as a partial vindication of the marshal's struggle to contain radicalism. In resisting this view, Bismarck acted both to persuade William and to pressure the French. From his family estate at Varzin he sent a confidential warning to William that "the ultramontane policy of coup d'état" would be "the soonest and surest way to war." Whether Gambetta or some other republican asserted leadership of the parliamentary opposition would not alter matters importantly; but MacMahon's retention of the Broglie-Fourtou cabinet would be "a serious symptom." The real danger, as Bismarck saw it, stood on the French Right. If William were unwilling to trust his judgment, he would resign. In a gesture practiced many times before, the Kaiser acceded: although he could still not feel that MacMahon had erred in defending his regime against the radicals, William would remain "solid and consistent" with Bismarck's opposition to ultramontanism in France.[83]

There is no need to detail the German press campaign, conducted as usual under exact instructions from the chancellor himself and pointed against the habitually alleged collusion of conservative and clerical elements in France. Fundamentally, this was but the logical extension of German propaganda during the electoral period. The focus alone was slightly altered to make it appear that one false step by MacMahon (rather than by the French voter, as before) might touch off an explosion.[84] Simultaneously, through his sometime financial adviser Henckel von Donnersmarck, Bismarck reiterated to Gambetta that "the republican form of state . . . is the only one in France which permits the peaceful functioning of enduring relations to Germany. . . . An *ultramontane* regime would be altogether incapable of avoiding a war." Not only the consistency of Bismarck's policy was obvious but also the persistence with which he encouraged French republican leaders to draw the appropriate conclusions.[85]

MacMahon's quandary deepened. Without a compromise there could be no cabinet—at least none acceptable to the president—and yet both sides were girding for a fight. Beginning in early November a committee of eighteen republicans began meeting daily at the residence of Léon Renault, Thiers's former prefect of police and now a key deputy of the Left Center. These men could justifiably claim to represent the majority of the French electorate, and they were adamant about extracting their due. They intended to begin by forcing a parliamentary investigation of administrative malpractices during the recent balloting. This would serve to embarrass the conservatives by exposing Fourtou's financial manipulations and, if possible, by overturning the narrow electoral margin of some conservative candidates. In preparation for meeting this challenge, Broglie went before a meeting of 120 conservative senators to plead for their united support of his ministry. The Legitimists and Bonapartists were amenable, but the Orleanist faction boggled: they would pledge allegiance only to MacMahon, not to Broglie and Fourtou. As one of their number said, he and his Orleanist colleagues "could not show themselves at home any more if they upheld the cabinet."[86]

All these doings were extensively reported to Berlin. Hohenlohe continued to believe that MacMahon would eschew the use of force but added that he "could easily be moved to a *masked* coup d'état." And if so, "the most adventurous decisions" might be expected.[87] These comments were not treated as routine. They were sent as coded dispatches, and they conveyed a more genuine sense of urgency than at any time since the war of 1870. No one was more excited than William, who scrawled across one of Hohenlohe's telegrams, "A catastrophe threatens!" As always, however, it was Bismarck who set the tone of German reaction. In view of the uncertainty and "high tension" in France, he wired from Varzin, the effects of direct intervention at that moment were incalculable; it was consequently advisable to "play dead *(faire le mort)*" and to leave MacMahon unmolested.[88]

As debate in Versailles on the establishment of a commission to investigate *seize mai* and the electoral results reached a climax, tempers were wearing thin. Broglie became bitter and acerbic in characterizing the republican strategy: "To disquiet the foreigner about the dispositions of France, then to intimidate France with the menace of the foreigner—that was the entire operation. . . . I feel ashamed for my country." Gambetta interjected, "You insult France, monsieur!" Even if Broglie's charge could not in all honesty be denied, the impact of repeated German threats remained a heavy liability for the French conservatives to bear. The most succinct explanation of that fact came from Hohenlohe: "Meanwhile dissatisfaction grows in the land. The elections went republican because the population wants peace and was motivated by a justified suspicion that a clerical-conservative regime would inaugurate a policy that would lead France to war. This feeling is so deeply rooted that all explanations of the regime and the conservatives to the contrary make no impression."[89] MacMahon and his associates were, in other words, suffering from a chronic crisis of public confidence which the marshal's maladroit efforts during and after the election had done nothing to dispel.

For anyone who would comprehend the political bankruptcy of the conservative tradition in France, the ensuing premiership of General de Rochebouët merits more attention than it has received. MacMahon's appointment of this provincial military commander as premier in November 1877 was a pitiful act of desperation. For weeks the president had attempted to devise some formula to constitute a new cabinet, only to founder each time on the intractability of one faction or another. His confusion was impossible to conceal. After collating contradictory reports from his Paris agents, Bleichröder could only assume that "MacMahon himself doesn't know at the moment what he intends to undertake in the near future." Yet for various reasons the marshal was unwilling to contemplate resignation. He was under pressure from the Church to remain in office at least until the election of a new pope; and he was implored by his wife to stay long enough to preside over the planned Paris exposition in 1878. Beyond these specific considerations, there was simply MacMahon's grinding sense of loyalty to his conservative cronies.[90]

And so appeared Rochebouët, a man known to hardly anyone outside professional army circles. As a corps commander, however, he had long been kept under surveillance by the German military attaché, who was now able to supply Berlin with pertinent biographical data. The new premier was sixty-five years of age, a Legitimist by inclination and personal connections, and potentially a "man of action" who harbored "a fundamental enmity against the republic." His most notable previous distinction was an award of the Legion of Honor for his services to Louis Bonaparte in the coup d'état of 1851. In addition to these discomforting details, Lieutenant Colonel von Bülow offered a correct prediction that Rochebouët, after keeping for himself the portfolio of war minister, would appoint as his adjutant in the Rue St. Dominque General Berge, an officer reputed for his "very intensive germanophobia."[91] This report could only corroborate the less precise impression already formed in the Wilhelmstrasse and passed on to the Kaiser: Rochebouët "did not seem to offer the same guarantees against a coup d'état as his predecessor," General Berthaut. In fact, Lieutenant Colonel von Bülow had previously warned that dismissal of the cautious and reliable Berthaut from the war ministry might be the signal for a show of force; and Bismarck was thus led to conclude that Rochebouët's appearance was "a significant step toward a coup d'état."[92]

For once German apprehensions were neither feigned nor greatly inflated. France was closer to civil disorder than at any moment between the Paris Commune and the Boulanger crisis. When the Chamber voted 315 to 207 to refuse any negotiations with the new regime, Hohenlohe described the situation as "a complete state of war."[93] In Berlin this seemed something more than a metaphor. In addition to appointing Berge to the war ministry, Rochebouët named as his chief of staff a protégé of General Ducrot, an officer to whom the German attaché ascribed a "restless military zealotry with a distinct religious bias." For Bismarck this was evidence sufficient to claim that the French high command was falling "completely into clerical hands." He therefore instructed the press to point out the encroaching dangers "should the French army thereby become 'vaticanized.'" The chancellor's neologism demonstrated his continuing awareness of propaganda as a political weapon; but his many marginal comments on dispatches from Paris also indicated the severity with which he judged the "ulterior thoughts of a coup d'état."[94]

We need not recapitulate in detail the denouement of Mac-

Mahon's anguished attempts to save his conservative friends. The marshal's dithering only made him appear foolish, even though he eventually displayed some self-assurance in refusing to associate his name with draconian political measures proposed by a rightist clique behind Senator Batbie. That refusal was instrumental in foreclosing the possibility of a military putsch, for which extensive preparations had already been made by Rochebouët, Ducrot, and presumably Broglie.[95]

In the end it was the combination of republican solidarity and German hostility that rendered hopeless the entire enterprise of *seize mai*. When Rochebouët's cabinet met for the last time on 12 December, the members heard a report from the acting foreign minister, the Marquis de Banneville, on the complications abroad that further resistance to the republican majority would create for France. In his briefcase he carried documents warning of "the gravest incidents" that might be provoked by Germany if the crisis continued.[96] With that, MacMahon was finally confronted with the hard choice Gambetta had predicted many months before. For the time being the marshal chose to submit rather than to resign. By doing so he was acknowledging that France had definitively become a republic and that the conservative opposition finally had failed beyond reprieve.

Chapter 7

The Opportunist Republic

The Afterglow of Victory

Rarely does a nation so self-consciously choose one course over another as did the French in 1877. Contemporaries of the event were fully aware of its significance. They did not require a later generation of historians to inform them that they had just witnessed, in the most accurate sense of the term, a political revolution. A longer perspective might have been useful, however, to realize that an era was finally closed which had opened on the day that Louis XVI was beheaded. The regicide of 1792 bequeathed to France many decades of uncertainty, a time during which each successive regime had erroneously believed itself to be the embodiment of a definitive form of state. Such an expectation had been revived once again on 4 September 1870, when the Government of National Defense proclaimed an end to the Second Empire. But in fact the republican principle was not securely established until the final month of 1877. During that interim the French state had remained fragile, distressingly vulnerable to outside pressures, and altogether tentative in its policies and personnel. In brief, the republic had passed through an initial phase of transition; now it was to begin a period of consolidation.

President MacMahon's capitulation had immediate and practical effects. Twenty-seven prefects resigned at once, forty-six were dismissed, and another seven were suspended. Therewith began the last of the abrupt and sweeping administrative purges of the 1870s. This change eventually reached into the highest and lowest echelons of the central government, permanently consolidating and further extending the advances of Gambetta's *nouvelle couche sociale*. Thus the political option reinforced the sociological composition of a bourgeois republic.[1] By comparison, the army was scarcely touched. After all, most military officers had conducted themselves with perfect propriety, maintaining both obedience to the commander-in-chief and discipline in the ranks. Naturally, Rochebouët and his closest associates disappeared from political view; and the main culprit in the estimation of most republicans, General Ducrot, was summarily discharged from military service. But demands for a court-martial, as well as for a criminal trial of Albert de Broglie, finally came to nothing. The essential matter was nevertheless settled: no major obstacle remained to the gradual, albeit imperfect, republicanization of the French army. Paradoxically, still less directly affected in personnel and institutional structure was the Church, even though the French episcopate had made no secret of its support for the losing cause. This insulation from reform which the clergy enjoyed, however, only increased the determination of bedrock anticlericals that Church be entirely separated from State.[2]

If the outcome of the *seize mai* crisis produced greater satisfaction anywhere than among French republicans, it was within the inner sanctum of the German government. "The feeling of being freed from a nightmare," as Hohenlohe described it, was no less evident in Berlin than in Paris. The overriding factors in favor of French stability could be easily enumerated: MacMahon was discredited, isolated, and unable to act alone; the new cabinet—in which the key figures were Dufaure, William Waddington, Freycinet, and Léon Say—was solidly yet moderately republican; the mounting economic stress during 1877 had left business and banking elites eager for a political respite; the strong possibility of a forthcoming negotiation of the Eastern question meant that France would require domestic calm in order to play an active diplomatic role. These considerations offset countervailing potentialities for instability: that, after biding their time, conservative and clerical elements might regroup behind MacMahon; that the Bonapartists might attempt to organize discontented radical elements of both Right and Left against the republican consensus; that the still antirepublican majority in the Senate might hamstring the parliament; or that the economy might slump so drastically as to shake the foundations of government. The evidence that these speculations were carefully weighed by the Germans is abundant. In general their prognostications were optimistic. But it is noteworthy that Bismarck himself continued to hold suspicions that MacMahon's conservative colleagues were only awaiting the first opportunity to revenge their "inner Sedan." The chancellor therefore ordered that the German press print "repeated and thorough discussions of the bellicosity of the French reactionary party. . . ."[3]

German approval consequently remained qualified and conditional. The new republican leaders were to be treated like truant schoolboys from whom exemplary behavior is expected lest they suffer reproof or punishment. Proper comportment would meanwhile be rewarded with words of praise and promises of a brighter future. After 1877 the Germans began to create the impression that a durable detente with France was well within reach. The natural way to begin was with a change of diplomatic personnel. Decazes, whom Bismarck did not fully trust after 1875, was gone from the Quai d'Orsay; and, at long last, Gontaut-Biron was relieved of his ambassadorial duties in Berlin. Any replacement for the conniving and incompetent Gontaut would be an improvement from Bismarck's point of view, but he let it be known by coded dispatch that he would be "especially gratified" by the selection of Saint-Vallier. Once this wish was granted by the new French foreign minister, Waddington, the chancellor innocently exclaimed his "extraordinary pleasure" at the fortunate news.[4]

In the exalted sphere of diplomatic protocol and courtly formalities, the appearance in Berlin of Thiers's former envoy to Nancy during the German occupation had much the same stabilizing effect as Harry von Arnim's replacement by Hohenlohe in Paris. Saint-Vallier's personal dedication and previous service to the republic made him an obviously appropriate representative after 1877 in a way that the frankly monarchist Gontaut was not. Whereas the latter had been altogether debarred from access to important political information in Berlin, the new French ambassador was ostentatiously included in discussions. Saint-Vallier's worry that the Kaiser, who had often shielded Gontaut from Bismarck's sarcasm, would be reticent to receive him was completely dispelled by his first visit with William and the imperial family. When the reception by press and public proved to be equally warm, Saint-Vallier had reason to boast that the change of guard had been "very satisfactory."[5]

Characteristic of the improved atmosphere was the facility with which one delicate problem was resolved soon after Saint-Vallier's arrival in Berlin. For more than a year preparations had been underway for an international exposition in Paris during the summer of 1878. Bismarck's refusal to permit German participation had been generally interpreted as a sign of strain between the Berlin government and the perpetrators of *seize mai*. But once the crisis in France had evaporated, the matter assumed a new cast. Hosting a German exhibit would be a mark of prestige for the new French regime and a conspicuous symbol of detente. The French were eager to request it but fearful of another public rebuff; and Bismarck wished to appear conciliatory but was unwilling to reverse his previous decision.[6] A graceful exit from this awkward circumstance was quickly discovered during two long interviews between the chancellor and Saint-Vallier: Germany would be represented by a special exhibition of paintings. In these discussions Bismarck proved to be as "forthcoming and amiable" in his attitude toward Waddington and Saint-Vallier as he was caustic in mentioning Decazes and Gontaut. Although "the damage has been done," Bismarck said of his negative response to the original invitation by Decazes ("the most ambiguous of men"), Germany recognized that "the past must be entirely liquidated."[7] Hence, the solution of a nonindustrial exhibit, *hors concours* and nonetheless unmistakably intended as a friendly gesture, was ideal. As a French agent pointed out, apart from the actual result of these talks, the very fact that they occurred was significant, considering that Gontaut had not been received by Bismarck in several years.[8] Both interlocutors were visibly pleased. The chancellor's positive evaluation of the "respectable course" being set by the new French regime was telegraphed to German legations throughout Europe; and Saint-Vallier's appreciation of the "many satisfactory symptoms" was amply reported to Paris.[9]

The diplomatic façade was thereby refurbished. Yet behind

it was a political reality that the Germans considered far more important. The emergence of Léon Gambetta as the true leader of the French republic had been the theme of innumerable German dispatches during the past year. We have documented both the contacts established by Bismarck with Gambetta and the German aid deliberately extended to his political campaign in 1877. In October of that year the possibility of a personal meeting between the two men had been vetoed by the chancellor for fear that a charge of collusion would only harm the Gambettist cause. But once the climax of *seize mai* had passed, the question was, not surprisingly, revived. Barely a week after MacMahon's concession, Henckel von Donnersmarck offered to bring Gambetta, either openly or secretly, to visit Bismarck in Varzin: "All that is required is a wink from you." This private bid was again declined on much the same grounds as before: although "entering into personal relations with [Gambetta] would be entirely welcome to me," Bismarck replied, the Kaiser was sure to be startled; and, besides, such an encounter might still be premature for Gambetta's own interests. It was therefore more prudent to assure that his position of authority in the republic not be shaken nor the usefulness of his "peaceful disposition" toward Germany be placed in jeopardy. Germany would therefore leave well enough alone.[10]

In the spring of 1878, however, the matter became more problematical. Rumors began to circulate in Paris that Gambetta was actively promoting a triple entente among France, Germany, and Italy; and Saint-Vallier disclosed that a pamphlet entitled "*L'alliance franco-allemande*" had been printed in Basel, distributed in Alsace-Lorraine, and even made available in the bookshops of Berlin.[11] In a version picked up by British newspapers and reprinted in the *Frankfurter Zeitung*, Gambetta wanted to accord Savoy to Italy, Lorraine and Belgium to France, Alsace and Holland to Germany. This was a fantastic scheme, no doubt, but it was also precisely the kind of *cauchemar* that chronically troubled the chancellor's sleep.[12] Beyond this press speculation we can verify the following details: that in early April Bismarck asked Henckel von Donnersmarck to arrange the previously deferred meeting; that Bismarck left for his Friedrichsruh estate only after offering to travel by rail for a rendezvous in Berlin on any day suitable to Gambetta; that Gambetta agreed to the trip immediately upon his return to Paris on 22 April after the funeral of his aunt in Nice; that reservations were made for Gambetta and Henckel at the Hotel Kaisershof in Berlin for the night of 29 April; that stories of the impending journey were somehow leaked to the French press; and that Bismarck canceled the visit at the last moment on grounds of his ill health.[13]

So far as we know, a summit meeting did not occur in 1878. Yet the near miss was in itself revealing. The likelihood that both the invitation and the cancellation of the Berlin interview originated with Bismarck provides some measure of the importance attached to Gambetta's potential role as a French statesman. No other republican politician received remotely as much attention. The future aside, as Henckel suggested, Gambetta's current status meant that he might be prepared to discuss two topics of considerable interest to Bismarck: a mutually agreeable limitation of the French military budget and "a united struggle of Germany and France against Rome." There is reason to believe, however, that Bismarck's immediate interest in sounding out Gambetta was kindled by the rumors of his efforts to find a way for France to emerge from diplomatic isolation. What better means to stifle an initiative than to smother it with kindness? If the French seriously wished a detente, in other words, they could not hope to sustain it while engaging in devious projects contrary to Germany's interests.[14]

What prompted the chancellor to cancel the Kaiserhof interview cannot be ascertained. His instable health may actually have been a factor; but it is more likely that a combination of public indiscretions and confidential reports changed his mind. Press releases in Paris dramatized the conservative allegation that Gambetta would henceforth be taking orders directly from Berlin and, if so, he would obviously disqualify himself as a worthy leader of the French nation. Bismarck's agents meanwhile confirmed that Gambetta had indeed disappeared for a time because of a family tragedy and that he had not been, as rumored, secretly conspiring in Vienna or elsewhere to promote some grand diplomatic design. The likely damage to Gambetta might therefore vitiate any possible advantage of a personal encounter, and the logical conclusion was further postponement.[15]

Both the manifest and the latent content of diplomacy thus revealed a German desire to encourage the current leadership of the French republic. Saint-Vallier's official and private correspondence back to Paris was ecstatic about the cordiality in Berlin ("je bois de la crème"); and the German press was unanimous in lavishing praise on the new regime.[16] The spirit of recovery and rapprochement thus preceded its most glamorous expressions in the summer of 1878: the Paris Exposition and the Berlin Congress. The intrinsic importance of these simultaneous gatherings was not more striking than their utter compatibility. Whereas the Exposition celebrated France's rehabilitation as the arbiter of European fashion, the Congress announced Germany's arrival as the broker of European politics.[17]

The invitation to Berlin was accepted by the French with alacrity. They had been secretly informed by Bleichröder to prepare for the trip; and there was no hestitation in regarding their delegation, headed by Waddington himself, as proof of France's rightful claim to rank again among the great powers. "My dear friend, I do not need to tell you," Saint-Vallier wrote to Waddington, "how happy I am for us, for our country, for our security, for our Exposition, because of the turn that events have taken."[18] Once the French arrived in the German capital, Bismarck took personal care to be "as amiable as possible" and evinced "an evident desire to produce a good impression." Waddington's letters back to Paris, many of them in English to his American wife, constitute a record of constant German catering to French feelings. By the conclusion of the Congress Waddington was convinced that France had played a role altogether commensurate with strict neutrality as well as with national interests; and he was persuaded that "Germany has a great need for peace [because] the chancellor made every effort to obtain it promptly in order to devote himself to the internal affairs of the Reich."[19]

The resulting calm in France after 1877 was deceptive. True, the public sense of crisis had abated almost entirely. For the first time in a decade neither civil nor foreign war threatened. But a profound and irreversible alteration was nonetheless occurring which formed the character of the Third Republic as it would essentially remain for more than half a century. Undramatic yet inexorable, this phenomenon was suggested in the sporadic by-elections held because of alleged malpractices by the Broglie-Fourtou cabinet in 1877. By May 1878 the following statistics were available: of 45 contested seats in the Chamber, 42 were redetermined; and in only 5 of these instances did a conservative candidate prevail. The subtraction of 37 deputies from the conservative column and their addition to the majority meant that the republicans were left only one short of their original total of 363, a figure they were certain to surpass in the near future. The repeated defeats and dwindling prospects of the rightist parties were regularly reported to Berlin, where it was correctly assumed that the process of republicanization would inundate the last conservative redoubt in the senatorial elections scheduled for the outset of 1879.[20]

No less indicative in its way was the new republican search for appropriate symbols and ceremonies. The stirring melody of the "Marseillaise" at official functions was becoming familiar despite the strong disapproval and repeated tantrums of President MacMahon ("sa petite colère habituelle," as Léon Say remarked). At the dedication of the great statue at the Place de la République the playing of the "Marseillaise" was forbidden by the Ministry of War but ordered by the Ministry of the Interior; to the delight of a huge crowd massed in the square, the anthem was sounded. The organization of a Voltaire jubilee proved less popular; but a Rousseau festival was attached to the national celebration of 14 July which had as its focus in Paris an American circus at the Place de la Bastille.[21] These tokens of the republic, like the tricolor itself, should not be underestimated in their psychological importance. Yet for sheer emotional impact none of them could eclipse the figure of Strasbourg, silently seated under a black shroud in the Place de la Concorde. Thus the mythology of the republic, just as every other aspect of its public life, had a disturbing German component to which the French could not be totally oblivious.[22]

After the termination of the *seize mai* crisis, however, the dominant mood remained one of detente. There was, of course, no shortage of diplomatic incidents, political episodes, caustic editorials, and tendentious reports from more or less reliable agents. But these did not seriously faze the composure of the republican leadership. Although still baffled by the "sphinx of Friedrichsruh," the French were far more inclined than in the past to ascribe difficulties to some ephemeral misunderstanding. The overriding consideration, as Saint-Vallier formulated it, was "the increasingly marked desire of Germany to be conciliatory with us and to collaborate in the majority of issues."[23] At the same time the French government was enjoying a better press in Germany than ever before. A strong preference for Waddington and a regime of the Left Center was conveyed, both publicly and privately, from Berlin to Paris.[24] Implicit in this message was a certain reluctance to favor Gambetta insofar as he might represent a further radicalization of the republic; yet even that hesitation fell far short of the imprecations and admonitions which had formerly been customary.[25]

The Franco-German diplomatic rapprochement thus inaugurated in 1878 was to endure into the middle of the succeeding decade. All those who have surveyed that period have insisted on the same obvious conclusion: that the spirit of detente was never sufficient to eradicate French resentment over the loss of Alsace-Lorraine nor to mitigate German suspicions of French unreliability and revanchism.[26] Although such observations are accurate enough, they should not obscure the fact that this respite precisely coincided with the consolidation of a republican regime acceptable to the Reich. In most regards, Frances's internal political development was henceforth able to take its own course—but only after the determination of that course had been incessantly and heavily influenced by Germany for many years.

The Outcome of Protectionism

One of the perennial conundrums of economic history is the relationship between growth and commerce. We have earlier examined the general growth patterns of France and Germany after 1870 and noted how the Reich perceptibly began to surpass the republic in the 1880s. We can now add with assurance that the growing volume of German production during that decade was accompanied by a high rate of exports; and it seems safe enough to assume that one could not have risen so steadily without the other. But the verb "accompanied" must be used advisedly, since definitive proof is still lacking to establish a firm causal sequence between foreign trade and economic growth.[27]

In broad terms we can characterize France's commercial relations with her principal European trading partners in the period after 1870 as a continued but declining surplus with England and Switzerland, virtual parity with Belgium, a slightly increasing deficit with Italy, and *with Germany alone* a drastic shift from a positive balance of trade in the 1870s to a negative balance in the 1880s. The annual average for the years from 1867 to 1876 (despite the transfer of Alsace-Lorraine) was 43.4 million francs to France's commercial advantage, whereas the annual average for the period from 1877 to 1883 shows a deficit for France in the amount of 77.5 million francs.[28] This was a crucial moment in the economic fortunes of France; and, especially with regard to Germany, it was an unsuccessful one. If it is ultimately impossible to prove exactly *why* the French failed to respond adequately and to keep pace in industry and commerce, we are at least able to determine *when* the wind went out of their sails and they began to fall seriously behind. In that same phase—presumably without coincidence—it was above all the Germans who were able to capitalize on French incapacity.

Let us take a closer look. Perhaps the best indicators are the figures for *commerce spécial*: goods specifically designated for import-export trade.[29] If we examine the annual average of French imports from the major European nations, we find that the value of products entering from Germany was rising much more rapidly than that of products from any other country (see table 6). It is evident that the rate of French imports from all these countries, with the exception of Germany, was slowing in the early 1880s. Yet meanwhile, France's exports to Germany were failing to accelerate at the same rhythm (see table 7).

Because the trade with Germany constituted about 10 percent of France's total commerce, and because the volume between the two was expanding more rapidly in the 1870s than that between France and any other nation, Germany was becoming increasingly more important to France both as a customer and as a competitor. Such a generalization would be more meaningful if we could with

Table 6 / French Imports (Special Commerce):
Annual Average, 1857–1883 (in millions of francs)

Country	1857–66	1867–76	1877–83
England	459.6	620.2	648.3
Belgium	230.7	396.6	451.9
Germany	158.1	283.1	433.6
Italy	193.8	339.5	381.4
Switzerland	64.2	107.7	113.3

Source: *Annuaire statistique de la France* 8 (1885): 390.

Table 7 / French Exports (Special Commerce):
Annual Average, 1857–1883 (in millions of francs)

Country	1857–66	1867–76	1877–83
England	694.3	932.9	925.5
Belgium	199.3	398.8	447.4
Germany	203.2	326.5	356.1
Italy	208.9	204.7	186.3
Switzerland	155.5	275.1	236.4

Source: Ibid., p. 391.

accuracy compare separate sectors of the two economies. But econometricians best equipped to do so agree that this is an exceedingly hazardous undertaking. Completely reliable trade statistics for Germany in the 1870s are unavailable; and those of the 1880s are difficult to reconcile altogether with official French tabulations.[30] Yet we do have some contemporary documents of the period that indicate what the situation was then thought to be and, in a general way, probably was (see table 8). France was, quite obviously, a regular customer for German goods. By comparison, purchases from the other nations tended to be very considerable in certain leading sectors but insignificant in others.

Table 8 / French Importation of Key Commodities, 1877
(in millions of francs)

Commodity	Germany	England	Belgium	Italy
Livestock	40.50	—	27.02	66.75
Lumber	33.59	—	11.69	8.65
Silks	23.70	29.37	1.65	0.11
Coal and coke	22.33	58.37	68.98	—
Furs and hides	18.37	8.11	4.80	5.00
Cottons	15.08	12.00	13.48	0.11
Linens	12.87	51.13	3.12	—
Machines	12.70	15.49	4.85	—
Beer	11.75	9.69	0.28	—
Grains and flour	10.79	1.80	3.50	11.27

Source: "Etat comparatif des principaux marchandises importées
d'Allemagne et des mêmes marchandises importées des autres pays
(valeurs exprimées en millions)," AN Paris, F¹² 6199. This was based
in part on statistics compiled by the Ministry of Commerce for the year
1877: "Importations d'Allemagne en France: principaux articles" and
"Exportations de France en Allemagne: principaux articles," ibid.

With this statistical information in mind, disclaimers not with-
standing, we may venture several hypotheses:

    1. Although the French balance of trade was positive
during the initial period of postwar recovery (and severe German slump) from 1872 to 1875, it became negative thereafter.

    2. The deficit of French commerce persisted beyond 1900.
In the entire period from the Franco-Prussian war to the First
World War, when the volume and value of world trade tre-
bled, France failed to participate in the commercial boom
nearly to the extent of the other industrialized nations.[31]

    3. The pattern of trade with Germany reflected this con-
dition and emphasized it. From a bilateral commercial surplus
of over 150 million francs in 1873, the French slid to a trade
deficit with Germany of almost 140 million francs in 1882.
Within a single decade France thus passed from a creditor to a
debtor nation, so far as Germany was concerned, at a difference of nearly 300 million francs.[32]

4. This shift in the Franco-German commercial relation-ship, far more marked than that with any of France's other trading partners, was both symptomatic of the languid French economic performance and an important contribution to it.

The last of these four points may not appear totally warranted by the evidence presented until one brings two further matters into focus. In the first place, we must bury a canard of nineteenth-century economic theory according to which increasing industri-alization meant a lessening dependence on foreign trade. Actually, within certain limits, the inverse was true for the period in ques-tion. Whereas the estimated commerce with other nations had amounted to only 13 percent of France's gross national product in 1830, by 1870 that figure was approaching 40 percent.[33] The exactitude of such calculations is dubious. But one may safely adopt the modest proposal that the aggregate value of exports and imports was equivalent to about one-third of the French GNP in the latter half of the nineteenth century. It follows that any sudden disequilibrium of the French commercial relationship with a prin-cipal trading partner could not occur without domestic economic repercussions.

In addition, it is crucial to note that the relative stagnation of the French economy, compared to Germany in the 1880s, did not simply mean a temporary statistical deficit but marked a per-manent change in the structure of the commercial relationship be-tween the two nations. To put a complex matter briefly, the share of finished goods among German exports grew while the per-centage of manufactures in the French export trade in Europe declined.[34] Only half of German exports were manufactured ar-ticles in the 1870s, but nearly three-quarters were by 1913. The rubric of metal products and machines alone, barely 6 percent of German exports in the 1870s, accounted for over 20 percent in the prewar years. The pattern of German imports mirrored that change: fewer industrial goods were brought into Germany while the quantity of nonagricultural raw materials purchased abroad was increased.[35]

Meanwhile, in global terms, France managed to keep a stable export trade: a fairly constant ratio of manufactures to other goods leaving the country. But doing so meant that an increasing quantity of such products had to seek protected outlets, such as colonies, in part because the French grew less competitive with Germany in the European market. One example will serve to illustrate the growing difference in the structure of the two economies. By the eve of the First World War both France and Germany exported about 330 million dollars' worth of textiles and clothing; but whereas that figure constituted 42 percent of France's export of manufactures, it represented only 18 percent of the comparable German total. Within Europe, and especially in relation to Germany, France was being transformed into a supplier of agricultural products, raw materials, and semifinished commodities.[36] To conclude that France was on the way to becoming no more than an economic satellite of Germany would be overwrought. Yet a new pattern was distinctly emerging that gave Germany the basis for an economic takeoff, while it left France to an inferior status.

For these developments the republican leadership was not completely blameless. Although, of course, imperfectly informed from a statistical point of view, the new opportunist regime was not unaware of the impending economic dangers when it took office. During 1877 a senatorial committee had already investigated reasons for the onset of a trade deficit and had recommended that French tariff rates be raised in order to reduce imports. But the government hesitated to impose higher duties, hoping instead that industry and commerce would be sufficiently buoyed by the Paris Exposition in 1878. The announcement in that February of Charles de Freycinet's plan to allocate nearly 5 billion francs for the construction of railway and harbor facilities was also conceived as a more palatable alternative to the adoption of stiff protectionist legislation.[37] In practice opportunism thereby lived up to its name, and that meant political compromise rather than hard economic choices. Yet the evidence also shows that republican leaders were not dogmatically committed to free trade and remained aware that France might have to respond to any decisive action by Germany. Before departing to spend several days at Bismarck's Friedrichsruh estate during the first week of January 1879, Saint-Vallier received special instructions from Waddington: "Take careful note of the economic and commercial views of the chancellor; that is important since all our commercial treaties will be terminated at the end of 1879 and we will be absolutely free."[38]

A month later the Reichstag debate on revision of Germany's tariff policy was opened. As had been anticipated for some time, and lately reconfirmed by Saint-Vallier, Bismarck threw the full weight of his office behind the protectionist cause, repeatedly intervening to support the proponents of a comprehensive tariff system. These proceedings were followed by the French in exhaustive detail, both in the form of lengthy summaries in French and of bulky dossiers of German newspaper clippings.[39] In complimenting Saint-Vallier for his efforts, Waddington emphasized the importance of obtaining the fullest information "because of the studies now being conducted in France of analagous subjects and the considerable influence that the new commercial policy of Germany may exercise on the economic system of other nations." In Paris there was consequently no surprise, although some consternation, when the Reichstag finished on 15 July 1879 by adopting the new tariff legislation advocated by Bismarck. This was, as Saint-Vallier privately commented, "a complete political triumph for him, surpassing by far the most favorable predictions."[40]

In France the tariff issue was less visible and the result less decisive. As we witnessed much earlier, the principle of protectionism had been contested from the outset of the republic. Adolphe Thiers and his finance minister, Pouyer-Quertier, had won an early round for higher tariffs; yet most of these increases were rescinded in 1873 when the French economy began to rebound and Thiers was dismissed from the presidency. But the prolonged German slump, the unfavorable shift in France's commercial balance, and the probability of a victory by the protectionists in Berlin all made imperative a reconsideration. The ensuing ideological and political struggle was conducted in varying degrees of secrecy among the republican leaders, as they meanwhile attempted to present a united front against the conservative opposition. Pouyer-Quertier again surfaced as an articulate proponent of high protective tariffs in direct response to the German legislation of 1879; but he was effectively countered in private and public by Léon Say, finance minister in the Dufaure and Waddington cabinets and a man well positioned in the banking world by his connections with the Rothschilds.[41] Simultaneously, there was another altercation within the ruling circle between Say and Gambetta over the twin issues of nationalizing the French railway system and financing the proposed new construction. Out of this complex of problems and personalities emerged Charles de Freycinet, at first in a role as informal arbiter, then in December 1879 as French premier. In face of Germany's protectionist legislation, he thought, his public works plan would be the appropriate riposte. A sweeping proposal for uniform tariff increases of 24 percent was therefore rejected in favor of selective raises of between 10 and 30 percent; the railways were not to be immediately nationalized; and Léon Say was to direct the operation of financing by public bonds. Hence the French republic entered the 1880s fully cognizant of the German economic challenge and yet still clinging to a mixed program of modest tariffs, public works, and "liberal" financing.[42]

Grandiose as it was, the Freycinet plan eventually proved to be no more than a palliative. Certainly the initial results were satisfactory: the metal and building trades flourished; the Paris Bourse, stimulated by huge government outlays of capital, was able to record a steady advance; commerce and industry generally seemed to respond.[43] But this was only the raising of the guillotine. In January 1882 the stock market began to break, and the remainder of the plan soon had to be abandoned. In the end, Freycinet's scheme probably produced more damage than benefit. At a critical economic juncture his project had the effect of staving off depression briefly, only to plunge the republic all the more helplessly into it thereafter; and though the plan gained a reprieve for the free traders at first, its results eventually sealed a more enduring victory for the protectionists.[44]

Thus, in the economic competition with Germany in the 1880s, France proved to be outmatched. This was not merely a matter of size, population, and resources—although these weighed of course in Germany's favor—but also of policy, organization, and consistency in implementation. Germany encountered the depression sooner and faced it more forthrightly. The passage of protectionist legislation in 1879 had a rapid and stunning effect in reducing German imports (see table 9). The perceptible rise of imports in the first postwar decade was manifestly halted not by

Table 9 / Volume of German Imports,
1870–1890 (1913 = 100)

Year	Volume	Year	Volume
1870	19.2	1880	25.5
1871	23.5	1881	27.5
1872	25.2	1882	29.4
1873	27.9	1883	31.3
1874	27.3	1884	32.8
1875	27.7	1885	31.8
1876	29.7	1886	31.6
1877	30.5	1887	34.2
1878	30.9	1888	35.1
1879	34.5	1889	41.9

Source: Walther G. Hoffmann, *Wachstum*, pp. 537–38.

the automatic mechanism of a depression but by the purposeful erection of tariffs. As a result, the 1879 import rate was not re-attained until 1888. Withdrawn behind the new trade barriers, German industry reduced prices and cut profit margins in order to maintain levels of production and exportation. It also sought new outlets by attempting, under government patronage, to construct a kind of central European customs union from which France might be excluded.[45] For Germany the treaty of Frankfurt thereby became an encumbrance to be jettisoned in order to achieve a favorable balance of trade and to sustain a fairly constant rate of growth. These objectives were in fact realized in the 1880s, and in this regard the German Reich advanced while the French republic faltered.

The Upsurge of Radicalism

As a summation of the senatorial balloting of January 1879, which assured republican control in both houses of the French Assembly, nothing could have been more apt than the cryptic remark of Léon Gambetta: "The period of dangers is closed; that of difficulties is about to begin." Most of the formal political debates that dominated the first postwar decade had at last been resolved. The years thereafter were not to be troubled by questions about the form of the state, the nature of the constitution, the prerogatives of the presidency, or the balance of parliamentary factions. The republic was established, and the possibility of its existence being once again placed in question seemed miniscule. That was primarily so because the resolution of the 1870s was in one regard decisive: it excluded a return to monarchism. Thus the "dangers" emanating from the political Right had ceased to be a credible threat, and henceforth the prevailing consensus would be plagued only by "difficulties" within the republican majority itself. Undeniably there was a justifiable measure of optimism in such a view. Yet it needed to be measured against a skeptical rejoinder by the German ambassador in Paris: "In time, however, these difficulties could become dangers again."[46]

Those finely balanced phrases at least indicated an awareness of fundamental changes occurring in the character of the Third Republic. The focus of political life was noticeably shifting toward the Left. Restoration was no longer an issue; radicalization was. In this process, Marshall MacMahon had become the relic of another era. All too obviously he had been installed as the caretaker of conservative ambitions; and once the republican composition of the Senate was confirmed, he was simply irrelevant. The president consequently began to prepare a graceful exit. His first opportunity was lost on 20 January when a compromise motion formulated by Jules Ferry attenuated immediate radical pressure on the Dufaure cabinet. Waddington later confided to Hohenlohe that the marshal actually appeared crestfallen on learning that a solution had been found: he already had a letter of resignation in his pocket.[47] But the wait to make use of it was not long. Ten days later a republican demand for dismissal of several army corps commanders provided MacMahon with the most appropriate adieu imaginable. If other distinguished military officers whose only sin was political conservatism were to be forced out, he would join them.[48]

The presidential succession of 1879 had little in common with that of 1873. Thiers was dismissed, MacMahon chose to resign; Thiers had been straining to lead, MacMahon was tired of following; Thiers's continuation would have meant a difference, Mac-Mahon's departure made none. In short, most of those matters that had been pending six years before were already resolved before Jules Grévy became the republic's third chief executive. Precisely such a thesis was expounded by Waddington in urging that this time Bismarck make no issue of diplomatic accreditation; it would be a sign of Germany's "friendly disposition" if Grévy were permitted, rather, to send only an official letter of notification to the courts of Europe. This request was accompanied by an assurance that the French foreign minister and his envoy in Berlin would remain at their posts.[49] The German response was unhesitatingly positive. A memorandum from the Wilhelmstrasse noted that the delays in 1873 had occurred "under somewhat different political circumstances"; and the chancellor wired from Friedrichsruh that he was in "complete agreement" with Waddington's proposal.[50] Evidently the presidency counted for relatively little—at least so long as it was occupied by a calm and colorless figure such as Grévy. But it escaped no one's attention that Grévy's successor as the presiding officer of the Chamber was Gambetta, who thereby positioned himself squarely at the head of the line. For once the Kaiser's commentary, penciled in French on a dispatch from Paris, was as perceptive as any: "All roads lead to the presidency."[51]

In the reshaping of the republic, a change at the Elysée might not have mattered as an isolated occurrence. But it was also the signal for an intensification of the administrative purge whose beginnings we have already recorded. By 1879 the prefectoral corps had become a blunt instrument in the hands of republican officials; and those who had two years earlier excoriated the political intervention of conservative prefects now demanded "vigilant control and strong discipline" in the execution of republican decrees.[52] Likewise, Saint-Vallier's replacement of Gontaut-Biron proved to be only the beginning of a shake-up in the diplomatic corps: the former French ambassadors in London, Vienna, and St. Petersburg were all retired in favor of loyal republicans. Similar changes were to some extent imposed on the military leadership, despite MacMahon's parting protest. A completely revised list of the army's eighteen corps commanders was published in February 1879, along with an announcement by the war ministry that France's military reorganization was thereby nearing completion, with only some details remaining to be settled.[53]

Most of these alterations could be categorized as unfinished business, neither unanticipated nor highly controversial. But the thrust of other reform issues, closely related, confronted the republic with essential problems of the future. "The current situation in France," as Hohenlohe remarked, "resembles more and more a struggle between the liberal bourgeoisie and the radical elements, the fourth estate."[54] The former was represented by the majority of republicans in the Chamber: the Left Center, some of the Gauche républicaine, and even part of the Union républicaine. The radicals could claim far less numerical support in the parliament but had gained control of the municipal council of Paris. From that political base they were demanding, first of all, a thorough purge of the Prefecture of Police, which, they argued, had become a tool of social repression. Leading this charge was Georges Clemenceau, whose remarkable oratorical and political talents now made him "even more dangerous for the moderate republicans and the cabinet than he already was." Clemenceau's clout was sufficient to fell both Minister of the Interior Marcère and Prefect of Police Lombard, evidence that there was no guarantee of immunity from radical demands.[55]

The cutting edge of radicalism was meanwhile sharpened by anticlericalism. Once again it was the municipal council of Paris that demanded immediate and drastic action—specifically, the dismissal of priests and nuns from the instructional staff of public schools—whereas the republican cabinet contemplated a more gradual procedure. The educational reforms inaugurated by the so-called Ferry laws soon showed that the effects of radical pressure on public policy would be far from negligible; and Hohenlohe was basically correct in predicting that the date of Ferry's first deposition to the Chamber, 15 March 1879, would henceforth be regarded as "the beginning of the Kulturkampf in France."[56]

These developments did not appear as threats to the Franco-German detente. In some regards, indeed, they were even welcomed in Berlin as belated repercussions of Germany's effort to influence the course of French affairs. Yet the worry was persistent that matters might spin out of control. That concern had been obliquely expressed by Bismarck to Saint-Vallier in January during their long winter walks along the dank pathways of the Sachsenwald near Friedrichsruh. In explaining Germany's recent adoption of antisocialist legislation, the chancellor emphasized the obligation of every European government to keep a firm grip on "the enemies of the social order."[57] This admonition was repeated once it became known that the French Assembly was preparing to pass a generous bill of amnesty for the communards of 1871. At the same time, a transfer of the Chamber and the Senate to Paris was proposed. Both measures were regarded by the Germans as a concession to radical demands and as a potential danger to the security of the republic. Following a remonstrance from Hohenlohe to President Grévy, Bismarck again intervened personally by arranging another formal interview with Saint-Vallier.[58] Their long conversation in Berlin was cordial but explicit. The chancellor restated his support for the existing French regime but deplored the amnesty and the Assembly's removal to the capital as "a peril for the future and the near future." If the Grévy government continued to compromise, it would "pass from the moderate republic to the radical republic." And should France thus become infected with "revolutionary virus," he warned, Germany would be forced to create a *cordon sanitaire* by fortifying the Vosgesian ridge with an additional one or two hundred thousand men.[59]

From these details we can easily extrapolate at least one general observation: that Germany's domineering practices would continue to disturb France in the 1880s nearly as much as they had before. But we can notice a fundamental difference as well as an underlying similarity in the exercise of German power. The distinction was that Bismarck's primary concern was no longer to combat conservatism in order to achieve a desired result—the moderate republic—but to preserve that result against the internal challenge of radicalism. The equally apparent similarity, however, lay in the inseparability of foreign and domestic politics. The French were given to understand that the detente with Germany could be maintained only by freezing the republic's internal affairs in their current condition. Hence, the consolidation of the Third Republic meant a transformation rather than a termination of Germany's direct influence in France.

This conclusion can also be confirmed by documenting the French response. The individual most exposed to German harassment was naturally Saint-Vallier. The ambassador was repeatedly harangued both by Bülow, speaking for the Kaiser, and by Bleichröder, who conveyed messages from Bismarck. The specter of a red menace in France was meanwhile being conjured daily in the German press. And Saint-Vallier's anxiety grew apace: "German public opinion—the court, the government, the salons, the journals—is unanimous in announcing our imminent collapse, the arrival of the radicals, the excess of the extremes, and the final revolution." His advice to the French government was to remain inflexible toward further radical demands and to pursue a "loyal and conciliatory policy" toward Germany. From the German standpoint, then, Saint-Vallier drew precisely the proper conclusions.[60]

Back in Paris the reaction was similar but somewhat less excited. Waddington, who in February became premier as well as foreign minister, insisted that the republic's dedication to peaceful coexistence with Germany was unaltered; and to Bismarck's allegation that he was becoming "a prisoner of the radicals," he ventured that his cabinet's concessions only proved that it was "sitting more firmly in the saddle."[61] Yet this reply provoked, in turn, more skepticism in Berlin. Bismarck continued to express his concern about the amnesty program and the parliament's return to Paris, which portended "the capitulation of the government to the radicals and the communards." No doubt was left to the French that a sudden disintegration of the moderate republic would be, in Bülow's words, "the mandatory signal for a complete change of Germany's policy toward France."[62]

The perpetual symbiosis of foreign and domestic affairs meant that France's internal development was part reason, part rationale for Germany's diplomatic strategy. Of course, the French were encouraged to believe that everything depended on their own comportment—a view toward which a certain national egocentrism perhaps already inclined them—as if the health of the detente were strictly a function of which regime held sway in Paris.

Yet we know in retrospect that the relationship with France was only one aspect of a general reorientation in 1879 of Germany's economic, political, and diplomatic arrangements. The changes which were occurring within Germany—such as the switch to protectionism, the termination of the Kulturkampf, the passage of antisocialist laws, and the formation of a defensive alliance with Austria-Hungary—all had implications for France that were of more than transitory significance.[63] One must consequently observe that French leaders' repeated expressions of anxiety concerning German capriciousness, however genuine, were partially the result of their myopic vision. In truth, they were probably far freer of German control by the end of the republic's first decade than they realized. Still, the perceived reality was what mattered. Accustomed as they were to the tone of German reprimands, the French continued to interpret them as a serious menace. Apprehension had become a well-conditioned reflex.

These observations provide the necessary context for an appraisal of Bismarck's most extensive and eloquent statement of his policy toward France since the republic became securely established. Delivered to Saint-Vallier, who had journied by train and carriage to the chancellor's East Prussian estate at Varzin in November 1879, Bismarck's long monologues on France constituted a kind of master diagnosis of the republic's past, present, and future. His principal intent, it is clear, was to reassure the French in confidence that the bilateral alliance between Berlin and Vienna was arranged solely against Russia; yet he took the occasion to worry aloud and at length about the possibility of France's succumbing to radicalism.[64] Either Grévy would set an example of determination to resist, Bismarck exclaimed, or else "one fine morning he will be *swept away like a dead leaf* by a Gambetta, a Clemenceau, or a communard." By exercising energetic leadership the moderates could still prevail. But they would need, for example, to block the Gambettist proposal to reintroduce a *scrutin de liste* that would favor popular radical candidates. "Mark my words, Gambetta will be in the Elysée within a few months if Grévy supports the electoral reform."[65] Bismarck thereupon unfolded a scenario of parliamentarians and communards returning simultaneously to Paris, the ensuing confusion, the conflicts, the collapse of authority. "Then we will see the radicals sieze the power left within their reach by the weakness of the moderates; farewell to the republic of Monsieur Thiers, farewell to correct policy, to good relations with European neighbors, to the regime which inspires confidence in us, which we support, which we hope to see maintained."[66]

Whether these words actually rolled so fluently off Bismarck's tongue as from Saint-Vallier's pen, we cannot be certain. For the Varzin interviews the French ambassador is our only detailed source. The chancellor's message nonetheless emerged clearly, and it was perfectly consistent with what preceded and followed. In essence, Bismarck had summed up his support of the regime which he had helped to create and which he regarded as the authentic heir of the Thierist republic. In Bismarck's perspective, then, the political evolution of France in the 1870s had been a consistent development to a fitting conclusion. The problem thereafter would be to retard the republican momentum sufficiently to achieve a safe and regular oscillation. "All our efforts," as he recapitulated his views after Saint-Vallier's departure from Varzin, "are directed toward keeping the current French statesmen at the helm."[67]

Climax and Anticlimax

If anyone seemed destined by force of circumstance and character to lead the republic, it was Léon Gambetta. Such was the apparent expectation of millions of Frenchmen; and such was, as we have often confirmed, the anticipation of most German officials and agents who dealt with France. The advent of a Gambettist regime was therefore an appropriate terminus of the republic's early history, but it also proved to be an inconclusive one. However logical Gambetta's rise may have been, his brief tenure of political power made little impression for good or ill.

Judging from the tenor of German propaganda and private warnings in 1879, one might have expected some sort of turbulence when the Waddington government fell in the final days of December—all the more so since the new premier was Charles de Freycinet, a man who had been Gambetta's lieutenant in the war of 1870 and who was regarded by the Germans as his faithful surrogate. Just a fortnight earlier, Field Marshal von Moltke had described to an incredulous British ambassador the havoc that Waddington's disappearance might create, adding that he was "tormented by nightmares in which he saw the Russians on the Spree and the French on the Main, penetrating from two sides into the heart of the Reich."[68] A notorious insomniac himself, Bismarck also wired to Berlin that the advance of "Gambetta and his engineer of the *guerre à outrance*," meaning Freycinet, would force the Germans "to shoulder arms and stay ready for anything." Although these indelicate hints immediately reached Saint-Vallier (as doubtless intended) and were transmitted by him to Paris, they were insufficient to spare Waddington. Upset and indeed overwrought to the point of submitting his resignation, Saint-Vallier complained that "the damage is great and the choice of Freycinet, a man of *guerre à outrance*, is deplorable for foreign affairs; he is regarded in Germany as a challenge and elsewhere as the harbinger of a policy of adventure."[69]

One is tempted to conclude that, after a full decade of war scares and cold showers, the French were simply too inured to quake at yet another shaking fist. But several other cogent reasons may be offered why, despite the German strictures, not even a minor tremor was felt. First, the Germans had long been aware that Gambetta's political and economic views were actually quite moderate. Otherwise they would have found it less easy to offer him support, not to say patronage, in the electoral campaign of 1877. Their misgivings had developed more recently, after conservatism was repulsed. Even then, they were able to reconfirm that Gambetta's convictions about French foreign policy still echoed those of Bismarck—"only the republic is capable of maintaining genuinely peaceful relations with Germany," he repeated to Bernhard von Bülow—and that his domestic political ambitions remained well under control.[70] Hohenlohe concluded that Gambetta had no intention of forcing his way into the premiership but preferred to await a suitable opportunity to replace Grévy in the presidency, even if that meant delaying for some time. Hohenlohe also imagined the most likely occasion for Gambetta's move: "In a moment when the country begins to be disquieted by the prospect of a Clemenceau cabinet, he will step forward as the savior of society, as the restorer of order." In that event, clearly, the Germans would have little reason to oppose Gambetta and the opportunist republic.[71]

Secondly, there were objective grounds to believe that the political system of France was stabilizing so as to preclude the extremes. By-elections to the Chamber continued to sustain republican moderates. Of twenty-one seats contested in April 1879, for exampe, only two fell to the Union républicaine. And at the other end of the ideological spectrum, the disunity of the conservatives was still as useful to the moderates as before: in the eighth arrondissement of Paris, once a pocket borough of the Right held by the Duc Decazes, the Orleanist and the Bonapartist candidates chose to see a republican moderate win, rather than to step aside one for the other.[72] In June the sensational announcement of the death of the Prince Imperial in Africa further dissipated the Bonapartist chimera. When Gambetta was asked by Hohenlohe for his reaction to the news, he replied that much time would elapse before any other imperial pretender could possibly attain the same importance for French voters: "The republic will have five or six years to consolidate itself, and that will be enough." Some Bonapartists would have had the Germans suppose that the prince's heroic sacrifice might actually enhance the Napoleonic legend. "But I believe," Hohenlohe responded, "that Gambetta is correct."[73] Not surprisingly, when the German government issued an official statement of condolence, the real significance lay in its "affirming more clearly than ever sentiments favorable to the moderate republic."[74]

Finally—an observation that should not escape an attentive reader—the Germans remained conspicuously imprecise in their notion of radicalism. The term has always been more frequently employed than defined, and the French republic was no exception. Part of the problem was linguistic: since all nouns are capitalized in German, there was no efficient way, as in French, to distinguish between a specific political faction and other free-floating elements of the Left. In itself, however, that explanation is inadequate, since the lack of semantic clarity was also partly deliberate. It afforded German propaganda the convenience of implying guilt by association. Thus references to radicals and communards could, on occasion, be indiscriminately attached to Gambetta's name—no matter what his historical record and political stance—for purposes of admonition. What the Germans wished to discourage was less Gambetta's own progress than the opening he might provide, even unwillingly, for less-disciplined fellow travelers who truly deserved the label of radicalism. Bismarck's own belated reservations can probably best be accounted for by noting unconfirmed reports from Paris, as early as November 1879, that "a reconciliation has taken place between Gambetta and Clemenceau."[75] But the chancellor's subsequent unflustered acceptance of the Freycinet ministry indicated his accurate if still tentative conclusion that, in reality, the moderate republic was in no immediate danger.

From that time until the beginning of the long-anticipated *grand ministère* in November 1881, French politics were dominated by what came to be known in Germanic fashion as "the Gambetta question." The parliamentary history of this period may be read elsewhere.[76] Here we need record only that, with one exception, German approval of Gambetta's public conduct was unstinting. Not since the final months of the Thiers presidency, in fact, had German reckoning of French affairs been so consistently focused on a single individual. Later in the 1800s, it can be added, the growing disorientation of German foreign policy toward France was partially a result of the original mistaken premise that Gambetta's personal influence on the republic would be decisive and durable.

Gambetta's demeanor before his accession to the premiership was in most regards a paragon of restraint. In contrast to times past, the Germans kept abreast of his thinking in the most direct manner: long interviews were conducted with him by Hohenlohe and also by Radowitz, who was sent to Paris for that purpose by Bismarck on a special assignment in the summer of 1880. These talks reconfirmed most of what was already assumed about Gambetta's intentions: that he was willing to allow the *seize mai* affair a decent political burial, although he felt that Broglie and Rochebouët should have been prosecuted earlier;[77] that he was gradually bolstering the republicanization of the army and furthering the military careers of certain personal protégés (among them a young officer named Boulanger);[78] that he supported Freycinet's economic plan of public works and mixed tariffs, a scheme he had helped to conceive; that his participation in anticlerical activities, including the Ferry educational reforms, would be firm but not fanatical; and that he was maintaining contact with new socialist and syndicalist movements in France but was encouraging organizational unity rather than erratic and intemperate outbursts.[79] If there was a blotch on this exemplary record of moderation, in the German view, it was an unfortunate tendency to rhetorical excess like that displayed at Cherbourg in August 1880: Gambetta's unabashed justification of French military rearmament, in order that the nation might "regain its place in the world," caused a stir of hostility in Berlin that reminded Saint-Vallier of 1875. Paris was advised that Bismarck denounced the speech as "a challenge and a provocation to Germany" and that "manifestly he has modified his policy, his language, the orientation of his newspapers."[80]

Although the repercussions of the Cherbourg episode cannot be written off solely to Saint-Vallier's habitual excitability, the incident loses importance when placed in the entire context of Germany's influence in French foreign and domestic affairs. The Franco-German detente, in effect since 1878, was not severely damaged and would endure for several more years. A reciprocity of limited self-interest, rather than mutual ties of friendship and genuine benevolence, held it together. Thus Gambetta's statements did more to keep the truth in perspective than to alter it; and in addition he provided the German chancellor and his propagandists with an excuse to suggest that, if the detente should one day collapse, the fault would not be theirs. As for the internal circumstances, it is important to recall that Gambetta's visit to Cherbourg was made with Grévy and that his oration was a deliberate exercise in hyperbole. Whereas the president carefully maintained an unruffled dignity befitting his office, Gambetta sought to make a display of his own passionate dedication to the French people and patrie. But this difference in style did not constitute a major distinction in substance. As the Germans were aware, Gambetta's off-stage behavior usually belied his platform performance. Scarcely less than Grévy, Gambetta incarnated the salient attributes of the opportunist republic: a middling polity, a hesitant economy, and a stalemate society.[81]

In the end, then, the onset of Gambetta's premiership presented the Reich with precisely the republic it wanted and deserved. Those who imagined that the creation of a *grand ministère* would provoke a drastic rupture were deluded. Berlin reacted to the new regime on 15 November 1881 with complete equanimity: Hohenlohe was blandly instructed that "the formation of a Gambetta cabinet will induce no change in our desire to maintain good relations with France."[82] Barely a month before, in early October, Gambetta had made one of his periodic voyages to Germany; and while there he may have engaged at last in secret conversation with Bismarck. That no record survives of their exchange relegates their encounter, perhaps appropriately, to the realm of legend.[83] One is left to speculate about how fittingly each articulated the aspirations, respectively, of the republic and the Reich. Neither could have known, of course, that Gambetta's ministry would last for less than three months, that it would end ingloriously and indecisively, or that within another year he would be dead at the age of forty-four. Yet in an important sense such events were no longer crucial. Personal tragedy did not significantly alter the political and economic reality any more than legend could enhance it. The irretrievable fact was that France had become a republic; and under the impact of German domination, moreover, France had become a certain kind of republic. True, the disruption caused by future conflicts with Germany, the irregular evolution of political institutions, and the effects of economic revitalization in this century have all conspired to mature the face of French society. But the character of the republic, essentially formed in the first decade after its inception, has ever since remained remarkably unaltered.

Notes

Abbreviations to the Notes

UNPUBLISHED SOURCES
AA / Auswärtiges Amt, Bonn
AN / Archives nationales, Paris
APP / Archives de la Préfecture de Police, Paris
BA / Bundesarchiv, Koblenz
BL / Baker Library, Harvard Business School, Cambridge, Mass.
BN / Bibliothèque nationale, salle des manuscrits, Paris
BT / Bibliothèque Thiers, Paris
BVC / Bibliothèque Victor Cousin, Sorbonne, Paris
CCP / Chambre de Commerce, Paris
DZA / Deutsches Zentralarchiv, Potsdam
DZA II / Deutsches Zentralarchiv, Historische Abteilung II, Merseburg
GStA / Geheimes Staatsarchiv, Munich
MAE / Ministère des affaires étrangères, Paris
SF / Schloss Friedrichsruh, near Hamburg

PUBLISHED SOURCES
DDF / *Documents diplomatiques français*
GP / *Die Grosse Politik der europäischen Kabinette*
GW / *Bismarck: die gesammelten Werke*
JORF / *Journal officiel de la république française*

Introduction

1. See the annotated bibliography in Allan Mitchell, *Bismarck and the French Nation, 1848–1890*, pp. 115–40.

2. A similar argument for the late eighteenth century is made by Robert R. Palmer, *The Age of Democratic Revolution*, 1:5–7.

3. Unduly pessimistic about the possibility of analyzing the "influence" of one nation on another is the recent work by Christoph Steinbach, *Die französische Diplomatie und das Deutsche Reich 1873 bis 1881*, pp. 9–10. As the title indicates, Steinbach attempts only to define Germany's role in French foreign policy; he consequently employs solely French archival sources, mainly from the Quai d'Orsay.

4. Most accounts rely heavily on Gabriel Hanotaux, *Histoire de la France contemporaine (1871–1900)*. See D. W. Brogan, *The Development of Modern France, 1870–1939*; Jacques Chastenet, *Histoire de la troisième république*; Guy Chapman, *The Third Republic of France*; and the new departure of Jean-Marie Mayeur, *Les débuts de la IIIe république, 1871–1898*.

5. Claude Digeon, *La crise allemande de la pensée française (1870–1914)*. This has been supplemented but not surpassed by such more recent studies as Harry W. Paul, *The Sorcerer's Apprentice*; Terry Nichols Clark, *Prophets and Patrons*; and William R. Keylor, *Academy and Community*. All of these confirm the intellectual impact of Germany on France after 1870. A considerable debt to Digeon has been acknowledged in my "German History in France after 1870," pp. 81–100.

6. The basic published collections are the *Documents diplomatiques française, 1871–1914*, and *Die Grosse Politik der europäischen Kabinette, 1871–1914*. Printed documents from these collections will be cited, respectively, DDF and GP; unprinted sources from the foreign office archives will be designated MAE Paris or AA Bonn.

7. This has been conclusively demonstrated for the Third Republic's final phase by Robert O. Paxton, *Vichy France*.

8. See Pierre Renouvin and Jean-Baptiste Duroselle, *Introduction à l'histoire des relations internationales*; and Charles Tilly, "Reflections on the History of European State-Making," in *The Formation of National States in Western Europe*, Charles Tilley, ed., pp. 3–83. Still the best general diplomatic history of the period is that of William L. Langer, *European Alliances and Alignments, 1871–1890*.

Chapter 1

1. The notion that the French republic was "the logical outcome of twenty centuries of history" was popularized by the *"petit Lavisse,"* a school textbook first published in 1876 and read by every French child for generations thereafter. See Raoul Girardet, ed., *Le nationalisme français, 1871–1914*, pp. 80–84. The historical debate has been examined by Paul Farmer, *France Reviews Its Revolutionary Origins*; and Pieter Geyl, *Napoleon, For and Against*. On the conflicting political traditions within a single national identity, also see Theodore Zeldin, *France, 1848–1945*, 2:24–28.

2. See Michael Howard, *The Franco-Prussian War*; and Wolfgang von

Groote and Ursala von Gersdorff, eds., *Entscheidung 1870*. In the absence
of an excellent recent treatment in French, one may consult Jacques
Desmarest, *La défense nationale, 1870–1871*; or Georges Roux, *La guerre
de 1870*.

3. For the background see Jacques Droz, *L'Allemagne et la révolution
française*; Sydney S. Biro, *The German Policy of Revolutionary France*; Owen
Connelly, *Napoleon's Satellite Kingdoms*, pp. 176–222; Karl Hammer, *Die
französische Diplomatie der Restauration und Deutschland, 1814–1830*; Ru-
dolph Buchner, *Die deutsch-französische Tragödie 1848–1864*; and Werner
E. Mosse, *The European Powers and the German Question, 1848–1871*.

4. See Heinz Otto Sieburg, *Deutschland und Frankreich in der Geschichtsschreibung des 19. Jahrhunderts*; André Armengaud, *L'opinion publique
en France et la crise nationale allemande en 1866*; and Klaus Malettke, *Die
Beurteilung der Aussen-und Innenpolitik Bismarcks von 1862–1866 in den
grossen Pariser Zeitungen*.

5. See the brief synthesis by J. P. T. Bury, *Napoleon III and the Second
Empire*; and monographs by Theodore Zeldin, *The Political System of
Napoleon III* and *Emile Ollivier and the Liberal Empire of Napoleon III*.

6. See Herbert Geuss, *Bismarck und Napoleon III.*; and William E.
Echard, "Conference Diplomacy in the German Policy of Napoleon III,
1868–1869," pp. 239–64.

7. Much of the recent literature is highly critical of the French initiatives: Jean Stengers, "Aux origines de la guerre de 1870," pp. 701–47;
Nancy Nichols Barker, "Napoleon III and the Hohenzollern Candidacy
for the Spanish Throne," pp. 431–50; Eberhard Kolb, *Der Kriegsausbruch
1870*; and Jochen Dittrich, "Ursachen und Ausbruch des deutsch-französischen Krieges 1870/71," pp. 64–94.

8. Bismarck to the Auswärtiges Amt (AA), 10 July 1870, GW 6b:
1588. See Georges Bonnin, *Bismarck and the Hohenzollern Candidature for
the Spanish Throne*; Jochen Dittrich, *Bismarck, Frankreich und die spanische
Thronkandidatur der Hohenzollern*; Lawrence D. Steefel, *Bismarck, the Hohenzollern Candidacy, and the Origins of the Franco-German War of 1870*;
Bastiaan Schot, "Die Entstehung des Deutsch-Französischen Krieges und
die Gründung des Deutschen Reiches," pp. 269–95; and the excellent
summary by Josef Becker, "Zum Problem der Bismarckschen Politik in
der spanischen Thronfrage 1870," pp. 529–607.

9. Probably the emperor would have preferred a glorious death in
action. See Howard, *The Franco-Prussian War*, pp. 133–34, 217–23.

10. See J. P. T. Bury, *Gambetta and the National Defence*; and Jacques
Chastenet, *Gambetta*. A useful overview of the period, with a judiciously
annotated bibliography, is provided by Roger L. Williams, *The French
Revolution of 1870–1871*.

11. "Proclamation du gouvernement de la défense nationale aux
parisiens," 4 Sept. 1870, *Archives diplomatiques 1871–1872*, 1: 504–5. "C'é-

tait le cri du salut public qui avait appelé Thiers au pouvoir comme l'homme nécessaire," wrote Charles de Rémusat, *Mémoires de ma vie*, 5:359.

12. Bismarck to Johanna von Bismarck, 6 Sept. 1870, GW 14b:1338. See other private messages from Bismarck to his wife in *Bismarcks Briefe an seine Gattin aus dem Kriege, 1870/71*.

13. Bismarck to Herbert von Bismarck, 7 Sept. 1870, GW 14b:1339.

14. On Favre's role see André Lambert, *Le siège de Paris*; and Robert I. Giesberg, *The Treaty of Frankfort*, pp. 17–36. Giesberg argues that the first Ferrières meeting represented "a missed opportunity" to end the war.

15. Bismarck to Herbert von Bismarck, 23 Sept. 1870, GW 14b:1344.

16. See Joachim Kühn, "Bismarck und der Bonapartismus im Winter 1870/71," pp. 49–100.

17. See Nancy Nichols Barker, *Distaff Diplomacy*, pp. 205–11.

18. See Geuss, *Bismarck und Napoléon III.*, pp. 294–312; and Giesberg, *The Treaty of Frankfort*, pp. 67–83.

19. Bismarck to Manteuffel, 17 Dec. 1870, GW 14b:1369.

20. Broglie to Thiers, 14 Oct. 1870, BN Paris, Papiers Thiers, NAR 20620.

21. See Henri Malo, *Thiers, 1797–1877*; and Charles Pomaret, *Monsieur Thiers et son siècle*.

22. Jules Favre, *Gouvernement de la défense nationale*, 1:383–86.

23. Favre to Thiers, 16 Sept. 1870, MAE Paris, Papiers Favre, 22; Adolphe Thiers, *Notes et souvenirs de M. Thiers, 1870–1873*, pp. 3–57.

24. Bismarck to Johanna von Bismarck, 28–29 Oct. 1870, GW 14b: 1353.

25. Bismarck to Johanna von Bismarck, 3 Nov. 1870, ibid., 1354; Bismarck to Herbert von Bismarck, 12 Nov. 1870, ibid., 1358; Thiers, *Notes et souvenirs*, pp. 61–106.

26. See R. A. Winnacker, "The French Election of 1871," pp. 477–83; Jacques Gouault, *Comment la France est devenue républicaine*, pp. 28–101; and Robert R. Locke, "A New Look at Conservative Preparations for the French Election of 1871," pp. 351–58.

27. Thiers, *Notes et souvenirs*, pp. 109–27. See Frank Herbert Brabant, *The Beginnings of the Third Republic in France*.

28. DDF 1:1; GP 1:1. See Hans Goldschmidt, *Bismarck und die Friedensunterhändler 1871*.

29. Favre to Gabrielle Favre, 3 Mar. 1871, BN Paris, Papiers Favre, NAF 24107; Bismark to Johanna von Bismarck, 5 Mar. 1871, GW 14b: 1410. See Aimé Dupuy, *1870–1871*, pp. 71–136.

30. Favre to Bismarck, 4 Mar. 1871, MAE Paris, Papiers Favre, 22.

31. Suzanne to Thiers, 5 Mar. 1871, BN Paris, Papiers Thiers, NAF 20623.

32. Favre to Thiers, 4 and 6 Mar. 1871, ibid., NAF 20622.

33. Thiers to Favre, 5 and 7 Mar. 1871, ibid., NAF 20623; Favre, *Gouvernement*, 3:185–87.

34. Favre to Thiers, 8 and 9 Mar. 1871, BN Paris, Papiers Thiers, NAF 20622.

35. Favre, *Gouvernement*, 3:189–98.

36. Favre to Thiers, 11 Mar. 1871, MAE Paris, Papiers Favre, 6.

37. Thiers to Favre, 12 Mar. 1871, ibid.

38. Suzanne to Thiers, 8 Mar. 1871, BN Paris, Papiers Thiers, NAF 20623.

39. Favre to Thiers, 10 Mar. 1871, ibid., NAF 20622.

40. Bismarck to Delbrück, 7 Mar. 1871, DZA Potsdam, XX gen. 43 adh. 13a, 1:1142; Favre to Thiers, 11 Mar. 1871, MAE Paris, Papiers Favre, 6. A text of the final agreement is printed in Favre, *Gouvernement*, 3:544–59. Since the accord was formally signed in Rouen, it is often designated as such.

41. Thiers to Broglie, 6 Mar. 1871, BN Paris, Papiers Thiers, NAF 20623.

42. Favre to Vinoy, 15 Mar. 1871, MAE Paris, Papiers Favre, 22; Favre to Fabrice, 19 Mar. 1871, AA Bonn, I.A.B.c 70, Fasc. 1, Nr. 11, Bd. 1; Favre, *Gouvernement*, 3:286.

43. Bismarck to Fabrice, 21 Mar. 1871, AA Bonn, I.A.B.c 70, Fasc. 1, Nr. 11, Bd. 1; Fabrice to Favre, 22 and 24 March, ibid., Bd. 2; Favre, *Gouvernement*, 3:287–91.

44. "Aux habitants de Lons-le-Launier," 23 Mar. 1871, BN Paris, Papiers Picard, NAF 24371.

45. Bismarck to Fabrice, 18 Apr. 1871, GP 1: 3. See Eberhard Kolb, "Der Pariser Commune-Aufstand und die Beendigung des deutsch-französischen Krieges," pp. 265–98.

46. Favre to Fabrice, 22 Mar. 1871, AA Bonn, I.A.B.c 70, Fasc. 1, Nr. 11, Bd. 1; Favre to Goeben, 11 Apr. 1871, MAE Paris, Papiers Favre, 6; Bismarck to Fabrice, 22 and 24 Apr. 1871, GP 1:7, 8. See Georges Bourgin, "Une entente franco-allemande," pp. 41–53.

47. Many such documents are to be found in BN Paris, Papiers Thiers, NAF 20640. See Louis M. Greenberg, *Sisters of Liberty*; Jeanne Guillard, *Communes de province, Commune de Paris, 1870–1871*; and Jacques Girault, *La commune et Bordeaux, 1870–1871*.

48. JORF, 20 Mar. 1871.

49. Ibid., 9 Apr. 1871.

50. Ibid., 29 Mar. 1871; Favre, *Gouvernement*, 3:291–94.

51. JORF, 11 Apr. 1871.

52. Gustave-Paul Cluseret, *Mémoires du général Cluseret*, 2:1–15; Norman Rich and M. H. Fisher, eds., *The Holstein Papers*, 1:83–90. See Kolb, "Der Pariser Commune-Aufstand," pp. 281–86.

53. Bismarck to Fabrice, 2 May 1871, GP 1:12. This charge was first made by Jules Valfrey, *Histoire du traité de Francfort et la libération du territoire français*, 2:71–73. But see Norman Rich, *Friedrich von Holstein*, 1:66–70.

54. Haye to Favre, 14 Apr. 1871, MAE Paris, Papiers Favre, 6; Fabrice to Bismarck, 24 Apr. 1871, AA Bonn, I.A.B.c 70, Fasc. 1, Nr. 11, Bd. 2.

55. Bismarck to Fabrice, 25 Apr. 1871, ibid.; Bismarck to Fabrice, 27 Apr. 1871, GP 1:9.

56. Favre to Fabrice, 29 Apr. 1871, MAE Paris, Papiers Favre, 6; Bismarck to Fabrice, 1 May 1871, GP 1:11; Bismarck to Favre, 2 May 1871, MAE Paris, Papiers Favre, 6. Thiers assured the Germans that a resumption of the war was "inconceivable" (Thiers to Fabrice, 4 May 1871, BN Paris, Papiers Thiers, NAF 20630).

57. Favre to Thiers, 6 and 7 May 1871, MAE Paris, Papiers Thiers, 1; Bismarck to Delbrück, 7 May 1871, GP 1:14. The economic rationale for German annexations has been minimized by Richard Hartshorne, "The Franco-German Boundary of 1871," pp. 209–50; whereas it is stressed by George W. F. Hallgarten, *Imperialismus vor 1914*, 1:151–59.

58. Favre to Thiers, 7 May 1871, MAE Paris, Papiers Thiers, 1; Thiers to Favre, 8 May 1871, ibid. The negotiations are detailed by Giesberg, *The Treaty of Frankfort*, pp. 157–67.

59. DDF 1:1, 2. From private correspondence we know that this distinction was consciously made, for example, Favre to Thiers, 10 May 1871, MAE Paris, Papiers Thiers, 1; Thiers to Duvergier, 16 May 1871, BN Paris, Papiers Thiers, NAF 20623.

60. Bismarck to Fabrice, 25 May 1871, AA Bonn, I.A.B.c 70, Fasc. 1, Nr. 11, Bd. 2; Haye to Favre, 17 May 1871, MAE Paris, Papiers Favre, 6.

61. Favre to Pontécoulant, 20 May 1871, ibid.; Thiers to Favre, 21 May 1871, ibid.; Favre, *Gouvernement*, 3:428–29. In view of this attitude it is hardly surprising that all efforts to promote negotiations collapsed. See David Robin Watson, *Georges Clemenceau*, pp. 34–55; and Gordon Wright, "The Anti-Commune," pp. 149–72.

62. Karl Marx, *The Civil War in France*, p. 81. For some recent versions of the Marxist interpretation see Henri Guillemin, *Les origines de la Commune*; Jean Bruhat et al., *La Commune de 1871*; and Jacques Rougerie, *Paris libre 1871*. A good balance between a sympathetic and a critical view of the communards is struck by Stewart Edwards, *The Paris Commune, 1871*. The bibliography is well reviewed by Jeanne Guillard, "La Commune," pp. 838–52.

Chapter 2

1. Among the easily accessible summaries are Shephard B. Clough, *France*; Rondo E. Cameron, *France and the Economic Development of Europe*;

Charles P. Kindleberger, *Economic Growth in France and Britain, 1851–1950*; Tom Kemp, *Economic Forces in French History*; and Alan S. Milward and S. B. Saul, *The Development of the Economies of Continental Europe, 1850–1914*. Still useful is the comparative study by J. H. Clapham, *The Economic Development of France and Germany, 1815–1914*.

2. On French banking and business see David S. Lanes, "French Entrepreneurship and Industrial Growth in the Nineteenth Century," pp. 45–61, and "Vieille banque et banque nouvelle," pp. 204–22; Jean Bouvier, *Le Crédit Lyonnais de 1863 à 1882*; Guy Palmade, *Capitalisme et capitalistes français au XIXe siècle*; and Bertrand Gille, *Histoire de la maison Rothschild*. The problem has been set in a broad context by David S. Landes, *The Unbound Prometheus*.

3. In particular see Rondo E. Cameron, "L'exportation des capitaux français, 1850–1880," pp. 346–53; François Crouzet, "Essai de construction d'un indice annuel de la production industrielle française au XIXe siècle," pp. 56–99; and Maurice Lévy-Leboyer, "La décélération de l'économie française dans la seconde moitié du XIXe siècle," pp. 485–507.

4. Roussy to Picard, 20 Dec. 1870, BN Paris, Papiers Picard, NAF 24371; Freycinet to Gambetta, 20 Dec. 1870, MAE Paris, Papiers Gambetta, 36.

5. Crémieux to Simon, Favre, and Picard, 28 Dec. 1870, BN Paris, Papiers Picard, NAF 24371; Roy and Roussy to Picard, 29 Dec. 1870, ibid.

6. "Note confidentielle sur les rapports financiers entre le Trésor et la Banque de France," 21 Feb. 1871, BN Paris, Papiers Thiers, NAF 20641; Rouland to Thiers, 24 Feb. 1871, ibid., NAF 20623.

7. Chambre de Commerce de Paris to Lambrecht, 28 Feb. 1871, CCP Paris, Correspondance, XV.

8. Rouland to Thiers, 3 and 4 Mar. 1871, BN Paris, Papiers Thiers, NAF 20623. Many letters from the provinces are to be found in AN Paris, F^{30} 214.

9. This request was submitted by Pouyer-Quertier on 31 Mar. and voted by the Assembly on 10 Apr. (JORF, 11 Apr. 1871).

10. Broglie to Thiers, 2 Mar. 1871, BN Paris, Papiers Thiers, NAF 20621.

11. Dutilleul to Picard, 17 Feb. 1871, BN Paris, Papiers Picard, NAF 24371. French investments abroad had risen from two billion francs in 1850 to fourteen billion by 1870 (see Kindleberger, *Economic Growth*, p. 58).

12. Rouland to Thiers, 8 Mar. 1871, BN Paris, Papiers Thiers, NAF 20623.

13. Thiers to Favre, 10 Mar. 1871, ibid.

14. Rouland to Thiers, 13 Mar. 1871, ibid.

15. Through an executive of the Rothschild bank in Paris, the Germans were informed in mid-March that the French loan would "see the

light of day" within a week (Emil Brandeis to Bleichröder, 17 Mar. 1871, BL Harvard, Bleichröder Nachlass, Box XVII).

16. Gutman (Bayerische Handelsbank) to Pouyer-Quertier, 9 June 1871, AN Paris, F³⁰ 215.

17. W. H. Burns (I. S. Morgan and Co.) to Pouyer-Quertier, 24 June 1871, ibid.

18. Texts of the two accords exchanged between Pouyer-Quertier and Rothschild Frères, 26 June 1871, are to be found in AN Paris, F³⁰ 216.

19. "Note sur l'emprunt de 2 milliards," 27 June 1871, BN Paris, Papiers Thiers, NAF 20641; Pouyer-Quertier to Thiers, [28?] June 1871, ibid., NAF 20622; Adolphe Thiers, *Notes et souvenirs de M. Thiers, 1870–1873*, p. 195. See Gabriel Hanotaux, *Histoire de la France contemporaine (1871–1900)*, 1:310–15; and Amant Louis Amagut, *Les emprunts et les impôts de la rançon de 1871*, p. 140. The latter's estimates vary slightly from those of Thiers. The entire matter has been superbly reviewed by Bertrand Gille, "Les emprunts de libération en 1871–1872," pp. 166–98.

20. Gedalia to Pouyer-Quertier, 29 June 1871, AN Paris, F³⁰ 215.

21. "Note sur l'emprunt de 2 milliards," 27 June 1871, BN Paris, Papiers Thiers, NAF 20641; Thiers, *Notes et souvenirs*, pp. 194–98.

22. Waldersee to Bismarck, 29 June and 1 July 1871, AA Bonn, I.A.B.c 71, Bd. 2; Thiers, *Notes et souvenirs*, pp. 173–75. See Jacques Chastenet, *Histoire de la troisième republique*, 1:164.

23. See Karl Linnebach, *Deutschland als Sieger im besetzten Frankreich 1871–1873*; and Hans Herzfeld, *Deutschland und das geschlagene Frankreich 1871–1873*.

24. Bismarck to Manteuffel, 6 Jan. 1871, GW 14b:1383.

25. Favre to Bismarck, 11 Feb. 1871, MAE Paris, Papiers Favre, 22. Paul von Hatzfeldt's minutes of the commission's seven sessions (11 Feb.–2 Mar. 1871) and other relevant papers are collected in AA Bonn, I.A.B.c 70, Bd.8.

26. Bismarck to Delbrück, 7 Mar. 1871, DZA Potsdam, XX gen. 43 adh. 13a, 1:1142; Favre to Thiers, 10 Mar. 1871, BN Paris, Papiers Thiers, NAF 20622.

27. "Sitzung des königlichen Staatsministeriums" (Abschrift), 4 May 1871, DZA Potsdam XX gen. 43 ach. 12, 2:1138; Saint-Vallier to Rému-sat, 24 and 26 Apr. 1871, MAE Paris, Papiers Thiers, 1.

28. Article VIII of the Frankfurt treaty of 10 May 1871, DDF 1:2; GP 1:17.

29. Favre to Fabrice, 4 June 1871, AA Bonn, I.A.B.c 70, Fasc. 1, Nr. 11, Bd. 2; Favre to Fabrice, 10 June 1871, MAE Paris, Papiers Favre, 6.

30. Favre to Bismarck, 16 June 1871, ibid., 7; Favre to MacMahon, 16 June 1871, ibid.

31. MacMahon to Thiers, 16 June 1871, ibid.; MacMahon to Grévy, 16 June 1871, ibid.

32. Favre to Bismarck, 16 June 1871, MAE Paris, Papiers Thiers, 1; Bismarck to Favre, 17 June 1871, ibid.; Saget to MacMahon, 17 June 1871, ibid.; MacMahon to Ladmirault, 17 June 1871, ibid.

33. Bismarck to Waldersee, 14 June 1871, GP 1:21; Jules Favre, *Gouvernement de la défense nationale*, 3:437–42.

34. "Instructions pour M. de Gabriac, chargé d'affaires de France à Berlin, " 30 June 1871, DDF 1:14; Marquis de Gabriac, *Souvenirs diplomatiques de Russie et d'Allemagne (1870–1872)*, pp. 133–92.

35. Favre to Gabriac (projet de note), [30?] June 1871, MAE Paris, Papiers Favre, 7; Waldersee to Bismarck, 28 June and 1 July 1871, AA Bonn, I.A.B.c 71, Bd. 2.

36. Gabriac to Favre, 9 July 1871, MAE Paris, CP Allemagne, 1.

37. Gabriac to Favre, 15 July 1871, MAE Paris, Papiers Favre, 7.

38. Manteuffel to Thiers, 16 May 1871, BN Paris, Papiers Thiers, NAF 20622. The negotiations conducted via Manteuffel and Saint-Vallier can be scanned in *Occupation et libération du territoire, 1871–1873*; yet, as indicated in the notes to this chapter, recently available archives contain much additional information.

39. Saint-Vallier to Favre, 15 July 1871, MAE Paris, Papiers Thiers, 1; Saint-Vallier to Favre, 16 July 1871, MAE Paris, Papiers Favre, 7.

40. Saint-Vallier to MAE, 19 July 1871, BN Paris, Papiers Thiers, NAF 20630; Saint-Vallier to Favre, 20 July 1871, MAE Paris, Papiers Thiers, 1.

41. Thiers to Manteuffel, 21 July 1871, ibid.; Manteuffel to Favre, 25 July 1871, MAE Paris, Papiers Favre, 7; Saint-Vallier to Thiers, 28 July 1871, BN Paris, Papiers Thiers, NAF 20630.

42. Favre to Waldersee, 22 July 1871, DZA Potsdam, XX gen. 43 adh. 13a, 2:1143; Waldersee to Bismarck, 24 July 1871, AA Bonn, I.A.B.c 71, Bd. 2; Favre to Gabriac, 26 July 1871, MAE Paris, CP Allemagne, 1; Gabriac to Favre, 29 July 1871, ibid.

43. Pouyer-Quertier to Manteuffel, 5 Aug. 1871, MAE Paris, Papiers Thiers, 1. See Fritz Machlup, "The Transfer Problem," pp. 374–95.

44. Pouyer-Quertier to Rémusat, 7 Aug. 1871, DDF 1:38; Saint-Vallier to Thiers, 11 Aug. 1871, BN Paris, Papiers Thiers, NAF 20630. The latter also contains a copy of the tentative accord.

45. Saint-Vallier to Rémusat, 13 Aug. 1871, MAE Paris, Papiers Favre, 7; Saint-Vallier to Rémusat, 13 Aug. 1871, BN Paris, Papiers Thiers, NAF 20630; Manteuffel to Bismarck, 13 Aug. 1871, GP 1:31; Bismarck to Manteuffel, 14 Aug. 1871, ibid., 32; Heinrich Otto Meisner, ed., *Denkwürdigkeiten des General-Feldmarschalls Alfred Grafen von Waldersee*, 1:130–66.

46. Saint-Vallier to Rémusat, 14 Aug. 1871, MAE Paris, Papiers Thiers, 1; Gabriac to Rémusat, 14 Aug. 1871, DDF 1:42; Saint-Vallier to Thiers, 15 Aug. 1871, BN Paris, Papiers Thiers, NAF 20630.

47. Waldersee to Bismarck, 15 Aug. 1871, AA Bonn, I.A.B.c 74;

Bismarck to Waldersee, 19 Aug. 1871, ibid.; Waldersee to Bismarck, 23 Aug. 1871, GP 1:33.

48. Arnim to Rémusat, 20 Sept. 1871, AA Bonn, I.A.B.c 74; Arnim to Bismarck, 30 Sept. 1871, ibid.; Lynaz to Bismarck, 11 Oct. 1871, ibid.

49. Rémusat to Gabriac, 20 Aug. 1871, MAE Paris, CP Allemagne, 1.

50. Bismarck to Arnim, 19 Sept. 1871, GP 1:47; "Text der zusätzlichen Uebereinkunft zu dem Friedensvertrage zwischen Deutschland und Frankreich vom 12. Oktober 1871," ibid., 55; "Text der Separat-Konvention vom 12. Oktober 1871," ibid., 56; Pouyer-Quertier to Thiers, 13 Oct. 1871, DDF 1:69.

51. Thiers to Broglie, 20 July and 8 Aug. 1871, BN Paris, Papiers Thiers, NAF 20623.

52. Thiers to Ozenne, 19 Aug. 1871, ibid.

53. Thiers to Ozenne, 25 Aug. 1871, MAE Paris, Papiers Favre, 7; "Note relative à la révision du traité de commerce conclu le 23 janvier 1860 entre la France et l'Angleterre," 31 Oct. 1871, BN Paris, Papiers Thiers, NAF 20622.

54. Gabriac to Rémusat, 26 Sept. and 1 Oct. 1871, MAE Paris, CP Allemagne, 1, 2.

55. "Mémoire du comité permanent du Handelstag allemand sur le traité franco-prussien du 2 avril 1862, adressé le 18 mars 1871 au conseil fédéral à Berlin," AN Paris, F^{12} 6435; Meurand to Lefranc, 29 Dec. 1871, ibid.

56. Rouland to Thiers, 14 Jan. 1871, BN Paris, Papiers Thiers, NAF 20625.

57. See Hanotaux, *Histoire*, 1:325–31, 381–89.

58. Saint-Vallier to Thiers, 7 Mar. 1872, *Occupation et libération*, 1:87. Pouyer-Quertier, although no longer a member of the French cabinet, was conveniently present in Berlin at the time and thus available for the negotiations.

59. Gontaut-Biron to Thiers, 2 Mar. 1872, DDF 1:113.

60. Bleichröder to Bismarck, 7 Apr. 1872, AA Bonn, I.A.B.c 70, Bd. 132; Gontaut-Biron to Rémusat, 19 Apr. 1872, MAE Paris, CP Allemagne, 5; Gontaut-Biron to Thiers, 12 June 1872, *Occupation et libération*, 1:155. Bleichröder's role as Bismarck's personal financial adviser during the war and the occupation has been lucidly detailed by Fritz Stern, *Gold and Iron*, pp. 134–56, 163–75, 318–27.

61. "Text der Spezialkonvention vom 29. Juni 1872 betreffend die Zahlung des Restes der französischen Kriegsentschädigung," GP 1:88.

62. Saint-Vallier to Thiers, 27 May 1872, *Occupation et libération*, 1:137.

63. Saint-Vallier to Thiers, 31 May 1872, ibid., 139.

64. France's lack of preparation was the subject of many military reports: e.g., Waldersee to Bismarck, 1 July 1871, AA Bonn, I.A.B.c 71,

Bd. 2; Roon to William, 16 Dec. 1871, ibid., I.D. 44; Roon to Bismarck, 3 May 1872, ibid., I.A.B.c 70, Bd. 132.

65. Gontaut-Biron to Rémusat, 30 June and 6 July 1872, MAE Paris, CP Allemagne, 6; Bleichröder to Bismarck, 10 July 1872, SF Hamburg, Bismarck Nachlass, B 15.

66. "Note confidentielle sur l'époche la plus opportune pour l'émission de l'emprunt des 3 milliards," signed by Rouland, 17 Apr. 1872, BN Paris, Papiers Thiers, NAF 20641; Thiers to Saint-Vallier, 15 July 1872, ibid., NAF 20631; JORF, 16 July 1872.

67. JORF, 17–27 July 1872. See Hanotaux, *Histoire*, 1:456–63.

68. "Note sur l'emprunt de 3 milliards," 28–29 July 1872, AN Paris, F^{30} 216. The festive atmosphere in Paris was described in a report from the Prefecture of Police to Thiers, 29 July 1872, BN Paris, Papiers Thiers, NAF 20641. See Gille, "Les emprunts," pp. 184–97.

69. "Emprunt de 3 milliards," July 1872, AN Paris, F^{30} 216. See Hanotaux, *Histoire*, 1:456–63.

70. A copy of the French budget and a detailed analysis of it were sent by Arnim to AA, 1 Dec. 1872, AA Bonn, I.A.B.c 75, Bd. 3.

71. Favre to Voguë, 12 June 1871, DDF 1:8.

72. Ministerial directives by Favre, 6 and 23 June 1871, MAE Paris, Papiers Favre, 7; Favre, *Gouvernement*, 3:480–93.

73. Gabriac to Favre, 13 July 1871, MAE Paris, CP Allemagne, 1; Favre to Gabriac, 15 July 1871, ibid.

74. Gabriac to Favre, 21 July 1871, ibid.

75. Rémusat to Gabriac, 7 Sept. 1871, ibid.; Gabriac to Rémusat, 11 Nov. 1871, ibid., 3. This problem is inadequately treated by Christoph Steinbach, *Die französische Diplomatie und das Deutsche Reich 1873 bis 1881*, pp. 31–32.

76. See William L. Langer, *European Alliances and Alignments, 1871–1890*, pp. 19–26; and Heinz Wolter, "Die Anfänge des Dreikaiserverhältnisses," 2:235–305.

77. Thiers to Banneville, 3 July 1871, BN Paris, Papiers Thiers, NAF 20623; Thiers to Le Flô, 4 Sept. 1871, ibid.; Rémusat to Thiers, 1 Sept. 1872, ibid., NAF 20625.

78. Thiers to Rémusat, 11 Sept. 1872, BT Paris, uncatalogued.

79. Harcourt to Thiers, 4 Aug. 1872, BN Paris, Papiers Thiers, NAF 20642; Ozenne to Thiers, 21 Sept. 1872, ibid.; Thiers to Le Flô, 26 Sept. 1872, DDF 1:157.

80. Thiers to Ozenne, 26 Oct. 1872, BN Paris, Papiers Thiers, NAF 20626; Thiers to Le Flô, 4 Nov. l872, ibid.

81. Saint-Vallier to Thiers, 24 and 28 June 1872, *Occupation et libération*, 1:164, 170; Saint-Vallier to Rémusat, 8 July 1872, BN Paris, Papiers Thiers, NAF 20631.

82. Saint-Vallier to Thiers, 19 Sept., 1 and 2 Oct. 1872, *Occupation et libération*, 2:204, 210, 211; Thiers to Saint-Vallier, 29 Sept. 1872, MAE

Paris, Papiers Thiers, 1. See Hans-Ulrich Wehler, "Das 'Reichsland' Elsass-Lothringen, 1870–79," pp. 431–37; Frederic H. Seager, "The Alsace-Lorraine Question in France, 1871–1914," pp. 111–26; Raymond Poidevin, ed., *Metz en 1870 et les problèmes des territoires annexés*; Dan P. Silverman, *Reluctant Union*; and Alfred Wahl, *L'option et l'émigration des Alsaciens-Lorrains (1871–1872)*. Wahl estimates that 128,000 persons (8.5 percent of the population) crossed from Alsace and Lorraine into France, of which all but 15,000 were natives of the two provinces (ibid., pp. 185–92).

83. Rémusat to Wesdehlen, 17 Aug. 1872, AA Bonn, I.A.B.c 74; Rouland to Thiers, 17 Aug. 1872, BN Paris, Papiers Thiers, NAF 20625; Moeller to Bismarck, 21 Aug. 1872, AA Bonn, II.B 10, Bd. 4.

84. Saint-Vallier to Thiers, 7 Oct. 1872, *Occupation et libération*, 2:213; Saint-Vallier to Thiers, 10 Oct. 1872, BN Paris, Papiers Thiers, NAF 20631; Saint-Vallier to Thiers, 6 Nov. 1872, DDF 1:158; Saint-Vallier to Thiers, 18 Nov. 1872, MAE Paris, Papiers Thiers, 1.

85. Hell to Rémusat, 14 Oct. 1872, MAE Paris, CCC Francfort, 8.

86. Montgascon to Rémusat, 12 Oct. 1872, MAE Paris, MD Allemagne, 172; Bleichröder to Bismarck, 20 Dec. 1872, SF Hamburg, Bismarck Nachlass, B 15.

87. Arnim to Bismarck, 3 Oct. 1872, GP 1:90; Bismarck to William, 14 Oct. 1872, ibid., 91; Balan to Arnim, 23 Nov. 1872, ibid., 92; Bismarck to Balan, 3 Dec. 1872, ibid., 93.

88. See Fritz Hartung, "Bismarck und Graf Harry Arnim," pp. 47–77; and George O. Kent, *Arnim and Bismarck*, pp. 89–106.

89. Saint-Vallier to Thiers, 5 Feb. 1873, DDF 1:169; Arnim to Bismarck, 5 and 7 Feb. 1873, GP 1:98, 99; Bismarck to Arnim, 17 Feb. 1873, ibid., 100. Further details can be gathered from *Occupation de libération*, 2:245 ff.

90. "Convention," 15 March 1873, DDF 1:191. See Kent, *Arnim and Bismarck*, pp. 107–16; and Robert I. Giesberg, *The Treaty of Frankfort*, pp. 228–40.

91. See Hanotaux, *Histoire*, 1:304–9; and the calculations of Jean Seguin, *Les emprunts contractés par la France à l'occasion de la guerre de 1870*, pp. 184–220.

92. Rondo E. Cameron, "Economic Growth and Stagnation in France, 1815–1914," pp. 1–13.

93. Robert Schnerb, "La politique fiscale de Thiers," 201:186–212, and 202:184–220.

Chapter 3

1. For the seminal formulation of these views, respectively, see François Goguel, *La politique des partis sous la IIIe république*; and André Siegfried, *Tableau des partis en France*.

2. From an extensive literature one may choose such standard works as Maurice Duverger, *Les partis politiques*; David Thompson, *Democracy in France since 1870*; and especially the second volume of René Rémond, *La vie politique en France depuis 1789*.

3. See René Rémond, *La droite en France de 1815 à nos jours*; Samuel Osgood, *French Royalism since 1870*; and Robert R. Locke, *French Legitimists and the Politics of Moral Order in the Early Third Republic*.

4. Bunsen to Manteuffel, 16 Dec. 1853, AA Bonn, I.A.B.c 41.

5. Hatzfeldt to William, 26 June 1856 and 31 Jan. 1857, ibid.

6. See Rudolf Buchner, *Die deutsch-französische Tragödie 1848–1864*, p. 81; and Marvin L. Brown, Jr., *The Comte de Chambord*, pp. 58–65.

7. Chambord to William, 1 Oct. 1870, AA Bonn, I.A.B.c 70 secr., Bd. 3.

8. Bismarck to the Countess zu Sayn-Wittgenstein, 11 Oct. 1870, GW 6b:1858. See François Laurentie, *Le comte de Chambord, Guillaume I et Bismarck en octobre 1870*.

9. "Setzen wir dem gallischen Hahn diesen Marder ins Nest, so wird er ihn so leicht nicht wieder los" (Bismarck to Manteuffel, 20 Feb. 1871, GW 14b:1405).

10. Secret report by "C. de B." sent via Fabrice to Bismarck, 22 Apr. 1871, AA Bonn, I.A.B.c 70, Fasc. 1, Nr. 11, Bd. 1. See J. P. T. Bury, "The identity of 'C. de B.,'" pp. 538–41.

11. Thiers to Duvergier, 16 May 1871, BN Paris, Papiers Thiers, NAF 20623; Adolphe Thiers, *Notes et souvenirs de M. Thiers, 1870–1873*, p. 169. See Gabriel Hanotaux, *Histoire de la France contemporaine (1871–1900)*, 1:226–37.

12. Bismarck to Fabrice, 4 June 1871, GP 1:19; Bismarck to Waldersee, 14 June 1871, ibid., 21; Haye to Pontécoulant, 10 June 1871, MAE Paris, Papiers Thiers, 1.

13. Waldersee to Bismarck, 26 June and 1 July 1871, AA Bonn, I.A.B.c 71, Bd. 2.

14. Alfred de Falloux, *Mémoires d'un royaliste*, 2: 380. See Brown, *Chambord*, pp. 87–93.

15. Waldersee to Bismarck, 11 July 1871, AA Bonn, I.A.B.c 41.

16. Ibid.

17. Arnim to Bismarck, 13 Nov. 1871, AA Bonn, I.A.B.c 71, Bd. 3; Bismarck to Arnim, 13 Nov. 1871, ibid.

18. Arnim to Bismarck, 19 Dec. 1871, ibid.; Arnim to William, 6 Jan. 1871, ibid., 75, Bd. 1.

19. Wesdehlen to Bismarck, 2 Aug. 1872, ibid., Bd. 2.

20. Wesdehlen to AA, 17 and 21 Sept. 1872, ibid.; Arnim to Bismarck, 25 Feb. 1873, ibid., 78, Bd. 1. See Jean Bouvier, "Aux origines de la IIIe république," pp. 271–301.

21. Typical expressions of that viewpoint are the Marquis de Roux, *La république de Bismarck*; and Jacques Bainville, *Bismarck et la France*. See

Allan Mitchell, "German History in France after 1870," pp. 91–92.

22. See John Rothney, *Bonapartism after Sedan*, pp. 12–15.

23. Bismarck to Manteuffel, 20 Feb. 1871, GW 14b:1405.

24. Reuss to Bismarck, 1 June 1871, AA Bonn, I.A.B.c 73, Bd. 1.

25. Thiers to Broglie, 10 May 1871, BN Paris, Papiers Thiers, NAF 20623; Bismarck to Fabrice, 4 June 1871, GP 1:19. See Rothney, *Bonapartism*, p. 15.

26. Adapting the terminology of the French Revolution, Rothney identifies these factions, respectively, as Coblence, the Plain, and the Mountain (ibid., pp. 22–35).

27. Waldersee to Bismarck, 2 Aug. 1871, AA Bonn, I.A.B.c 71, Bd. 2; Waldersee to Bismarck, 23 Aug. 1871, ibid., 73, Bd. 1; Arnim to Bismarck, 10 Sept. 1871, ibid.; Renault to Thiers, 1 Dec. 1871, BN Paris, Papiers Thiers, NAF 20658.

28. Reuss to Bismarck, 29 Nov. and 10 Dec. 1871, AA Bonn, I.A.B.c 73, Bd. 1; Bismarck to Reuss, 5 Dec. 1871, ibid.

29. Bernstorff to Bismarck, 10 Dec. 1871, ibid., 71, Bd. 3; Bernstorff to Bismarck, 24 Dec. 1871, ibid., 73, Bd. 1.

30. Reuss to Bismarck, 10 Jan. 1872, ibid.; Bismarck to Reuss, 19 Jan. 1872, ibid.

31. Thiers's confidence was based on Manteuffel's assurance that the Bonapartist claims to Berlin's favor were "absolutely contrary to the truth." See Saint-Vallier to Thiers, 25 Jan. 1872, *Occupation et libération du territoire, 1871–1873*, 1:65; Arnim to Bismarck, 6 Feb. 1872, AA Bonn, I.A.B.c 75, Bd. 1; Thiers to Harcourt, 7 Feb. 1872, BN Paris, Papiers Thiers, NAF 20626.

32. Broglie to Barthélémy Saint-Hilaire, 10 Feb. 1872, BVC Paris, Papiers Barthélémy Saint-Hilaire, 260; police reports of 12 and 25 Feb. 1872, APP Paris, B A/86. *Le Gaulois* and *L'Etoile* were temporarily suspended; *L'Ordre* was allowed to continue printing if it maintained a respectful tone toward the government.

33. Police report of 22 Apr. 1872, APP Paris, B A/86.

34. Arnim to Bismarck, 6 May 1872, GP 1:69.

35. Bismarck to Arnim, 12 May 1872, ibid., 71. As late as Christmas 1872, German agents were led to believe that "next to the Thiers regime, that of the Emperor Napoleon III is the most desirable for Germany because it would be the weakest abroad and at home" (Reuss to Bismarck, 22 Dec. 1872, AA Bonn, I.A.B.c 73, Bd. 1).

36. Arnim to AA, 25 Nov. 1872, ibid., 75, Bd. 2. See Jacques Gouault, *Comment la France est devenue républicaine*, pp. 141–51; and Rothney, *Bonapartism*, pp. 35–42.

37. Reuss to Bismarck, 20 Jan. 1873, AA Bonn, I.A.B.c 73, Bd. 1.

38. Favre to Picard, [15?] Feb. 1871, BN Paris, Papiers Picard, NAF 24370.

39. JORF, 28 March 1871.

40. Waldersee to Bismarck, 17 June 1871, AA Bonn, I.A.B.c 71, Bd. 2.

41. Waldersee to Bismarck, 28 July and 3 Aug. 1871, ibid.

42. Waldersee to Bismarck, 23 Aug. 1871, ibid.; Bismarck to Waldersee, 26 Aug. 1871, GP 1:35.

43. Bismarck to AA, 24 Aug. 1871, AA Bonn, I.A.B.c 71, Bd. 2. The chancellor threatened the immediate mobilization of five hundred thousand troops (Bismarck to Waldersee, 27–28 Aug. 1871, GP 1:36–38). See Eberhard Naujoks, "Bismarck und die Organisation der Regierungspresse," pp. 46–80, and "Rudolf Lindau und die Neuorientierung der auswärtigen Pressepolitik Bismarcks (1871/78)," pp. 299–344.

44. Keudell to Bleichröder, 28 Aug. 1871, BL Harvard, Bleichröder Nachlass, Box XXI.

45. Bismarck to Waldersee, 27 Aug. 1871, GP 1:37; Manteuffel to Padbielski, 31 Aug. 1871, AA Bonn, I.A.B.c 71, Bd. 2.

46. Gabriac to Rémusat, 6 Sept. 1871, MAE Paris, CP Allemagne, 1. The message from Thiers was sent directly by Pouyer-Quertier to Bismarck (12 Oct. 1871, AA Bonn, I.A.B.c 71, Bd. 2).

47. Arnim to Bismarck, 2 and 6 Sept. 1871, ibid.; Bismarck to Arnim, 16 Nov. 1871, ibid., Bd. 3. See George O. Kent, *Arnim and Bismarck*, pp. 63–95.

48. The dispatches from Arnim on which this paragraph is based are located in AA Bonn, I.A.B.c 75, Bde. 1–3; quoted are those of 1 Oct. and 25 Nov. 1872.

49. Bismarck to William, 31 Jan. 1872, GP 1:66.

50. This twenty-five page memorandum was entitled "Ist, was in Frankreich auf militärischem Gebiet geschieht, Reorganisation oder Rüstung?" (Roon to Bismarck, 3 May 1872, AA Bonn, I.A.B.c 70, Bd. 132).

51. Bleichröder to Bismarck, 13 May 1872, ibid., 75, Bd. 1.

52. Bleichröder to Bismarck, 10 July 1872, SF Hamburg, Bismarck Nachlass, B 15.

53. Arnim to Bismarck, 3 Oct. 1872, GP 1:90.

54. Balan to Arnim, 23 Nov. 1872, ibid., 92.

55. Arnim to Bismarck, 12 Nov. 1872, AA Bonn, I.A.B.c 75, Bd. 2.

56. Bismarck to Balan, 3 Dec. 1872, GP 1:93; Balan to Bismarck, 4 Dec. 1872, AA Bonn, I.A.B.c 75, Bd. 3.

57. Balan to Arnim, 14 Dec. 1872, ibid.

58. Bismarck to Manteuffel, 15 Mar. 1873, GW 14b:1482.

59. See J. P. T. Bury, *Gambetta and the National Defense*, pp. 116–58.

60. Waldersee to Bismarck, 14 July 1871, AA Bonn, I.A.B.c 71, Bd. 2.

61. After interruption by the Commune, the regular practice of daily reports from the Prefecture of Police to the Ministry of the Interior was resumed in late November 1871. The first of these made an observation, henceforth often repeated, that "the dominating trait of the physiogamy

of Paris is still indifference toward purely political objects and questions" (police report of 28 Nov. 1871, APP Paris, B A/86).

62. Dozens of such letters are collected in MAE Paris, Papiers Gambetta, 55–58.

63. Manteuffel to William, 11–13 Sept. 1871, AA Bonn, I.A.B.c 71, Bd. 2; Saint-Vallier to Thiers, 25 Jan. and 2 Mar. 1872, *Occupation et libération*, 1:65, 84.

64. Thiers to Saint-Vallier, 4 Mar. 1872, ibid., 86; Saint-Vallier to Thiers, 12 Apr. 1872, ibid., 101.

65. Waldersee to Bismarck, 14 and 23 July 1871, AA Bonn, I.A.B.c 71, Bd. 2; reports by agent Belina, 12 and 16 Aug. 1872, ibid., 77, Bd. 1.

66. Saint-Vallier to Thiers, 20 July 1872, *Occupation et libération*, 1:184.

67. Wesdehlen to Bismarck, 26 Aug. and 7 Sept. 1872, AA Bonn, I.A.B.c 75, Bd. 2. See Hanotaux, *Histoire*, 1:404–6.

68. Hanotaux, *Histoire*, 1:479–81. See Joseph Reinach, *La vie politique de Léon Gambetta*, pp. 31–37.

69. Arnim to Bismarck, 3 Oct. 1872, GP 1:90; Saint-Vallier to Thiers, 1 Oct. 1872, *Occupation et libération*, 2:110; Thiers to Saint-Vallier, 5 Oct. 1872, ibid., 112; Arnim to AA, 7 Oct. 1872, AA Bonn, I.A.B.c 75, Bd. 2.

70. Thiers to Casimir-Périer, 7 Oct. 1872, BN Paris, Papiers Thiers, NAF 20626.

71. Wesdehlen to AA, 11 and 14 Oct. 1872, AA Bonn, I.A.B.c 75, Bd. 2. The latter dispatch enclosed a detailed report by the German military attaché in Paris, Major von Bülow.

72. Saint-Vallier to Thiers, 14 Oct. 1872, *Occupation et libération*, 2:218; Thiers to Saint-Vallier, 17 Oct. 1872, ibid., 220.

73. Wesdehlen to AA, 26 Oct. 1872, AA Bonn, I.A.B.c 75, Bd. 2; Thiers to Le Flô, 4 Nov. 1872, BN Paris, Papiers Thiers, NAF 20626; Arnim to AA, 19 Nov. 1872, AA Bonn, I.A.B.c 75, Bd. 3.

74. Saint-Vallier to Thiers, 29 Oct. 1872, *Occupation et libération*, 2:231; Arnim to Balan, 10 Nov. 1872, AA Bonn, I.A.B.c 75, Bd. 2; Arnim to Bismarck, 12 and 14 Nov. 1872, ibid.; Arnim to AA, 25 and 29 Nov. 1872, ibid., Bd. 3.

75. Saint-Vallier to Thiers, 6 Nov. 1872, *Occupation et libération*, 2:236; Arnim to Balan, 30 Nov. 1872, AA Bonn, I.A.B.c 75, Bd. 3.

76. Bismarck to Arnim, 20 Dec. 1872, GP 1:95; Gontaut-Biron to Rémusat, 28 Dec. 1872, MAE Paris, CP Allemagne, 7.

77. Reports by agent "C. de B.," 16 May and 1 June 1871, AA Bonn, I.A.B.c 70, Fasc. 2, Nr. 24; Thiers, *Notes et souvenirs*, pp. 145–50; Général Du Barail, *Souvenirs*, 3:275–77; manuscript of Rémusat's memoirs, 5:33–34, BN Paris, Papiers Rémusat, NAF 14468 (in this passage, expurgated from the published version, MacMahon is described as "a simple and timid man"); Waldersee to Bismarck, 20 June 1871, AA Bonn, I.A.B.c 71, Bd. 2. See Jacques Silvestre de Sacy, *Le maréchal de MacMahon, duc de*

Magenta (1808–1893), a biography based on MacMahon's unpublished memoirs.

78. Waldersee to Bismarck, 3 and 27 Aug. 1871, AA Bonn, I.A.B.c 71, Bd. 2; Arnim to Bismarck, 11 Dec. 1871, ibid., Bd. 3. One Bonapartist was heard to utter an appropriate remark: "Ah, si MacMahon voulait, mais il ne veut pas" (police report of 29 Feb. 1872, APP Paris, B A/86). The same sentiment was expressed by the Duc Decazes to Metternich, 3 Feb. 1872, BT Paris, Papiers Decazes, 728.

79. JORF, 14 Nov. 1872.

80. Arnim to AA, 21 and 25 Nov. 1872, AA Bonn, I.A.B.c 75, Bd. 3; Arnim to Bismarck, 24 Nov. 1872, ibid.

81. Activity on the Paris Bourse was regularly evaluated in daily police reports, now on file in APP Paris, B A/86. See Hanotaux, *Histoire*, 1:516–29.

82. See Brown, *Chambord*, pp. 99–100.

83. Police reports of 15 and 22 Jan. 1873, APP Paris, B A/86. See Rothney, *Bonapartism*, pp. 42–52.

84. See Allan Mitchell, "Thiers, MacMahon, and the Conseil Supérieur de la Guerre," pp. 232–52.

85. Rémusat to Picard, 30 Mar. 1872, BN Paris, Papiers Picard, NAF 24370. See Charles de Rémusat, *Mémoires de ma vie*, 5:455–62.

86. Barodet to Gambetta, 7 and 9 Apr. 1873, BN Paris, NAF 24900. Gambetta defended his strategy ("to have done with the republic without republicans" and to demonstrate that "no government can rule without the support of Paris") at a meeting of the Union républicaine for which minutes were kept by Scheurer-Kestner (21 Apr. 1873, AN Paris, AP 276:1).

87. Picard to Madame Picard, [23?] Apr. 1873, BN Paris, Papiers Picard, NAF 24369. See Hanotaux, *Histoire*, 1:581–85; and Daniel Halévy, *La fin des notables*, pp. 230–49.

88. Rouland to Barthélémy Saint-Hilaire, 29 Apr. 1873, BVC Paris, Papiers Barthélémy Saint-Hilaire, 122; Picard to Rémusat, 1 May 1873, BN Paris, Papiers Picard, NAF 24369; Arnim to AA, 2 May 1873, AA Bonn, I.A.B.c 78, Bd. 1.

89. Manteuffel to Bismarck, 6 May 1873, ibid.

90. William's comment was entered on the margin of a dispatch from Bismarck to William, 11 May 1873, ibid.

91. Arnim to Bismarck, 24 May 1873, ibid., Bd. 2. See Kent, *Arnim and Bismarck*, pp. 117–22.

92. E.g., Chastenet, *Histoire de la troisième republique*, 1:150–51. But MacMahon is described as "a good president in an extremely difficult period" by Guy Chapman, *The Third Republic of France*, p. 43. See Rémond, *La vie politique en France*, 2:317–49.

Chapter 4

1. Arnim to AA, 23 May 1873, AA Bonn, I.A.B.c 78, Bd. 2; Arnim to Bismarck, 24 May 1873 (4:25 A.M. and 12:20 P.M.), ibid.; Arnim to Bismarck, 24 May 1873 (received in Berlin at 6 a.m. on the twenty-fifth), ibid. See Christoph Steinbach, *Die französische Diplomatie und das Deutsche Reich 1873 bis 1881*, pp. 52–54.

2. William to Bismarck, 25 May 1873, AA Bonn, I.A.B.c 78, Bd. 2; Bismarck to Arnim, 25 May 1873, ibid.

3. Bismarck to Manteuffel, 2 June 1873, GP 1:114.

4. Bismarck to Arnim, 26 May 1873, AA Bonn, I.A.B.c 78, Bd. 2; Bismarck to Reuss, 26 May 1873, ibid.; Bismarck to Wesdehlen, 26 May 1873, ibid.

5. Bismarck to Reuss, 27 May 1873, ibid.

6. Reuss to Bismarck, 27 May 1873, ibid.; Bismarck to Arnim, 28 May 1873, ibid.

7. Broglie to Rudhart, 26 May 1873, MAE Paris, CP Bavière, 252; Arnim to AA, 27 May 1873, AA Bonn, I.A.B.c 78, Bd. 2; Broglie to Gontaut-Biron, 28 May 1873, DDF 1:207; Gontaut-Biron to Bismarck, 29 May 1873, AA Bonn, I.A.B.c 78, Bd. 2; Vicomte de Gontaut-Biron, *Mon ambassade en Allemagne (1872–1873)*, pp. 346–73.

8. Bismarck to Reuss, 29 and 30 May 1873, AA Bonn, I.A.B.c 78, Bd. 2; Gontaut-Biron to Broglie, 1 June 1873, DDF 1:213.

9. Bismarck to Manteuffel, 2 June 1872, GP 1:114; Bismarck to Arnim, [2?] June 1873, AA Bonn, I.A.B.c 78, Bd. 2. The latter document was marked "secret" and may not have been sent to Paris; later, however, it became the basis for a highly critical reprimand from Bismarck to Arnim (19 June 1873, GP 1:115). See Werner Pöls, "Bleichröder und die Arnim Affäre," pp. 65–76.

10. Arnim to AA, 1 and 2 June 1873, AA Bonn, I.A.B.c 78, Bd. 2; Bismarck to Arnim, 1 and 3 June 1873, ibid.

11. Bray-Steinburg to Ludwig, 4 June 1873, GStA Munich, MA 83277; Bismarck to Gontaut-Biron, 6 June 1873, GW 14b:1490.

12. Broglie to Lefebvre de Béhaine, 19 June 1873, CP Bavière, 252.

13. See Gerhard Ritter, *Staatskunst und Kriegshandwerk*, 1: 239–329; and George O. Kent, *Arnim and Bismarck*, pp. 184–85.

14. Bismarck to William, [19?] June 1873, AA Bonn, I.A.B.c 78, Bd. 2. This message, also marked "secret," was not immediately conveyed to the Kaiser; see the editorial comments in GP 1:189–91.

15. See Eckhart Kehr, *Der Primat der Innenpolitik*; Hans-Ulrich Wehler, *Bismarck und der Imperialismus*; and Michael Stürmer, *Regierung und Reichstag im Bismarckstaat 1871–1880*.

16. Manteuffel to Bismarck, 16 June 1873, AA Bonn, I.A.B.c 78, Bd. 2.

17. Arnim to Bismarck, 13 June 1873, ibid.; Manteuffel to Bismarck,

16 June 1873, ibid.; Wesdehlen to Bismarck, 16 July 1873, ibid., Bd. 3. See André Latreille et al., *Histoire du catholicisme en France*, 3:383–414; Adrien Dansette, *Histoire religieuse de la France contemporaine*, pp. 340–59; and Jacques Gadille, *La pensée et l'action politiques des évêques français au début de la IIIe république 1870/1883*.

18. Comte de Paris to Haussonville, 3 Aug. 1873, MAE Paris, Papiers Hanotaux, 4; Harcourt to Haussonville, 5 Aug. 1873, ibid.

19. Wesdehlen to AA, 17 July and 2 Aug. 1873, AA Bonn, I.A.B.c 78, Bd. 3; Wesdehlen to Bismarck, 11 and 14 Aug. 1873, ibid.

20. Bismarck to Manteuffel, 7 Aug. 1873, GW 14b:1495.

21. Wesdehlen to Bismarck, 16, 26, and 28 Aug. 1873, AA Bonn, I.A.B.c 78, Bd. 3. The last of these dispatches contained a military report from Major von Bülow, dated 24 Aug. 1873.

22. Bismarck to Wesdehlen, 3 Sept. 1873, GP 1:131; Wesdehlen to Bismarck, 12 Sept. 1873, ibid., 132; Balan to Arnim, 20 Sept. 1873, ibid., 133; Gontaut-Biron to Broglie, 6 and 11 Sept. 1873, MAE Paris, CP Allemagne, 11.

23. Notification of this order was sent from Bismarck to Arnim, 29 Sept. 1873, AA Bonn, I.A.B.c 78, Bd. 3.

24. Arnim to Bismarck, 29 Sept. 1873, GP 1:134.

25. Gontaut-Biron to Broglie, 2 Oct. 1873, DDF 1:240. See William L. Langer, *European Alliances and Alignments, 1871–1890*, pp. 34–35.

26. Although the Kaiser had no objection to Aumale's petition, Bismarck discouraged any German cooperation: for example, Wesdehlen to AA, 22 Sept. 1873, AA Bonn, I.A.B.c 78, Bd. 3; Bismarck to William, 27 Sept. 1873, ibid.; Bucher to AA, 7 Oct. 1873, ibid.

27. Bismarck to William, 11 Oct. 1873, ibid., 82, Bd. 1; Bismarck to Arnim, 30 Oct. 1873, GP 1:137.

28. Decazes to Chaudordy, 26 Sept. 1873, MAE Paris, Papiers Chaudordy, 1; Arnim to Bismarck, 29 Sept. 1873, AA Bonn, I.A.B.c 78, Bd. 3; Comte de Paris to Haussonville, 6 Oct. 1873, MAE Paris, Papiers Hanotaux, 4; Bismarck to AA, 8 Oct. 1873, AA Bonn, I.A.B.c 78, Bd. 3.

29. Simon to Thiers, 12 Oct. 1873, BN Paris, Papiers Thiers, NAF 20627.

30. Landsberg to Bleichröder, 10 Oct. 1873, BL Harvard, Bleichröder Nachlass, Box XXIII; Arnim to Bismarck, 11 Oct. 1873, AA Bonn, I.A.B.c 78, Bd. 3; Decazes to Broglie, 11 Oct. 1873, BT Paris, Papiers Decazes, 716; Bleichröder to Bismarck, 13 Oct. 1873, AA Bonn, II.B. 10, Bd. 5.

31. Compare the accounts of Marvin L. Brown, Jr., *The Comte de Chambord*, pp. 120–29; and Jacques Chastenet, *Histoire de la troisième république*, 1:161. The latter quotes Chambord as saying, "Jamais je ne renoncerai au drapeau blanc." Whichever version is literally correct, the effect was the same. See Robert R. Locke, *French Legitimists and the Politics of Moral Order in the Early Third Republic*, pp. 49–53.

32. Arnim to Bismarck, 17 Oct. 1873, AA Bonn, I.A.B.c 78, Bd. 3; Arnim to AA, 20 Oct. 1873, ibid.

33. Bismarck to Alvensleben, 25 Oct. 1873, ibid. For the backdrop see Langer, *European Alliances and Alignments*, pp. 31–39.

34. Arnim to AA, 30 and 31 Oct. 1873, AA Bonn, I.A.B.c 78, Bd. 3. See Helmuth Rogge, ed., *Holstein und Hohenlohe*, pp. 63–67.

35. See Gabriel Hanotaux, *Histoire de la France contemporaine (1871–1900)*, 2:257–310; and Brown, *Chambord*, pp. 129–38.

36. Debains to Broglie, 11 and 12 Oct. 1873, MAE Paris, CP Allemagne, 11.

37. Bucher to Bülow, 15 Nov. 1873, AA Bonn, I.A.B.c 82, Bd. 1. See Eberhard Naujoks, "Rudolf Lindau und die Neuorientierung der auswärtigen Pressepolitik Bismarcks," pp. 322–28.

38. Unsigned agent's report, 9 Nov. 1873, APP Paris, B A/320.

39. Otto Pflanze, *Bismarck and the Development of Germany*, pp. 8–14, 87–92.

40. Holstein to Herbert von Bismarck, 20 Nov. 1873, SF Hamburg, Bismarck Nachlass, B 56; Landsberg to Bleichröder, 24 Nov. 1873, AA Bonn, II.B 10, Bd. 5.

41. Arnim to Decazes, 11 Dec. 1873, BT Paris, Papiers Decazes, 687; Decazes to Arnim, 11 Dec. 1873, ibid., 716; "Notiz z. d. Akten betr. einen Artikel in der *Volkszeitung*, " 11 Dec. 1873, AA Bonn. I.A.B.c 78, Bd. 4; Arnim to AA, 14 Dec. 1873, ibid.; Bismarck to Arnim, 19 Dec. 1873, ibid. The threatening passage was deleted from the coded telegram sent to the German embassy in Paris.

42. Bismarck to Arnim, 30 Dec. 1873, ibid.; Arnim to Bismarck, 7 Jan. 1874, ibid., 79, Bd. 1. Rothschild's call on Arnim followed an intercession by MacMahon's personal secretary, Bernard d'Harcourt. See Jacques Silvestre de Sacy, *Le maréchal de MacMahon, duc de Magenta (1808–1893)*, pp. 301–2.

43. Bülow to Arnim, 11 Dec. 1873, AA Bonn, I.A.B.c 82, Bd. 1; Gontaut-Biron to Decazes, 2 Dec. 1873, BT Paris, Papiers Decazes, 687; "Aufzeichnung des Staatssekretärs des Auswärtigen Amtes von Bülow," 31 Dec. 1873, GP 1:141.

44. Bülow to Arnim, 31 Dec. 1873, AA Bonn, I.A.B.c 82, Bd. 1; Gontaut-Biron to Decazes, 31 Dec. 1873, DDF 1:253.

45. Decazes to Gontaut-Biron, 16 Dec. 1873, 2 and 10 Jan. 1874, BT Paris, Papiers Decazes, 716. Bismarck's sources indicated that the French army was still completely unprepared for combat (excerpt from a military report by Major von Bülow, 4 Dec. 1873, AA Bonn, I.A.B.c 78, Bd. 4; and military reports from Major von Brandt, 9 and 16 Dec. 1873, ibid., II.B. 10, Bd. 5).

46. Bülow to Arnim, 11 Jan. 1874, GP 1:143. The dispatches from Gontaut-Biron can be read in DDF 1:259–64.

47. Gontaut-Biron to Decazes, 3 Jan. 1874, BT Paris, Papiers Decazes,

688; Gontaut-Biron to Decazes, 14 Jan. 1874, MAE Paris, CP Allemagne, 12.

48. Gontaut-Biron to Decazes, 15 Jan. 1874, BT Paris, Papiers Decazes, 688.

49. Decazes to Gontaut-Biron, 18 Jan. 1874, ibid., 716; Decazes to the French ambassadors in London, Saint Petersburg, and Vienna, 18 Jan. 1874, DDF 1:265.

50. Bismarck to Arnim, 9 Jan. 1874, AA Bonn, I.A.B.c 82, Bd. 2.

51. Decazes to Broglie, [19?] Jan. 1874, BT Paris, Papiers Decazes, 717.

52. JORF, 21 Jan. 1874; Decazes to Harcourt, 19 Jan. 1874, MAE Paris, Papiers Hanotaux, 6; Decazes to Gontaut-Biron, 20 Jan. 1874, DDF 1:268; Gontaut-Biron to Decazes, 21 and 22 Jan. 1874, ibid., 269, 272.

53. Decazes to Gontaut-Biron, 28 Jan. 1874, BT Paris, Papiers Decazes, 688; Gontaut-Biron to Decazes, 7 and 14 Feb. 1874, ibid., 716; unsigned report of a French agent in Berlin, 8 Feb. 1874, APP Paris, B A/320; Bülow to Arnim, 17 Feb. 1874, GP 1:150. On the suspension of *L'Univers* see E. Malcolm Carroll, *French Public Opinion and Foreign Affairs, 1870–1914*, pp. 51–53; Bert Böhmer, *Frankreich zwischen Republik und Monarchie in der Bismarckzeit*, pp. 183–87; and Steinbach, *Die französische Diplomatie*, pp. 59–65.

54. An apt analogy between Bismarck's constant intimidation of the French during the 1870s and his threat in the 1880s to discard the German constitution is suggested by Michael Stürmer, "Staatsstreichgedanken im Bismarckreich," pp. 556–615.

55. Landsberg to Bleichröder, 21 Jan. 1874, BL Harvard, Bleichröder Nachlass, Box XXIII. See Chastenet, *Histoire de la troisième république*, 1:175–93.

56. Decazes to Harcourt, 1 Feb. and 9 Mar. 1874, BT Paris, Papiers Decazes, 716.

57. Decazes to Chaudordy, 21 Feb. 1874, MAE Paris, Papiers Chaudordy, 1; Decazes to Corcelle, 2 Apr. 1874, BT Paris, Papiers Decazes, 716.

58. Landsberg to Bleichröder, 5 and 14 Apr. 1874, BL Harvard, Bleichröder Nachlass, Box XXIII.

59. Decazes to Gontaut-Biron, 25 Apr. 1874, BT Paris, Papiers Decazes, 716.

60. Decazes to Gontaut-Biron, 13 May 1874, ibid., 717.

61. This story made the rounds from Orlov to Tsar Alexander to the Kaiser, who jotted it in the margin of a dispatch from Hohenlohe to Bismarck, 23 May 1874, AA Bonn, I.A.B.c 79, Bd. 2.

62. Holstein to Herbert von Bismarck, 23 May 1874, SF Hamburg, Bismarck Nachlass, B 56; Hohenlohe to Bismarck, 30 May 1874, AA Bonn, I.A.B.c 79, Bd. 2. See Chlodwig zu Hohenlohe, *Denkwürdigkeiten des Fürsten Chlodwig zu Hohenlohe-Schillingsfürst*, 2:122–24. Hohenlohe's

private papers, including the unexpurgated manuscript of his memoirs, are now in BA Koblenz.

63. Hohenlohe to Bismarck, 19 Aug. 1874, AA Bonn, I.A.B.c 79, Bd. 3.

64. The foregoing list is based on Hohenlohe's *Denkwürdigkeiten* and on his ambassadorial reports to Berlin in the summer of 1874, AA Bonn, I.A.B.c 79, Bd. 2, 3.

65. Hohenlohe to William, 16 June 1874, ibid., Bd. 2. In addition to his frequent contacts with Thiers and Decazes, Hohenlohe was also approached on several occasions by Orleanists, Bonapartists, and Gambettists.

66. JORF, 24 July 1874; Hohenlohe to Bismarck, AA Bonn, I.A.B.c 79, Bd. 3.

67. Wesdehlen to Bülow, 30 Oct. 1874, ibid., Bd. 4.

68. Manipulation of the German press was indicated, e.g., by Bülow to Hohenlohe, 5 and 7 Aug. 1874, ibid.; and by Wesdehlen to Bülow, 29 Oct. 1874, ibid. An explanation of Arnim's arrest and impending trial was sent from Bülow to William, 4 Oct. 1874, DZA II Merseburg, Rep. 89 H VI, 3b. The French reaction was summarized by Decazes to Gontaut-Biron, 7 Dec. 1874, BT Paris, Papiers Decazes, 717. See Kent, *Arnim and Bismarck*, pp. 150–71.

69. Münster to Bismarck, 14 Dec. 1874, AA Bonn, I.A.B.c 79 secr., Bd. 1. A copy of this confidential message, relayed by Münster from a Russian source, is also to be found in SF Hamburg, Bismarck Nachlass, B 81.

70. Bülow to Münster, 16 Dec. 1874, AA Bonn, I.A.B.c 79 secr., Bd. 1.

71. Hohenlohe to Bismarck, 26 Dec. 1874 and 12 Jan. 1875, ibid.

72. Hohenlohe to AA, 21 and 23 Jan. 1875, ibid.; AA to Hohenlohe, 21 Jan. 1875, ibid.; Hohenlohe to Bismarck, 29 Jan. 1875, ibid.

73. JORF, 30–31 Jan. 1875.

74. Hohenlohe to Bismarck, 25 Feb. 1875, AA Bonn. I.A.B.c 79, Bd. 5. See Hanotaux, *Histoire*, 3:171–215.

75. See Daniel Halévy, *La république des ducs*.

76. Hohenlohe to Bismarck, 25 Feb. 1875, AA Bonn, I.A.B.c 79. Bd. 5. This observation accorded with the prediction of one of the most trusted German agents in Paris that France would soon experience a "bellum omnium contre omnes" (Landsberg to Bleichröder, 19 Feb. 1875, BL Harvard, Bleichröder Nachlass, Box XXIII).

Chapter 5

1. These changes and their implications for France are summarized in Allan Mitchell, *Bismarck and the French Nation*, pp. 89–93. See Helmut

Böhme, *Deutschlands Weg zur Grossmacht*, pp. 419–20, 587–604; Rudolf Lill, *Die Wende im Kulturkampf*; and Bruce Waller, *Bismarck at the Crossroads*.

2. See W. W. Rostow, ed., *The Economics of Take-Off into Sustained Growth*; and Hans Rosenberg, *Grosse Depression und Bismarckzeit*.

3. The former view is exemplified by a review of Rosenberg's work by Alexander Gerschenkron in the *Journal of Economic History* 28 (1968): 154–56; and the latter by David S. Landes, *The Unbound Prometheus*, pp. 231–37. Note that neither critic necessarily infers depression from deflationary prices. A comprehensive refutation of the Rostow-Rosenberg position has been attempted by S. B. Saul, *The Myth of the Great Depression, 1873–1896*. Yet the controversy continues, especially over Germany. See Hans-Ulrich Wehler, *Bismarck und der Imperialismus*, pp. 39–111; Jürgen Kocka, "Theoretical Approaches to Social and Economic History of Modern Germany," pp. 101–19; and, in summary, Knut Borchardt, "Wirtschaftliches Wachstum und Wechsellagen 1800–1914," pp. 198–275.

4. For example, see a critique of the attempt by Wehler and others to derive parallels between France and Germany from a theory of economic cycles, in Allan Mitchell, "Bonapartism as a Model for Bismarckian Politics," pp. 181–209. An analysis of the entire problem by Simon Kuznets suggests that the economic patterns for Britain and Germany in the later nineteenth century were roughly similar, albeit with some significant variations, whereas Sweden and the United States conformed less well; it is noteworthy that he does not even discuss France in this context (Kuznets, *Economic Growth of Nations*, pp. 43–50). A more recent study of economic fluctuations and cycles ends by admitting frankly that "we do not know sufficient about these long swings" (Alan S. Milward and S. B. Saul, *The Development of the Economies of Continental Europe, 1850–1914*, pp. 505–13).

5. Rosenberg, in *Grosse Depression*, pp. 38–51, presents his statistical data in such a way as to emphasize the long swings of Germany's economic growth. Thus he shows that the *amount* of investment in new joint-stock companies was (in billions of marks):

1851–73	5.5
1874–96	2.9
1897–1914	5.2

But if we calculate an *annual rate* of investment for the same years and divide the entire period into four segments rather than three, the resulting pattern (given here in millions of marks) appears quite otherwise:

1851–70	120
1871–73	967
1874–96	132
1897–1914	306

6. See the references in Chapter 2, nn. 1–3. The entire question is capably reviewed by Claude Fohlen, "The Industrial Revolution in France," pp. 201–25.

7. That Germany's economic performance in the postwar decades had "few points in common with France" is underscored by Milward and Saul, *Development*, pp. 137–39. This observation bears out their general tenet that "processes of development would vary more widely in accordance with national historical backgrounds than with anything else" (ibid., p. 526). Although noting similar rates of productivity of mining operations in French and German Lorraine in the period 1871 to 1914, William N. Parker argues that important differences of technique and organization nonetheless emerged: "National economies may rather be delicately compared to national cuisines" (Parker, "National States and National Development," pp. 201–12).

8. Gould's calculations follow Angus Maddison, *Economic Growth in the West*, and Walther G. Hoffmann, *Das Wachstum der deutschen Wirtschaft seit der Mitte des 19. Jahrhunderts*.

9. To read further on Germany's rapid and massive industrialization, "one of the commonplaces of contemporary history," see J. H. Clapham, *The Economic Development of France and Germany*, pp. 178–338. A comparison with Britain is more central to Landes, *The Unbound Prometheus*, pp. 326–58.

10. But see the critical discussion of this problem (what is a "product"?) by Borchardt, "Wirtschaftliches Wachstum," pp. 204–10. Viewed in such a long perspective, it does not appear that the large reparations imposed by Germany in 1871 represented a major handicap for French growth; in fact, they may have briefly stimulated exports. "But the annexation of Alsace and part of Lorraine by Germany proved a heavy blow," mainly because of losses in the iron and cotton industries (Milward and Saul, *Development*, p. 75).

11. See Rondo E. Cameron, "Economic Growth and Stagnation in France, 1815–1914," pp. 1–13; and David S. Landes, "French Entrepreneurship and Industrial Growth in the Nineteenth Century," pp. 45–61. We stand warned about "the virtual impossibility of proving anything positive about theories of growth through the use of history, and the propensity of economic historians, with rare exceptions, to overgeneralize" (Charles P. Kindleberger, *Economic Growth in France and Britain, 1851–1950*, p. 324).

12. It should be obvious that there is no precise analytic method of assigning weight to the various factors mentioned. One expert on the subject has proposed for heuristic purposes a formula for determining total income or output: $Y = f(P, R, T, X)$, where P is population, R is resources, T is technology, and X is the "great unknown" inherent in the "socio-cultural context" of economic activity; as he readily concedes,

this formula falls notably short of scientific exactitude (Rondo E. Cameron, "Economic History, Pure and Applied," pp. 3–27). Likewise, one British authority has reviewed the complexity of factors making up France's "particular inherited environment" and has concluded that "there are no simple or monocausal answers" (Tom Kemp, *Industrialization in Nineteenth-Century Europe*, pp. 52–80.

13. Police report of 3 Apr. 1873, APP Paris, B A/86.

14. The current state of the economy and the various attitudes toward increased protectionism were outlined in a report from the Chamber of Commerce to the president of the French Assembly, Jules Grévy, 18 June 1873, CCP Paris, Correspondence, XV. See Michael S. Smith, "Free Trade versus Protection in the Early Third Republic," pp. 293–314.

15. Arnim to Bismarck, 11 Oct. 1873, AA Bonn, I.A.B.c 78, Bd. 3.

16. Bleichröder to Bismarck, 25 July 1873, SF Hamburg, Bismarck Nachlass, B 15.

17. Dervieu to Broglie, 2 Oct. 1873, MAE Paris, CCC Hambourg, 43; Hell to Broglie, 19 Nov. 1873 and 14 Jan. 1874, MAE Paris, CCC Francfort, 9.

18. Bleichröder to Bismarck, 23 Apr. 1874, SF Hamburg, Bismarck Nachlass, B 15.

19. Hohenlohe to Bismarck, 18 July 1874, AA Bonn, I.A.B.c 78, Bd. 3; Hoehne to AA, 4 Nov. 1874, DZA Potsdam, Kons. Fr. 11, Bd. 2, 51812; Chambre de Commerce de Paris to the Vicomte de Meaux, 19 Mar. 1875, CCP Paris, Correspondence, XVI.

20. Minutes of the third general assembly of the Crédit Mobilier, 14 Jan. 1873, AN Paris, 25 AQ 7. On the background see Rondo E. Cameron, "The Crédit Mobilier and the Economic Development of Europe," pp. 461–88.

21. Minutes of the fifth general assembly of the Crédit Mobilier, 30 June 1874, AN Paris, 25 AQ 7.

22. Minutes of the sixth general assembly of the Crédit Mobilier, 2–3 Mar. 1875, ibid.

23. See Ivo Nikolai Lambi, *Free Trade and Protection in Germany, 1868–1879*; and Böhme, *Deutschlands Weg*, pp. 341–59.

24. E.g., Fontenay to Decazes, 21 May 1875, AN Paris, F^{12} 6435.

25. Bleichröder to Bismarck, 7 Nov. 1875, SF Hamburg, Bismarck Nachlass, B 15. See Fritz Stern, *Gold and Iron*, pp. 181–97.

26. Hell to Decazes, 20 Nov. 1875 and 13 Jan. 1876, MAE Paris, CCC Francfort, 10.

27. Rothschild to Bleichröder, 21 Jan. and 7–8 Feb. 1876, BL Harvard, Bleichröder Nachlass, Box XIII.

28. See Hans Herzfeld, *Die deutsch-französische Kriegsgefahr von 1875*; William L. Langer, *European Alliances and Alignments, 1871–1890*, pp. 31–55; Martin Winckler, "Der Ausbruch der 'Krieg-in-Sicht'-Krise vom

Frühjahr 1875," pp. 671–713; Andreas Hillgruber, "Die 'Krieg-in-Sicht' Krise," pp. 239–53; and Christoph Steinbach, *Die französische Diplomatie und das Deutsche Reich, 1873 bis 1881*, pp. 68–69, 81–109, 258–59.

29. Dechend to Bismarck, 31 Jan. 1875, AA Bonn, I.A.B.c 79 secr., Bd. 1; Hohenlohe to Bismarck, 4 Feb. 1875, ibid.; Bülow to Hohenlohe, 13 Feb. 1875, ibid.

30. Schencking to Hohenlohe, 12 Feb. 1875, ibid., 79, Bd. 5; Bismarck to Hohenlohe, 26 Feb. 1875, GP 1:155.

31. Hohenlohe to Bülow, 14 Mar. 1875, AA Bonn, I.A.B.c 79, Bd. 5.

32. "Bericht des Militärattachés Major von Bülow, zufolge Erlasses vom 26. Februar, die französischen Pferdeankäufe betreffend," 1 Mar. 1875, GP 1:156.

33. Krause to Moltke, 18 Mar. 1875, ibid., 157.

34. Holstein to Hohenlohe, 22 and 23 Mar. 1875, BA Koblenz, Hohenlohe Nachlass, XB H 22.

35. See the apologia for Bismarck by the editors of the *Grosse Politik*, 1:253–54.

36. Decazes to Harcourt, 9 Apr. 1875, MAE Paris, Papiers Hanotaux, 6.

37. Hohenlohe to AA, 18 Apr. 1875, GP 1:160; Bismarck to Hohenlohe, 18 Apr. 1875, ibid., 161.

38. This view was advocated by E. Malcolm Carroll, *French Public Opinion and Foreign Affairs, 1870–1914*, pp. 54–65; and by Langer, *European Alliances and Alignments*, pp. 53–55; and it has more recently been adopted by Walter Bussmann, *Das Zeitalter Bismarcks*, pp. 130–32.

39. Lord Edmond Fitzmaurice, *The Life of Granville George Leveson Gower, Second Earl Granville*, 2:49; Münster to Bülow, 7 June 1875, GP 1:187. See Gerhard Ritter, *Staatskunst und Kriegshandwerk*, 1:275–99.

40. Hohenlohe to Bismarck, 21 Apr. 1875, AA Bonn, I.A.B.c 83, Bd. 1.

41. Compare Gontaut-Biron to Decazes, 21 Apr. 1875, DDF 1:395; and "Promemoria des Gesandten im Auswärtigen Amt von Radowitz," 12 May 1875, GP 1:177. Hohenlohe's source for Radowitz's personal opinion was the Countess Dönhoff-Seydwitz, as is revealed in unexpurgated portions of Hohenlohe's diary, entries for 21 May and 5 Aug. 1875, BA Koblenz, Hohenlohe Nachlass, XX C 2. A share of the blame was also placed on Radowitz by the London *Times* correspondent, Henri Stephan de Blowitz, *My Memoirs*, pp. 100–127. See Hajo Holborn, *Bismarcks europäische Politik zu Beginn der siebziger Jahre und die Mission Radowitz*; and Langer, *European Alliances and Alignments*, pp. 46–47.

42. Hohenlohe to Bismarck, 12 Apr. 1875, GP 1:164.

43. Hohenlohe to Bülow, 25 Apr. 1875, AA Bonn, I.A.B.c 83, Bd. 1; Hohenlohe to Bismarck, 25 and 29 Apr. 1875, GP 1:167, 169; Decazes to French diplomatic representatives in the major capitals, 29 Apr. 1875,

DDF 1:399; Wesdehlen to AA, 14 May 1875, AA Bonn, I.A.B.c 79, Bd. 6.

44. Bülow to Reuss, 4 May 1875, ibid., 79 secr., Bd. 1; Hohenlohe to Bismarck, 5 May 1875, ibid.

45. "A French Scare," London *Times*, 6 May 1875. Contrast the defense of Decazes by Gabriel Hanotaux, *Histoire de la France contemporaine (1871–1900)*, 3:234–94; and the attack on him in the editorial commentary of GP 1:278.

46. William to Bülow, 11 May 1875, ibid., 175; Bülow to William (with the Kaiser's marginalia), ibid., 181.

47. Bismarck to Münster, 9 May 1875, AA Bonn, I.A.B.c 83, Bd. 1; Bismarck to Münster, 12 and 14 May 1875, GP 1:176, 180. See Klaus Hildebrand, "Von der Reichseinigung zur 'Krieg-in-Sicht'-Krise," pp. 205–34.

48. See Stanley Hoffmann, ed., *In Search of France*, pp. 1–117.

49. Leon Trotsky, *The History of the Russian Revolution*, 1:206–15.

50. In addition to the works previously cited on French politics, see the merciless critique by Herbert Lüthy, *Frankreichs Uhren gehen anders*, translated as *France against Herself*.

51. Hohenlohe to Bülow, 9 and 14 Mar. 1875, AA Bonn, I.A.B.c 79, Bd. 5. The censored journal was the *Libéral de l'Est*.

52. Wesdehlen to Bülow, 20 Sept. 1875, AA Bonn, I.A.B.c 79, Bd. 6. See Robert R. Locke, *French Legitimists and the Politics of Moral Order in the Early Third Republic*, pp. 224–61.

53. Hohenlohe to Bismarck, 12 Apr. 1875, AA Bonn, I.A.B.c 79, Bd. 5. The French government's crackdown on Bonapartist propaganda had been inaugurated in January by Prefect of Police Léon Renault; this action was routinely reported to Berlin (Hohenlohe to Bismarck, 27 Jan. 1875, ibid., 73, Bd. 2; Hohenlohe to Bülow, 2 Mar. 1875, ibid.). See Theodore Zeldin, *France, 1848–1945*, 1:560–69.

54. Manuscript of Hohenlohe's diary, entry for 13 Apr. 1875, BA Koblenz, Hohenlohe Nachlass, XX C 2; Hohenlohe to Bismarck, 13 Apr. 1875, AA Bonn, I.A.B.c 73, Bd. 2; Bülow to Hohenlohe, 27 Apr. 1875, ibid.

55. Keudell to Bülow, 15 Nov. 1875, ibid., 79, Bd. 7; Hohenlohe to Bismarck, 4 Dec. 1875, ibid., 73, Bd. 2.

56. Hohenlohe to Bismarck, 9 Jan. 1876, ibid., 79, Bd. 8. See Henri Malo, *Thiers, 1797–1877*, pp. 578–88.

57. Hohenlohe to Bismarck, 23 June 1875, AA Bonn, I.A.B.c 79, Bd. 6.

58. Hohenlohe to Bismarck, 14 Jan. 1876, ibid., Bd. 8.

59. Hohenlohe to Bismarck, 25 May 1875, ibid., Bd. 6.

60. Bleichröder to Bismarck, 10 Feb. 1876, ibid., Bd. 8.

61. E.g., police report of 12 Mar. 1876, APP Paris, B A/87; Hohen-

lohe to Bismarck, 15 Mar. 1876, AA Bonn, I.A.B.c 79, Bd. 9. Gambetta's police dossiers are in APP Paris, B A/917–24.

62. Hohenlohe to Bülow, 12 Nov. and 13 Dec. 1875, AA Bonn, I.A.B.c 79, Bd. 7.

63. Report of a Paris agent, forwarded from Bleichröder to Bismarck, 24 Dec. 1875, SF Hamburg, Bismarck Nachlass, B 15.

64. JORF, 13 Jan. 1876; Hohenlohe to Bismarck, 11 Mar. 1876, AA Bonn, I.A.B.c 79, Bd. 8. See Jacques Silvestre de Sacy, *Le maréchal de MacMahon, duc de Magenta (1808–1893)*, pp. 323–25.

65. Wesdehlen to Bülow, 2 Nov. 1875, AA Bonn, I.A.B.c 79, Bd. 7.

66. MacMahon to Decazes, 9 Dec. 1875, BT Paris, Papiers Decazes, 699; Beckmann to Hohenlohe, 23 Dec. 1875, BA Koblenz, Hohenlohe Nachlass, XB B 7; Hohenlohe to Bismarck, 9 Jan. 1876, AA Bonn, I.A.B.c 79, Bd. 8.

67. Abzag to Decazes, 24 Jan. 1876, BT Paris, Papiers Decazes, 728; Hohenlohe to Bismarck, 29 Jan. 1876, AA Bonn, I.A.B.c 79 secr., Bd. 1; Hohenlohe to Bismarck, 5 Feb. 1876, ibid., 79, Bd. 8.

68. Gontaut-Biron to Decazes, 9 Mar. 1876, BT Paris, Papiers Decazes, 701; Report by agent "Ancien 5," 13 Mar. 1876, APP Paris, B A/962.

69. Hohenlohe to Bismarck, 30 Mar. 1876, AA Bonn, I.A.B.c 73, Bd. 2; Bülow to Schleinitz, Münster, Dönhoff, and Keudell, 4 Apr. 1876, ibid.

70. Alexis de Tocqueville, *Recollections*, pp. 16–19.

71. E.g., police reports of 7 and 11 Aug. 1876, APP Paris, B A/87. That Gambetta's own formulation ("le cléricalisme? voilà l'ennemi!") was actually coined by an obscure politician in 1863 is noted by Gordon Wright, *France in Modern Times*, p. 141. See René Rémond, *L'anticléricalisme en France de 1815 à nos jours*, pp. 175–87.

72. Police reports of 28 July, 21 Aug., and 23 Sept. 1876, APP Paris, B A/87.

73. Police report of 28 Oct. 1876, ibid.

74. Police reports of 5 and 11 Oct. 1876, ibid.

75. On students, e.g., police reports of 21 May and 8 June 1876, ibid.; and on women, e.g., police reports of 1–9 Dec. 1876, ibid. See Madelaine Guilbert, *Les femmes et l'organisation syndicale avant 1914*; and Zeldin, *France*, 1:343–62.

76. Police reports of 28 Apr., 25 July, and 20 Aug. 1876, APP Paris, B A/87.

77. Police report of 25 Aug. 1876, ibid. See Adrien Dansette, *Histoire religieuse de la France contemporaine*, pp. 360–68; and Jean Palou, *La franc-maçonnerie*.

78. E.g., police reports of 9 and 20 Mar., 3 Apr., 11 May, 17 June, and 4 Aug. 1876, APP Paris, B A/87. See Aaron Noland, *The Founding of*

the French Socialist Party; Edward Shorter and Charles Tilly, *Strikes in France, 1830–1968*, pp. 46–75; and Michelle Perrot, *Les ouvriers en grève*, 1:15–199.

79. Police report of 4 Apr. 1876, APP Paris, B A/87.

80. Police reports of 1 and 16 Aug. 1876, ibid.

81. E.g., police reports of 12 Apr., 14 June, 25 July, 18 Sept., 14 Oct., and 26 Nov. 1876, ibid.

82. See Claude Digeon, *La crise allemande de la pensée française*, pp. 48–112; and K. W. Swart, *The Sense of Decadence in Nineteenth-Century France*, pp. 123–38.

83. These figures were first published in the *Annuaire de l'économie politique* in 1876 and were discussed in dispatches from Hohenlohe to Bismarck, 30 Aug. and 23 Sept. 1876, AA Bonn, I.A.B.c 79, Bd. 10, 11. The number of marriages continued to decline, hovering about 280,000 annually in the late 1870s (*Annuaire statistique de la France* 6 [1883]: 48–49).

84. Police report of 27 Mar. 1876, APP Paris, B A/87. The themes of this section will be elaborated in a sequel to the present volume.

Chapter 6

1. Wesdehlen to Bülow, 20 Oct. 1876, AA Bonn, I.A.B.c 79, Bd. 11.

2. Hohenlohe to Bismarck, 30 Aug. 1876, ibid., Bd. 10. Ten days earlier a meeting of some five hundred Belleville workers had adopted with near unanimity the following motion: "The assembly declares that M. Gambetta has lost the confidence of the voters of the twentieth arrondissement and that he is unworthy to represent them" (police report of 21 Aug. 1876, APP Paris, B A/87).

3. See Jean T. Joughin, *The Paris Commune in French Politics, 1871–1880*; and J. P. T. Bury, *Gambetta and the Making of the Third Republic*, pp. 297–302, 326–27.

4. Wesdehlen to Bismarck, 29 and 31 Dec. 1876, AA Bonn, I.A.B.c 79, Bd. 12. See Gabriel Hanotaux, *Histoire de la France contemporaine (1871–1900)*, 3:625–32.

5. Hohenlohe to Bismarck, 5 and 9 Dec. 1876, AA Bonn, I.A.B.c 79, Bd. 11. See Fresnette Pisani-Ferry, *Le coup d'état manqué du 16 mai 1877*, pp. 123–45.

6. JORF, 15 Dec. 1876; Hohenlohe to Bismarck, 15 Dec. 1876, AA Bonn, I.A.B.c 79, Bd. 12. See Philip A. Bertocci, *Jules Simon*, pp. 184–91.

7. Decazes to Gontaut-Biron, 23 Jan. 1877, BT Paris, Papiers Decazes, 718; Decazes to Harcourt, 16 Feb. 1877, ibid.

8. Gontaut-Biron to Decazes, 24 and 26 Jan. 1877, MAE Paris, CP Allemagne, 20; Gontaut-Biron to Decazes, 27 Jan. 1877, BT Paris, Papiers Decazes, 709; report of agent "No. 32," APP Paris, B A/962.

9. Hohenlohe to Bismarck, 20 Feb. 1877, AA Bonn, I.A.B.c 79 secr.,

Bd. 1; manuscript of Hohenlohe's diary, entry for 8 Mar. 1877, BA Koblenz, Hohenlohe Nachlass, XX C 4; Hohenlohe to Bismarck, 16 Mar. 1877, AA Bonn, I.A.B.c 79, Bd. 13.

10. Keudell to Bülow, 17 Feb. 1877, ibid., 73, Bd. 2; Hohenlohe to Bismarck, 23 Feb. 1877, ibid., 79, Bd. 13; Bülow to Hohenlohe, 24 Mar. 1877, ibid.

11. E.g., Lefebvre de Béhaine to Decazes, 14 Apr. 1877, BT Paris, Papiers Decazes, 711. According to this report from Munich, "L'idée se répand ici que la guerre qui commence va de nouveau mettre aux prises la France et l'Allemagne. Cela se dit partout: aussi bien dans les comptoirs des banquiers que dans les brasseries; dans les salons comme dans les casernes. . . . "

12. Decazes to Gontaut-Biron, 21 Apr. 1877, BT Paris, Papiers Decazes, 719; Simon to Decazes, 21 Apr. 1877, ibid., 728.

13. *L'année politique*, 1877, pp. 115–16; Gontaut-Biron to Decazes, 18 Apr. 1877, MAE Paris, CP Allemagne, 20; Lindau to Bismarck, 29 Apr. 1877, AA Bonn, I.A.B.c 79, Bd. 14.

14. JORF, 5 May 1877; Hohenlohe to Bismarck, 5 May 1877, AA Bonn, I.A.B.c 79, Bd. 14.

15. Hohenlohe to Bülow, 17 May 1877, ibid.

16. Hohenlohe to Bülow, 14 May 1877, ibid.

17. For the background see Brian Chapman, *The Prefects and Provincial France*; Edward A. Whitcomb, "Napoleon's Prefects," pp. 1089–118; Nicholas J. Richardson, *The French Prefectoral Corps, 1814–1830*; Bernard Le Clère and Vincent Wright, *Les préfets du second empire*; and Jeanne Siwek-Pouydesseau, *Le corps préfectoral sous les IIIe et IVe républiques*.

18. Quoted by Robert Dreyfus, *De Monsieur Thiers à Marcel Proust*, p. 284. See Dreyfus's essay "Maires et fonctionnaires: bouleversements administratifs et municipaux (1870–1880)," in ibid. pp. 253–326.

19. According to Bury, *Gambetta and the Making*, p. 407, outright dismissals during the first month after 16 May were enforced for 484 prefects and subprefects, 184 magistrates, 83 mayors, and 381 justices of the peace.

20. Directive from the Ministry of the Interior to all prefects, 2 July 1877, AN Paris, F^{1a} 2135; Fourtou to the prefect of Alpes-Maritimes, 19 Sept. 1877, ibid., F^7 12681.

21. E.g., Fourtou to the prefects of Nord and Cher, 5 July 1877, ibid.; Fourtou to the prefect of Loire, 3 and 8 Sept. 1877, ibid.; Ministry of the Interior to all prefects, 9–10 Oct. 1877, ibid. A parliamentary investigation in 1878 revealed that eight million francs had been spent by the Broglie government on electoral propaganda. See Claude Bellanger et al., *Histoire générale de la presse française*, 3:159; and, for specific examples of official pressure, Georges Dupeux, *Aspects de l'histoire sociale et politique du Loir-et-Cher, 1848–1914*, pp. 476–79; Pierre Barral, *Le département de l'Isère sous la troisième république, 1870–1940*, pp. 398–99; and Jacques

Basso, *Les élections législatives dans le département des Alpes-Maritimes de 1860 à 1939*, pp. 112–15.

22. Fourtou to the prefect of Aisne, 22 May 1877, AN Paris, F⁷ 12681; Fourtou to the prefect of Basses-Alpes, 12 June 1877, ibid., 12682; Fourtou to the prefect of Seine-Inférieure, 11 July and 4 Sept. 1877, ibid., 12683, 12684; Hohenlohe to Bismarck, 22 July 1877, AA Bonn, I.A.B.c 79, Bd. 17.

23. Ministry of the Interior (Direction de la presse) to the prefect of Haute Garonne, [?] 1877, AN Paris, F⁷ 12681; Fourtou to police prefects of Paris, Lille, Arras, and Rouen, [?] Sept. 1877, ibid.; Ministry of the Interior (Directeur de sureté) to all prefects, 7 Oct. 1877, ibid., 12682.

24. Fourtou to the prefect of Allier, 31 May 1877, ibid., 12681; Fourtou to the prefect of Rhône, 6 June 1877, ibid., 12682; Fourtou to the prefect of Meurthe-et-Moselle, 30 June and 1 July 1877, ibid., 12683, 12684. One historian specifically notes that the republicans were aided by German threats: "C'était accréditer le bruit que voter pour Broglie, c'était voter pour la guerre" (Jean-Paul Charnay, *Les scrutins politiques en France de 1815 à 1962*, pp. 81–83). Also see Auguste Soulier, *L'instabilité ministerielle sous la troisième république (1871–1938)*, pp. 49–51; and Jean-Marie Mayeur, *Les débuts de la IIIe république*, pp. 39–40.

25. Hohenlohe to Bülow, 28 May and 7 June 1877, AA Bonn, I.A.B.c 79, Bd. 15; Ministry of the Interior (chef du cabinet) to the prefects of Ain and Ande, 13 July 1877, AN Paris, F⁷ 12681. See Bellanger et al., *Presse française*, 3:158–62.

26. *Le maréchal devant l'opinion* (Paris, 1877). A copy was forwarded from Hohenlohe to Bülow, 8 and 11 June 1877, AA Bonn, I.A.B.c 79, Bd. 15.

27. Hohenlohe attended a soirée in the Thiers residence at the Place St. Georges along with such prominent centrist politicians as Léon Say, Barthélémy Saint-Hilaire, Marcère, Grévy, and Jules Simon (police agent's report of 16 June 1877, APP Paris, B A/1280).

28. For an analysis of this and other issues developed in the campaign, see Dupeux, *Aspects*, pp. 479–89.

29. Manuscript of Hohenlohe's diary, entry for 14 June 1877, BA Koblenz, Hohenlohe Nachlass, II C 4; Hohenlohe to Bülow, 14, 22, and 26 June 1877, AA Bonn, I.A.B.c 79, Bd. 15, 16; Hohenlohe to Bismarck, 27 June 1877, ibid. See Pisani-Ferry, *Coup*, pp. 201–71.

30. According to one German source, Aumale had written to Broglie and accused him of allowing preparations for a "Bonapartist orgy" (Hohenlohe to Bismarck, 29 June 1877, AA Bonn, I.A.B.c 79, Bd. 16).

31. Hohenlohe to Bismarck, 11 and 31 July, 17 Aug. 1877, ibid., Bd. 17, 18.

32. Bleichröder to Bismarck, 18 July and 16 Aug. 1877, ibid., Bd. 17. Distressed by Fourtou's tactics, Decazes wanted to resign; but Broglie prevailed on him to remain in office in order to avert "certain defeat" if

the cabinet disintegrated (Decazes to Broglie, 24 July 1877, BT Paris, Papiers Decazes, 728; Broglie to Decazes, 25 July 1877, ibid.).

33. Joseph Reinach, *La vie politique de Léon Gambetta*, pp. 62–64; Hohenlohe to Bismarck, 17 Aug. 1877, AA Bonn, I.A.B.c 79, Bd. 18. See Bury, *Gambetta and the Making*, pp. 421–24.

34. Fourtou to the prefect of Allier, [?] 1877, AN Paris, F⁷ 12681.

35. Gambetta to Barthélémy Saint-Hilaire, 19 Aug. 1877, BVC Paris, Papiers Barthélémy Saint-Hilaire, 260.

36. Hohenlohe to Bülow, 20 Aug. 1877, AA Bonn, I.A.B.c 79, Bd. 18. Most French police informers continued to believe that Thiers would prevail. As one of them commented, "Everywhere, in all classes and in all departments, no one seems to doubt for an instant that he will soon regain the place he was forced to vacate on May 24 [1873]" (Report by agent "Yves," 25 Aug. 1877, APP Paris, B A/1280).

37. Decazes to Gontaut-Biron, 26 Aug. 1877, BT Paris, Papiers Decazes, 719. See Henri Malo, *Thiers, 1797–1877*, pp. 588–97.

38. Beauvoir to Decazes, 4 and 5 Sept. 1877, BT Paris, Papiers Decazes, 730; Wesdehlen to Bülow, 4 and 6 Sept. 1877, AA Bonn, I.A.B.c 79, Bd. 18.

39. Bismarck's informants in France, as one of them wrote, uniformly continued to assume that "the elections will turn out very republican" (Brandeis to Bleichröder, 27 Sept. 1877, BL Harvard, Bleichröder Nachlass, Box XVII).

40. *Le Français*, 14 Sept. 1877, sent by Wesdehlen to Bülow, 21 Sept. 1877, AA Bonn, I.A.B.c 79, Bd. 19.

41. Quoted by the *Journal des débats*, 30 Sept. 1877. The *triduum* had been proposed to the pope by a French priest, François Picard, whose request was granted in Rome on 11 Sept.

42. Wesdehlen to Bülow, 2 Oct. 1877, I.A.B.c 79, Bd. 19. See Jacques Gadille, *La pensée et l'action politiques des évêques français au début de la IIIe république 1870/1883*, 2:58–78.

43. JORF, 6 Oct. 1877; *Journal des débats*, 14 Oct. 1877.

44. JORF, 12 Oct. 1877.

45. Hohenlohe to Bismarck, 23 Feb. 1877, AA Bonn, I.A.B.c 79, Bd. 13.

46. Hohenlohe to Bülow, 17 May 1877, ibid, Bd. 14; police report of 16 May 1877, APP Paris, B A/71.

47. Hohenlohe to Bülow, 17, 18, and 21 May 1877, AA Bonn, I.A.B.c 79, Bd. 14. The French envoy to Italy shared the apprehension: "I am really disturbed and the spectre of an Italo-German alliance now haunts me" (Noailles to Decazes, 19 May 1877, BT Paris, Papiers Decazes, 712).

48. Tiby to Decazes, 18 May 1877, ibid.

49. Bülow to Bismarck, 17 May 1877, GP 1:209; memorandum by

Bülow (annotated by Bismarck), 18 May 1877, AA Bonn, I.A.B.c 79, Bd. 14; Bülow to Hohenlohe, 22 May 1877, ibid. Editorials in the German press warned, e.g., that "the new ultramontane campaign is beginning in France" and that the French cabinet "can maintain its position only through acts of violence" (*Bösenzeitung*, 20 May 1877). The question of Bismarck's relation to the press during the *seize mai* crisis is unfortunately ignored by E. Malcolm Carroll, *Germany and the Great Powers, 1866–1914.*

50. "Militärischer Bericht Nr. 131 des Oberlieutenants v. Bülow, betreffend den Sturz des Ministeriums, vom militärischen Gesichtspunkt aus betrachtet," sent from Hohenlohe to AA, 19 May 1877, AA Bonn, I.A.B.c 79, Bd. 14.

51. Bülow to German embassies in Saint Petersburg, Rome, Vienna, London, and Constantinople, 23 May 1877, ibid.

52. Hohenlohe to Bülow, 24 May 1877, ibid., Bd. 15; Bülow to Hohenlohe, 4 June 1877, ibid. Hartmann's probable identity has been established by Bury, *Gambetta and the Making*, p. 438.

53. Hohenlohe to Bülow, 24 May 1877, AA Bonn, I.A.B.c 79, Bd. 15.

54. Herbert von Bismarck to Bülow, 29 May 1877, ibid.

55. Ibid.; Bülow to Keudell, 30 May 1877, AA Bonn, I.A.B.c 79, Bd. 15. In the directive to Keudell in Rome the phrase "sehr schnell in den Krieg kommen" was modified to "bald in den Krieg gerathen."

56. Bleichröder to Bismarck, 3 June 1877, AA Bonn, I.A.B.c 81, Bd. 2; Bismarck to Bülow, 4 June 1877, ibid.

57. Draft of a message from Herbert von Bismarck to Bülow, 18 June 1877, ibid., 79, Bd. 15.

58. E.g., Tiby to Decazes, 9 June 1877, MAE Paris, CP Allemagne, 21; Tiby to Decazes, 22 June 1877, BT Paris, Papiers Decazes, 713.

59. Hohenlohe to Bülow, 11 June 1877, AA Bonn, I.A.B.c 79 secr., Bd. 2; Herbert von Bismarck to Bülow, 13 June 1877, ibid.; Bülow to Hohenlohe, 15 June 1877, GP 1:211.

60. Decazes to Ring, 24 June 1877, BT Paris, Papiers Decazes, 719; Decazes to Tiby, 24 June 1877, ibid.

61. One of Bismarck's marginal comments read, "Wenn das 16.5 gelingt, so *wird* Krieg mit Fr. so gut wie 70" (Bülow to Bismarck, 25 June 1877, AA Bonn, I.A.B.c 79, Bd. 16).

62. Bismarck to Hohenlohe, 29 June 1877, GP 1:212; Bismarck to Hohenlohe, 29 June 1877, AA Bonn, II.B 12. "In his unofficial connections—with Thiers, for example—Hohenlohe should speak more on this matter in order to attempt to influence the elections in our interest"; so wrote Herbert von Bismarck to Radowitz, 29 June 1877, AA Bonn, I.A.B.c 79 secr., Bd. 2.

63. Hohenlohe to Bismarck, 2 July 1877, ibid.

64. "Bemerkungen des Herrn Reichskanzlers," 9 July 1877, ibid., 79, Bd. 16.

65. Keudell to Bismarck, 11 July 1877, ibid., Bd. 17; Bucher to Keudell, 15 July 1877, ibid.; Keudell to Bismarck, 28 July 1877, ibid.

66. Because of his preoccupation with foreign affairs, this point is overlooked by William L. Langer, *European Alliances and Alignments, 1871–1890*, pp. 156–57, 225–27; and for want of attention to German evidence, the same omission occurs in Hanotaux's *Histoire*, 4:159–63.

67. Hohenlohe to Bismarck, 3 July 1877, AA Bonn, I.A.B.c 79, Bd. 16. The French were alerted by the Catholic Reichstag deputy Windhorst that "Gambetta was in constant communication with the chancellor" (Gontaut-Biron to Decazes, 9 July 1877, BT Paris, Papiers Decazes, 713).

68. "Que signiferait le triomphe de la politique du maréchal MacMahon dans les prochaines élections?. . . . A l'étranger, ce succès n'aurait qu'une signification: la guerre. C'est du reste ainsi que la presse allemande envisage la question. En effect si la France hesiterait, la prudence conseillerait à l'Allemagne et à l'Italie de prendre l'initiative d'une lutte qu'aucune force humaine ne pourrait plus éviter" (*La république française*, 15 July 1877).

69. In the words of a master: "L'orientation de l'opinion publique ne trouve presque jamais son explication dans un facteur unique, mais dans les combinaisons variées de plusieurs facteurs, dont il s'agit justement de préciser le nombre et le caractère" (André Siegfried, *Tableau politique de la France de l'ouest sous la troisième république*, pp. 361–62). The fundamental and enduring importance of regional characteristics is also stressed by Alain Lancelot, *L'abstentionnisme électoral en France*, p. 55. The division after 1870 between the largely pro-republican east and the more conservative west is documented by François Goguel, *Géographie des élections françaises sous la troisième et la quatrième république*, pp. 20–23. To establish a secure causal chain is probably impossible, but it is nonetheless statistically conspicuous that the eastern territories had a greater tendency to republicanism than those sections of France less exposed to past or future conflicts with Germany or Italy. But for a further complicating factor, see Stuart R. Schram, *Protestantism and Politics in France*, pp. 62–79.

70. René Rémond, *La vie politique en France depuis 1789*, 2:236–37.

71. "C'était accuser le gouvernement de compromettre la paix: les déclarations prodiguées a cet égard par le duc Decazes . . . ne purent annuler l'effet de cette accusation sur l'opinion publique" (François Goguel, *La politique des partis sous la IIIe république*, 1:55. The very slow awakening of the countryside to national issues is discussed in an important chapter, "Peasants and Politics," in Eugen Weber's *Peasants into Frenchmen*, pp. 241–77. Weber cautions: "The impact of all this should not be exaggerated; knowledge of the wider world remained vague,

interest in its details slight and at best anecdotal. But the growing awareness that international affairs were capable of affecting one's life and the life of the locality carried with it a growing awareness of the nation. Willy-nilly, the inward-looking rural islands, self-sufficient at least in their own view, were being forced to attend to wider complications" (ibid., p. 268). On this general theme also see Jacques Kayser, *La presse en province sous la troisième république*, pp. 27–38, 118–35.

72. The cases briefly presented here have not been selected to suit the thesis of this chapter. To the contrary, the areas discussed are located in southern and western France, i.e., in the areas geographically distant from those eastern departments most vulnerable to direct German pressure. It is more than a historical curiosity that a French customs official by the name of Schnaebelé, involved in a famous border incident in 1887, was among those who reported to Paris concerning the imposing German menace in the east. These provinces could not remain unaware, he observed, that "on the other side of the frontier they are still convinced that the security of Germany urgently requires that France remain republican and not tolerate for long 'the government of priests' which the 16th of May has bestowed on it" (Schnaebelé to the Ministry of the Interior [Directeur de la sureté générale], 20 Aug. 1877, AN Paris, F⁷ 12566).

73. André Gorgues, *Les élections législatives et sénatoriales en Inde-et-Loire de 1871 à 1879*, pp. 203–6.

74. *Journal d'Indre-et-Loire*, 12 Oct. 1877, cited by Gorgues, ibid., p. 182.

75. Noël Landou and Jean-Paul Landrevie, *De l'empire à la république: structures politiques et sociales du Tarn-et-Garonne (1869–1877)*, pp. 159–94.

76. JORF, 20 Nov. 1877.

77. Ibid., 24 Feb. 1878. I am indebted to Dr. Karen M. Offen for references concerning the department of Gers.

78. Cited by Jean Micheu-Puyou, *Histoire électorale du département des Basses-Pyrénées sous la IIIe et la IVe république*, pp. 125–39.

79. This editorial in *La publicateur*, 10 Oct. 1877, continued, "Et maintenant choissisez: si vous voulez le retour en France des communards qui sont au bagne; si vous voulez la ruine du pays et votre propre ruine; si enfin vous voulez attirer sur vous le fléau de la guerre, votez pour les républicains!" The attack was resumed on 14 Oct. 1877: "Si vous voulez faire les affaires de la Prusse; si enfin vous voulez que M. de Bismarck montre bientôt notre pays à l'Europe monarchique comme un foyer de pestilence révolutionnaire et qu'il obtienne l'assentiment des puissances pour nous déclarer de nouveau la GUERRE, votez pour les candidats républicains!" (quoted by the *Journal des débats*, 17 Nov. 1877).

80. JORF, 15–16 Oct. 1877.

81. Hanotaux, *Histoire*, 4:185–94.

82. Manuscript of Hohenlohe's diary, entry for 31 Oct. 1877, BA

Koblenz, Hohenlohe Nachlass, XX C 4; Hohenlohe to Bismarck, 1 and 5 Nov. 1877, AA Bonn, I.A.B.c 79, Bd. 20.

83. Holstein to Bülow, 21 Oct. 1877, ibid., 79 secr., Bd. 2; Bülow to Bismarck, 29 Oct. 1877, ibid.; Bismarck to Bülow, 24 Oct. 1877, SF Hamburg, Bismarck Nachlass, B 24.

84. Bismarck to AA, 20 Oct. and 1 Nov. 1877, AA Bonn, I.A.B.c 79, Bd. 20.

85. Herbert von Bismarck to Henckel von Donnersmarck, 30 Oct. 1877, SF Hamburg, Bismarck Nachlass, B 52.

86. Hohenlohe to AA, 8 Nov. 1877, AA Bonn, I.A.B.c 79, Bd. 20. See Hanotaux, *Histoire*, 4:195, for a list of the eighteen leading republicans.

87. Hohenlohe to AA, 7 and 9 Nov. 1877, AA Bonn, I.A.B.c 79, Bd. 20.

88. Hohenlohe to AA, 14 Nov. 1877, ibid.; Bismarck to AA, 15 Nov. 1877, ibid.

89. Hohenlohe to Bismarck, 11 Nov. 1877, ibid., Bd. 21; JORF, 15–16 Nov. 1877.

90. Bleichröder to Bismarck, 13 Nov. 1877, SF Hamburg, Bismarck Nachlass, B 15. Bismarck had planted a story in the French press that MacMahon was hanging on until the election of a new pope. From Paris it was soon reported that this "had made an impression in all political circles" (Hohenlohe to Bismarck, 1 and 11 Dec. 1877, AA Bonn, I.A.B.c 79, Bd. 21, 22).

91. "Militärischer Bericht Nr. 146 des Oberstlieutenants von Bülow, betreffend den Wechsel im Kriegs-Ministerium," 24 Nov. 1877, ibid., Bd. 21.

92. "Militärischer Bericht Nr. 145 des Oberstlieutenants v. Bülow, betreffend die politische Krise," 17 Nov. 1877, ibid.; Bülow to William, 23 Nov. 1877, ibid.; Herbert von Bismarck to Bülow, 28 Nov. 1877, ibid.

93. Hohenlohe to Bismarck, 25 Nov. 1877, ibid. Bleichröder also warned that "a forcible disruption could occur at any moment" (Bleichröder to Bismarck, 30 Nov. 1877, AA Bonn, I.A.B.c 81, Bd. 2).

94. "Militärischer Bericht Nr. 148 des Oberstlieutenants v. Bülow, betreffend Personal-Veränderung," 1 Dec. 1877, ibid., 79, Bd. 21; Herbert von Bismarck to Bülow, 5 Dec. 1877, ibid.; Hohenlohe to Bismarck, 8 Dec. 1877, ibid.

95. "Cinq jours de crise: les journées des 8, 9, 10, 11, et 12 décembre à l'Elysée," first published in *L'Estafette*, 6 Jan. 1878, and forwarded by Wesdehlen to Bülow, 8 Jan. 1878, AA Bonn, I.A.B.c 81, Bd. 22.

96. Compare the narratives of Hanotaux, *Histoire*, 4:206–17; Pisani-Ferry, *Coup*, pp. 292–308; and Jacques Silvestre de Sacy, *Le maréchal de MacMahon, duc de Magenta (1808–1893)*, pp. 351–57. A summary of the subsequent parliamentary investigations is gathered in *L'année politique*, 1879, pp. 80–89, 360–79. See Charnay, *Scrutins*, pp. 83–86.

Chapter 7

1. JORF, 19, 27, and 31 Dec. 1877. See Gabriel Hanotaux, *Histoire de la France contemporaine (1871–1900)*, 4:221–25; Mattei Dogan, "Les filières de la carrière politique en France," pp. 461–71; and Jean Charlot, "Les élites politiques en France de la IIIe à la Ve république," pp. 78–92.

2. On changes in the army see especially Raoul Girardet, *La société militaire dans la France contemporaine, 1815–1939*; and David B. Ralston, *The Army of the Republic*. Useful guides to the voluminous literature on the Church have been provided by Aline Coutrot and François Dreyfus, *Les forces religieuses dans la société française*; and by John McManners, *Church and State in France, 1870–1914*. The military question and the religious question in France after 1870 will constitute the central themes of the sequel to the present volume.

3. Hohenlohe to Bismarck, 15 Dec. 1877, AA Bonn, I.A.B.c 79, Bd. 22; Bülow to Hohenlohe, 16 Dec. 1877, ibid.; Hohenlohe to Bülow, 19 Jan. 1878, ibid., Bd. 23; Herbert von Bismarck to Bülow, 4 Feb. 1878, ibid.

4. Bismarck to AA, 15 Dec. 1877, ibid., II.B 12; Bismarck to Henckel von Donnersmarck, 28 Dec. 1877, GW 14b:1579. See Fritz Stern, *Gold and Iron*, pp. 327–30.

5. Saint-Vallier to Waddington, 31 Jan. and 6 Feb. 1878, MAE Paris, CP Allemagne, 22; Saint-Vallier to Hohenlohe, 5 Feb. 1878, BA Koblenz, Hohenlohe Nachlass, XB V 1.

6. Hohenlohe to Bismarck, 19 Jan. 1878, AA Bonn, I.A.B.c 79 secr., Bd. 2; Bismarck to Hohenlohe, 26 Jan. 1878, ibid. Bismarck's desire to find a solution was confirmed by Bleichröder and communicated from Saint-Vallier to Waddington, 26 Feb. 1878, MAE Paris, Papiers Waddington, 8.

7. Saint-Vallier to Waddington, 16 and 24 Feb. 1878, ibid., MD Allemagne, 166.

8. Report by agent "Frédéric," 18 Feb. 1878, AN Paris, F⁷ 12566. In fact, the chancellor had granted occasional interviews to the French ambassador in the Wilhelmstrasse, usually to issue a reprimand. See André Dreux, ed., *Dernières années de l'ambassade de M. de Gontaut-Biron, 1874–1877*, pp. 174–86.

9. Bülow to Hohenlohe et al., 22 Feb. 1878, AA Bonn, I.A.B.c 79, Bd. 23; Saint-Vallier to Waddington, 5 Apr. 1878, MAE Paris, MD Allemagne, 166. See also GP 3:651–53; and DDF 2:259–76.

10. Henckel von Donnersmarck to Bismarck, 23 Dec. 1877, SF Hamburg, Bismarck Nachlass, B 52; Bismarck to Henckel von Donnersmarck, 28 Dec. 1877, GW 14b:1579.

11. Manuscript of Hohenlohe's diary, entry for 8 Feb. 1878, BA Koblenz, Hohenlohe Nachlass, XX C 5; Saint-Vallier to Waddington, 19 Apr. 1878, MAE Paris, CP Allemagne, 23.

12. Bülow to Bismarck, 13 Feb. 1878, AA Bonn, I.A.B.c 81, Bd. 2.

13. Henckel von Donnersmarck to Bismarck, 12 and 23 Apr. 1878, SF Hamburg, Bismarck Nachlass, B 52; Bismarck to Henckel von Donnersmarck, 14 Apr. 1878, ibid.; Hohenlohe to Bismarck, 20 Apr. and 1 May 1878, AA Bonn, I.A.B.c 79, Bd. 24; Bismarck to Hohenlohe, 28 Aug. 1878, ibid., 79 secr., Bd. 2. According to another version it was Gambetta who asked that the meeting be postponed (Joseph Reinach, *La vie politique de Léon Gambetta*, pp. 245–60). See E. Malcolm Carroll, *French Public Opinion and Foreign Affairs, 1870–1914*, pp. 72–76.

14. Henckel von Donnersmarck to Bismarck, 23 Dec. 1877, SF Hamburg, Bismarck Nachlass, B 52.

15. Bülow to Stolberg, 28 Apr. 1878, AA Bonn, I.A.B.c 79, Bd. 24; Hohenlohe to Bülow, 1 May 1878, ibid.; Stolberg to Bülow, 9 May 1878, ibid.

16. Saint-Vallier to Waddington, 13 May 1878, MD Allemagne, 166.

17. See W. N. Medlicott, *The Congress of Berlin and After*; William L. Langer, *European Alliances and Alignments, 1871–1890*, pp. 150–66; and the chapter "L'année de l'exposition" in Daniel Halévy, *La république des ducs*, pp. 331–66.

18. Saint-Vallier to Waddington, 25 May 1878, MAE Paris, MD Allemagne, 166.

19. Waddington to Dufaure, 10 June 1878, ibid., Papiers Waddington, 1; Waddington to Madame Waddington, 11 and 13 June 1878, ibid.; Waddington to Voguë, 10 July 1878, ibid., 4.

20. Hohenlohe to Bülow, 7 May and 1 June 1878, AA Bonn, I.A.B.c 79, Bd. 24; Wesdehlen to Bülow, 10 July 1878, ibid.

21. Say to Waddington, 2 July 1878, MAE Paris, Papiers Waddington, 2; Wesdehlen to Bülow, 13 and 17 July, AA Bonn, I.A.B.c 79, Bd. 24. See Maurice Agulhon, "Esquisse pour une archéologie de la république," pp. 5–24; and Charles Rearick, "Festivals in Modern France," pp. 435–60.

22. In Germany, meanwhile, the French chargé noted that Sedan Day was being celebrated with "less fanaticism than formerly" (Moüy to Waddington, 3 Sept. 1878, MAE Paris, CP Allemagne, 25).

23. Saint-Vallier to Waddington, 17 Nov. and 26 Dec. 1878, ibid., MD Allemagne, 166.

24. An editorial in the *Kölnische Zeitung*, 7 Dec. 1878, advised the French to observe the old English adage "leave well alone [*sic*]". See Hohenlohe to Bismarck, 9 Dec. 1878, AA Bonn, I.A.B.c 79, Bd. 27; Saint-Vallier to Waddington, 12 and 21 Dec. 1878, MAE Paris, MD Allemagne, 166.

25. Bismarck's contact with Gambetta was maintained through Blowitz, who once again offered to arrange a meeting of the two (Blowitz to Hohenlohe, 18 July 1878, BA Koblenz, Hohenlohe Nachlass, XB B 20; Hohenlohe to Bismarck, 20 Aug. 1878, AA Bonn, I.A.B.c 79 secr., Bd. 2; Bismarck to Hohenlohe, 28 Aug. 1878, ibid.).

26. See Robert H. Wienefeld, *Franco-German Relations, 1878–1885*; and Pearl Boring Mitchell, *The Bismarckian Policy of Conciliation with France, 1875–1885*.

27. See Charles P. Kindleberger, *Foreign Trade and the National Economy*, pp. 195–211. Another historian adds this thoroughly pessimistic comment: "But how far, and in what ways, was pre-1914 growth *dependent* on foreign trade? Regrettably, no firm answer can be given to this question" (J. D. Gould, *Economic Growth in History*, pp. 257; see also pp. 287–90).

28. *Annuaire statistique de la France* 8 (1885):379–92. Among the still useful standard treatments of the subject are Shephard B. Clough, *France*, pp. 214–17; Harry D. White, *The French International Accounts, 1880–1913*; Walter B. Harvey, *Tariffs and International Relations in Europe, 1860–1914*; and Frank A. Haight, *A History of Commercial Policies*, pp. 43–60. A reconsideration is attempted by Sanford Elwitt, *The Making of the Third Republic*, pp. 230–72.

29. For the distinction between "general" and "special" trade, as well as a remark on the pitfalls of computing the two types, see B. R. Mitchell, *European Historical Statistics, 1750–1970*, p. 485.

30. Walther G. Hoffmann, *Das Wachstum der deutschen Wirtschaft seit der Mitte des 19. Jahrhunderts*, p. 151. Here is a word of caution: "The records of no two countries tell precisely the same story about their trade with each other. The chief cause of this is confusion between countries of shipment, of consignment, and of origin. Different systems have been used at various times in most countries; and even when allowance is made for this, it is clear that the system supposedly in use has not always been followed with precise accuracy in every case. It would be extremely useful to have statistics showing a breakdown of the trade of the various countries by major commodity groups. Unfortunately, changes in definition occur in the published statistics of every country with very great frequency, and to produce consistent and comparable series for even one country is a considerable enterprise" (B. R. Mitchell, *Statistics*, pp. 485–86).

31. Alan S. Milward and S. B. Saul, *The Development of the Economies of Continental Europe, 1850–1914*, pp. 472–73. It has been estimated that world trade increased at a decennial rate of about 33 percent throughout the nineteenth century, whereas world product expanded much more slowly: from 1800 to 1913 the former grew 25 times over but the latter only 2.21 times (Simon Kuznets, "Quantitative Aspects of the Growth of Nations," pp. 3–8).

32. *Annuaire statistique de la France* 38 (1922):95.

33. Maurice Lévy-Leboyer, "La croissance économique en France au XIXe siècle," pp. 788–807. The comparable figure for Germany in the period 1880–84 is set at 35.1 percent by Walther G. Hoffmann, *Wachstum*, p. 151. See Kuznets, "Quantitative Aspects," pp. 98–103.

34. This point is elaborated by Raymond Poidevin and Jacques Bariéty, *Les relations franco-allemandes 1815–1975*, pp. 133–35. Inexplicably, however, they make no mention whatever of changes in the balance of trade.

35. Kuznets, "Quantitative Aspects," pp. 126–27. There are some discrepancies in the data, adapted from Walther G. Hoffmann, depending on whether constant (1913) or current prices were employed.

36. Kuznets, "Quantitative Aspects," pp. 126–27. The data for France, corrected by Kuznets, are based on Jacques Duvaux and Jean Weiller, "Economie française, échanges extérieurs et structures internationales." See Milward and Saul, *Development*, pp. 123–24; Gould, *Economic Growth*, pp. 255–56; and Poidevin and Bariéty, *Relations*, p. 134.

37. Hohenlohe to Bismarck, 15 Dec. 1877, AA Bonn, I.A.B.c 79, Bd. 22; Hohenlohe to Bülow, 4 Feb. 1878, ibid., Bd. 23; Charles de Freycinet, *Souvenirs, 1848–1893*, 2:7–22. See Yasuo Gonjo, "Le 'Plan Freycinet,' 1878–1882," pp. 49–86.

38. Waddington to Saint-Vallier, 1 Jan. 1879, MAE Paris, Papiers Waddington, 2.

39. E.g., the thirty-seven-page report from Saint-Vallier to Waddington, 10 May 1879, AN Paris, F¹² 6199.

40. Waddington to Saint-Vallier, 2 June 1879, MAE Paris, CP Allemagne, 27; Saint-Vallier to Waddington, 13 July 1879, ibid., MD Allemagne, 166 bis.

41. Say to Waddington, 3 Feb. 1879, ibid., Papiers Waddington, 2. See Jean Bouvier, *Les Rothschilds*, pp. 205–21. Pouyer-Quertier and Bismarck corresponded in the spring of 1879 and found themselves in accord on the tariff issue (Bismarck to Saint-Vallier, 11 May 1879, AA Bonn, I.A.B.c 87, Bd. 4; Pouyer-Quertier to Bismarck, 12 June 1879, ibid.).

42. JORF, 7 May 1880. See Hanotaux, *Histoire*, 4:524–27; Clough, *France*, pp. 214–17; Gonjo, "Le 'Plan Freycinet,'" pp. 78–79; and Milward and Saul, *Development*, pp. 116–20.

43. For a different perspective see Elwitt, *Making*, pp. 136–69.

44. "In this manner, the reforms of 1881–82, far from re-establishing protection—as most textbooks still suggest they did—actually extended the free trade system of the Second Empire for ten more years. Unfortunately for the free traders, they were not able to preserve this victory in the midst of changing economic and political circumstances at home and abroad after 1882" (Michael S. Smith, "Free Trade versus Protection in the Early Third Republic," pp. 309–14). The "baisse brutale" in January 1882 is described by Jean Bouvier, *Le Krach de l'Union Générale (1878–1885)*, pp. 140–87. On the depression of prices in the agricultural sector and the eventual impact on trade policy, see Eugene Owen Golob, *The Méline Tariff*; Tom Kemp, *Economic Forces in French History*, pp. 227–43; and Milward and Saul, *Development*, pp. 103–16.

45. Saint-Vallier to Waddington, 21 Oct. and 3 Nov. 1879, AN Paris, F^{12} 6199; Reichskanzleramt to Reichsschatzamt, 14 Nov. 1879, BA Koblenz, R 2/1455. See Helmut Böhme, *Deutschlands Weg zur Grossmacht*, pp. 525–29, 597–604.

46. Gambetta's remark, "La période des dangers est close, celle des difficultés va commencer," and Hohenlohe's rejoinder, "Diese Schwierigkeiten können aber mit der Zeit wieder zu Gefahren werden," are quoted in Hohenlohe to Bismarck, 6 Jan. 1879, AA Bonn, I.A.B.c 87, Bd. 1.

47. Hohenlohe to Bismarck, 1 Feb. 1879, ibid.

48. See Jacques Silvestre de Sacy, *Le maréchal de MacMahon, duc de Magenta (1808–1893)*, pp. 363–71.

49. Hohenlohe to AA, 31 Jan. 1879, AA Bonn, I.A.B.c 87, Bd. 1.

50. "Pro Memoria betreffend die Notifikations- und Creditivfrage bei französichen Präsidentenwechseln," 31 Jan. 1879, AA Bonn, I.A.B.c 87, Bd. 1; Bismarck to Bülow, 1 Feb. 1879, ibid. Waddington's personal expression of gratitude for the expeditious settlement was passed on from Hohenlohe to Bismarck, 5 Feb. 1879, SF Hamburg, Bismarck Nachlass, B 54. The entire affair and the surprise it occasioned in Berlin were summarized in a letter from Saint-Vallier to Waddington, 18 Feb. 1879, MAE Paris, MD Allemagne, 166 bis.

51. Bernhard von Bülow to AA, 30 Jan. 1879, AA Bonn, I.A.B.c 87, Bd. 1. Bleichröder's informants in Paris led him to conclude that Grévy would be only an interim figure; this opinion was shared by Blowitz, who predicted the eventual return of Bonapartism (Bleichröder to Bismarck, 2 Feb. 1879, SF Hamburg, Bismarck Nachlass, B 15; manuscript of Hohenlohe's diary, entry for 5 Feb. 1879, BA Koblenz, Hohenlohe Nachlass, XX C 7).

52. Directive from Lepère (minister of the interior) to all prefects, 3 June 1879, AN Paris, F^{1a} 2140a.

53. JORF, 12 Feb. 1879; "Militärischer Bericht Nr. 179 des Oberstlieutenants v. Bülow, betreff: Die Personal-Veränderunger unter den kommandierenden Generalen," 13 Feb. 1879, AA Bonn, I.A.B.c 87, Bd. 2. See Hanotaux, *Histoire*, 4:448–49.

54. Hohenlohe to Bismarck, 18 Feb. 1879, AA Bonn, I.A.B.c 87, Bd. 2.

55. "L'importance de M. Clémenceau grandit tous les jours. . . . Sa manière est seche, expéditive comme celle d'un chirurgien. Il ne parle pas, il opère. Et quelle rigeur, quelle logique, quelle dureté!" (*Moniteur universel*, 3 Mar. 1879, forwarded by Hohenlohe to Bismarck, 4 March 1879, AA Bonn, I.A.B.c 87, Bd. 2. See David Robin Watson, *Georges Clemenceau*, pp. 66–73).

56. Hohenlohe to Bismarck, 4 and 18 Mar. 1879, AA Bonn, I.A.B.c 87, Bd. 2, 3. See Evelyn Acomb, *The French Laic Laws, 1879–1889*; Adrien Dansette, *Histoire religieuse de la France contemporaine*, pp. 413–

30; and Jean-Marie Mayeur, *Les débuts de la IIIe république, 1871–1898*, pp. 111–19, 134–53.

57. Saint-Vallier to Waddington, 6 Jan. 1879, MAE Paris, CP Allemagne, 27; Saint-Vallier to Waddington, 7 Jan. 1879, ibid., MD Allemagne, 166 bis.

58. Hohenlohe to AA, 3 Feb. 1879, AA Bonn, I.A.B.c 87, Bd. 1; Saint-Vallier to Waddington, 25 Feb. 1879, MAE Paris, CP Allemagne, 27.

59. Saint-Vallier to Waddington, 26 Feb. 1879, ibid., MD Allemagne, 166 bis.

60. Saint-Vallier to Waddington, 21 and 22 Feb. 1879, ibid., CP Allemagne, 27; Saint-Vallier to Waddington, 27 Feb. and 4 Mar. 1879, ibid., MD Allemagne, 166 bis.

61. Saint-Vallier to Waddington, 29 and 31 Mar. 1879, ibid.; "Bülow (Aufzeichnung) betr. die inneren Zustände Frankreichs," 4 Apr. 1879, AA Bonn, I.A.B.c 87, Bd. 3.

62. Saint-Vallier to Waddington, 5 Apr. and 6 May 1879, MAE Paris, MD Allemagne, 166 bis.

63. See above, Chapter 5, n. 1.

64. Saint-Vallier to Waddington, 14 Nov. 1879, MAE Paris, Papiers Waddington, 6. This important dispatch remained undiscovered by the editors of the French diplomatic documents, who printed instead two other communiqués from Saint-Vallier to Waddington (14 Nov. 1879, DDF 2:476, 477).

65. Saint-Vallier to Waddington, 14 Nov. 1879, MAE Paris, Papiers Waddington, 6. Bismarck had been informed at least eight months earlier of the consultations among Waddington, Ferry, and Gambetta concerning electoral reform in France (Hohenlohe to Bismarck, 24 Mar. 1879, AA Bonn, I.A.B.c 87, Bd. 3).

66. Saint-Vallier to Waddington, 14 Nov. 1879, MAE Paris, Papiers Waddington, 6.

67. Bismarck to Ballhausen, 24 Nov. 1879, GW 14b:1623.

68. Moltke's outburst to Odo Russell was reported by Saint-Vallier to Waddington, 5 Dec. 1879, MAE Paris, Papiers Waddington, 8.

69. Saint-Vallier to Waddington, 28 and 29 Dec. 1879, ibid., 7, 8.

70. Bernhard von Bülow to Hohenlohe, 10 Mar. 1879, BA Koblenz, Bülow Nachlass, Nr. 21.

71. Hohenlohe to Bismarck, 14 Jan. and 14 Mar. 1879, AA Bonn, I.A.B.c 87, Bd. 1, 2.

72. Hohenlohe to Bismarck, 7 Apr. 1879, ibid., Bd. 3.

73. Hohenlohe to Bismarck, 20 June 1879, ibid., 73, Bd. 3.

74. Saint-Vallier to Waddington, 23 June 1879, MAE Paris, MD Allemagne, 166 bis.

75. Hohenlohe to Bismarck, 8 Nov. 1879, AA Bonn, I.A.B.c 73, Bd. 3.

76. See Hanotaux, *Histoire*, 4:619–24.

77. Hohenlohe to Bismarck, 13 Feb. 1880, BA Koblenz, Hohenlohe Nachlass, XX B 2.

78. Billot to Gambetta, 29 Feb. and 27 Mar. 1880, BN Paris, NAF 24900; Boulanger to Gambetta, 5 July 1880, ibid.

79. Radowitz to AA, 30 July 1880, AA Bonn, Europa-Generalia 82, Nr. 5, Bd. 1; Radowitz to Bismarck, 26 Oct. 1880, ibid.; Thielmann to Bismarck, 24 Nov. 1880, ibid. During the autumn, Bismarck recalled Radowitz to Berlin, explaining that "a worsening of our international relations is not presently to be feared" (Bismarck to Radowitz, 31 Oct. 1880, SF Hamburg, Bismarck Nachlass, B 90). See Hajo Holborn, ed., *Aufzeichnungen und Erinnerungen aus dem Leben des Botschafters Joseph Maria von Radowitz*, 2:124–56.

80. Odo Russell to Saint-Vallier, 23 Sept. 1880, BVC Paris, Papiers Barthélémy Saint-Hilaire, 260; Saint-Vallier to Barthélémy Saint-Hilaire, 25 Sept. 1880, ibid.

81. Until the publication of the final volume of J. P. T. Bury's biography of Gambetta, the authoritative account remains Joseph Reinach's *Le ministère Gambetta*. Also see Stanley Hoffmann, ed., *In Search of France*, pp. 14–21; and S. A. Ashley, "The Failure of Gambetta's *Grand Ministère*," pp. 105–24.

82. Hatzfeldt to Hohenlohe, 15 Nov. 1881, GP 3:669; "Aufzeichnung des Legationsrats Herbert von Bismarck," ibid., 670.

83. See Hanotaux, *Histoire*, 4:708.

Bibliography

Manuscript Sources

Archives nationales, Paris
 F^1 Administration générale
 F^7 Police générale
 F^{12} Commerce et industrie
 F^{30} Finances. Administration centrale
 AP Archives privées
 AQ Archives d'entreprises
Archives de la Préfecture de Police, Paris
 B A/86–87 Rapports quotidiens
 B A/311–37 Rapports de correspondants de la Préfecture de Police
  principalement à l'étranger
 B A/917–24 Dossiers Gambetta
` Miscellaneous
Auswärtiges Amt, Bonn
 I.A.B.c Frankreich (70–87)
 I.D. 44
 II.B. 10, 12
 Europa-Generalia
  See *A Catalogue of Films and Microfilms of the German Foreign Ministry Archives, 1867–1920.* Edited by George O. Kent. Oxford, 1959.
Baker Library, Harvard Business School, Cambridge, Mass.
 Bleichröder Nachlass
Bibliothèque nationale (salle des manuscrits), Paris
 Papiers Favre (NAF 24107–26)
 Papiers Picard (NAF 24369–73)
 Papiers Rémusat (NAF 14414–71)
 Papiers Thiers (NAF 20601–84)
 Miscellaneous

Bibliothèque Thiers, Paris
  Papiers Decazes (681–751)
  Fonds Thiers (24–40)
Bibliothèque Victor Cousin, Paris
  Papiers Barthélémy Saint-Hilaire
Bundesarchiv, Koblenz
  Bülow Nachlass
  Hohenlohe Nachlass
  R2/1455 Acta betr: Der deutsch-französische Handelsvertrag (Nov.
    1879–Dez. 1898)
Chambre de Commerce, Paris
  Correspondance (XV–XVI)
Deutsches Zentralarchiv. Potsdam
  Auswärtiges Amt, Politische Abteilung: Deutsche Konsulate (Kons.
    Fr. 1–37)
  Reichskanzleramt
  Beziehungen zum Ausland (II gen. Frankr.)
  Finanzielle Angelegenheiten aus dem Kriege 1870/71, Militaria (II gen.
    43)
Deutsches Zentralarchiv, Historische Abteiling II, Merseburg
  Krieg mit Frankreich (Rep. 77, Tit. 134a)
  Okkupationen (Rep. 77, Tit. 875)
  Auswärtige Angelegenheiten (Rep. 89 H VI.)
  Frankreich (Rep. 120 C XIII.)
Geheimes Staatsarchiv, Munich
  Politisches Archiv (MA I: 745–49)
  Die diplomatischen Berichte (MA III: 2128–37, 2651–58)
  Deutsches Reich (MA 77942–49)
  Auswärtige Staaten (MA 83277)
Ministère des affaires étrangères, Paris
  Correspondance consulaire et commerciale, Francfort (8–12)
  Correspondance consulaire et commerciale, Hambourg (43–46)
  Correspondance politique, Allemagne (1–38)
  Correspondance politique, Bavière (250–60)
  Correspondance politique des consuls, Allemagne (1–7)
  Mémoires et documents, Allemagne (156–67 bis, 172–73)
  Papiers Chaudordy
  Papiers Favre
  Papiers Gambetta
  Papiers Hanotaux
  Papiers Thiers
  Papiers Waddington
Schloss Friedrichsruh, near Hamburg
  Bismarck Nachlass

Published Documents

Année politique.
Annuaire statistique de la France
Archives diplomatiques 1871–1872. Paris, n.d.
Bismarck: die gesammelten Werke. Edited by Herman von Petersdorf et al. 15 vols. Berlin, 1924–35.
Die Grosse Politik der europäischen Kabinette, 1871–1914. Edited by Johannes Lepsius et al. 40 vols. Berlin, 1922–27.
Documents diplomatiques français, 1871–1914. Edited by the Ministère des affaires étrangères. 1re série (1871–1900). 15 vols. Paris, 1929–59.
Journal officiel de la république française.
Occupation et libération du territoire, 1871–1873. 2 vols. Paris, 1903.

Memoirs and Letters

Bismarck, Otto von. *Bismarcks Briefe an seine Gattin aus dem Kriege, 1870/71.* Stuttgart and Berlin, 1903.
Blowitz, Henri Stephan de. *My Memoirs.* London, 1903.
Cluseret, Gustave-Paul. *Mémoires du général Cluseret.* 3 vols. Paris, 1887–88.
Dreux, André, ed. *Dernières années de l'ambassade de M. de Gontaut-Biron, 1874–1877.* Paris, 1907.
Du Barail, Général. *Souvenirs.* 3 vols. Paris, 1894–96.
Falloux, Alfred de. *Mémoires d'un royaliste.* 2 vols. Paris, 1888.
Favre, Jules. *Gouvernement de la défense nationale.* 3 vols. Paris, 1871–75.
Fitzmaurice, Lord Edmond. *The Life of Granville George Leveson Gower, Second Earl Granville.* 2 vols. London, 1905.
Freycinet, Charles de. *Souvenirs, 1848–1893.* 2 vols. Paris, 1912–13.
Gabriac, Marquis de. *Souvenirs diplomatiques de Russie et d'Allemagne (1870–1872).* Paris, 1896.
Gontaut-Biron, Vicomte de. *Mon ambassade en Allemagne (1872–1873).* Paris, 1906.
Hohenlohe, Chlodwig zu. *Denkwürdigkeiten des Fürsten Chlodwig zu Hohenlohe-Schillingsfürst.* 2 vols. Stuttgart and Leipzig, 1907.
Holborn, Hajo, ed. *Aufzeichnungen und Erinnerungen aus dem Leben des Botschafters Joseph Maria von Radowitz.* 2 vols. Berlin, 1925.
Meisner, Heinrich Otto, ed. *Denkwürdigkeiten des General-Feldmarschalls Alfred Grafen von Waldersee.* 2 vols. Stuttgart and Berlin, 1922.
Rémusat, Charles de. *Mémoires de ma vie.* 5 vols. Paris, 1958–67.
Rich, Norman and Fisher, M. H., eds. *The Holstein Papers: The Memoirs, Diaries and Correspondence of Friedrich von Holstein, 1837–1909.* 4 vols. Cambridge, 1955–63.
Rogge, Helmuth, ed. *Holstein und Hohenlohe: neue Beiträge zu Freidrich von Holsteins Tätigkeit als Mitarbeiter Bismarcks und als Ratgeber Hohenlohes.* Stuttgart, 1959.

Thiers, Adolphe. *Notes et souvenirs de M. Thiers, 1870–1873*. Paris, 1903.
Tocqueville, Alexis de. *Recollections*. New York, 1971.

Books and Articles

Acomb, Evelyn. *The French Laic Laws, 1879–1889: The First Anti-Clerical Campaign of the Third French Republic*. New York, 1941.
Agulhon, Maurice. "Esquisse pour une archéologie de la république: l'allégorie civique feminine." *Annales* 28 (1973):5–34.
Amagut, Amant Louis, *Les emprunts et les impôts de la rançon de 1871*. Paris, 1889.
Armengaud, André. *L'opinion publique en France et la crise nationale allemande en 1866*. Paris, 1962.
Ashley, S. A. "The Failure of Gambetta's *Grand Ministère*." *French Historical Studies* 9 (1975):105–24.
Bainville, Jacques. *Bismarck et la France*. Paris, 1907.
Barker, Nancy Nichols. *Distaff Diplomacy: The Empress Eugénie and the Foreign Policy of the Second Empire*. Austin, 1967.
————. "Napoleon III and the Hohenzollern Candidacy for the Spanish Throne." *Historian* 29 (1967):431–50.
Barral, Pierre. *Le département de l'Isère sous la troisième république, 1870–1940*. Paris, 1962.
Basso, Jacques. *Les élections législatives dans le département des Alpes-Maritimes de 1860 à 1939*. Paris, 1968.
Becker, Josef. "Zum Problem der Bismarckschen Politik in der spanischen Thronfrage 1870." *Historische Zeitschrift* 212 (1971):529–607.
Bellanger, Claude, et al. *Histoire générale de la presse française*. 3 vols. Paris, 1969–72.
Bertocci, Philip A. *Jules Simon: Republican Anticlericalism and Cultural Politics in France, 1848–1886*. Columbia, 1978.
Biro, Sydney, S. *The German Policy of Revolutionary France*. 2 vols. Cambridge, Mass., 1957.
Böhme, Helmut. *Deutschlands Weg zur Grossmacht: Studien zum Verhältnis von Wirtschaft und Staat während der Reichsgründungszeit 1848–1881*. Cologne and Berlin, 1966.
Böhmer, Bert. *Frankreich zwischen Republik und Monarchie in der Bismarckzeit: Bismarcks Antilegitimus in französischer Sicht (1870/1877)*. Kallmünz, 1966.
Bonnin, Georges. *Bismarck and the Hohenzollern Candidature for the Spanish Throne*. London, 1957.
Borchardt, Knut. "Wirtschaftliches Wachstum und Wechsellagen 1800–1914." In *Handbuch der deutschen Wirtschafts und Sozialgeschichte*, edited by Hermann Aubin and Wolfgang Zorn. Stuttgart, 1976.
Bourgin, Georges. "Une entente franco-allemande: Bismarck, Thiers,

Jules Favre et la répression de la Commune de Paris (mai 1871)." *International Review of Social History* 1 (1956):41–53.

Bouvier, Jean. "Aux origines de la IIIe république: les réflexes des milieux d'affaires." *Revue historique* 210 (1953):271–301.

_____. *Le Crédit Lyonnais de 1863 à 1882.* 2 vols. Paris, 1961.

_____. *Le Krach de l'Union Générale (1878–1885).* Paris, 1960.

_____. *Les Rothschilds.* Paris, 1967.

Brabant, Frank Herbert. *The Beginnings of the Third Republic in France: A History of the National Assembly (February-September 1871).* London, 1940.

Brogan, D. W. *The Development of Modern France, 1870–1939.* 2d ed. New York, 1966.

Brown, Marvin L., Jr. *The Comte de Chambord: The Third Republic's Uncompromising King.* Durham, N.C., 1967.

Bruhat, Jean, et al. *La Commune de 1871.* 2d ed. Paris, 1970.

Buchner, Rudolf. *Die deutsch-französische Tragödie 1848–1864: Politische Beziehungen und Psychologisches Verhältnis.* Würzburg, 1965.

Bury, J. P. T. *Gambetta and the Making of the Third Republic.* London, 1973.

_____. *Gambetta and the National Defence.* London, 1936.

_____. *Napoleon III and the Second Empire.* London, 1964.

_____. "The Identity of 'C. de B.'" *French Historical Studies* 3 (1964):538–41.

Bussmann, Walter. *Das Zeitalter Bismarcks.* 4th ed. Frankfurt, 1970.

Cameron, Rondo E. "Economic Growth and Stagnation in France, 1815–1914." *Journal of Modern History* 30 (1958):1–13.

_____. "Economic History, Pure and Applied." *Journal of Economic History* 36 (1976):3–27.

_____. *France and the Economic Development of Europe, 1800–1914.* Princeton, 1961.

_____. "L'exportation des capitaux français, 1850–1880." *Revue d'histoire économique et sociale* 33 (1955):346–53.

_____. "The Crédit Mobilier and the Economic Development of Europe." *Journal of Political Economy* 61 (1953):461–88.

Carroll, E. Malcolm. *French Public Opinion and Foreign Affairs, 1870–1914.* New York and London, 1931.

_____. *Germany and the Great Powers, 1866–1914: A Study in Public Opinion and Foreign Policy.* New York, 1938.

Chapman, Brian. *The Prefects and Provincial France.* London, 1955.

Chapman, Guy. *The Third Republic of France: The First Phase, 1871–1894.* New York, 1962.

Charlot, Jean. "Les élites politiques en France de la IIIe à la Ve république." *Archives européennes de sociologie* 14 (1973):78–92.

Charnay, Jean-Paul. *Les scrutins politiques en France de 1815 à 1962.* Paris, 1964.

Chastenet, Jacques. *Gambetta*. Paris, 1968.

———. *Histoire de la troisième république*. 7 vols. Paris, 1952–63.

Clapham, J. H. *The Economic Development of France and Germany, 1815–1914*. 4th ed. Cambridge, 1955.

Clark, Terry Nichols. *Prophets and Patrons: The French University and the Emergence of the Social Sciences*. Cambridge, Mass., 1973.

Clough, Shephard B. *France: A History of National Economics, 1789–1939*. New York, 1939.

Connelly, Owen. *Napoleon's Satellite Kingdoms*. New York, 1965.

Coutrot, Aline, and Dreyfus, François. *Les forces religieuses dans la société française*. Paris, 1965.

Crouzet, François. "Essai de construction d'un indice annuel de la production industrielle française au XIXe siècle." *Annales* 25 (1970):56–99.

Dansette, Adrien. *Histoire religieuse de la France contemporaine*. 2d ed. Paris, 1965.

Desmarest, Jacques. *La défense nationale, 1870–1871*. Paris, 1949.

Digeon, Claude. *La crise allemande de la pensée française (1870–1914)*. Paris, 1959.

Dittrich, Jochen. *Bismarck, Frankreich und die spanische Thronkandidatur der Hohenzollern: die "Kriegsschuldfrage" von 1870*. Munich, 1970.

———. "Ursachen und Ausbruch des deutsch-französischen Krieges 1870/71." In *Reichsgründung 1870/71: Tatsachen, Kontroversen, Interpretationen*, edited by Theodor Schieder and Ernst Deuerlein. Stuttgart, 1970.

Dogan, Mattei. "Les filières de la carrière politique en France." *Revue française de sociologie* 7 (1967):461–71.

Dreyfus, Robert. *De Monsieur Thiers à Marcel Proust: histoire et souvenirs*. Paris, 1939.

Droz, Jacques. *L'Allemagne et la révolution française*. Paris, 1949.

Dupeux, Georges. *Aspects de l'histoire sociale et politique du Loir-et-Cher, 1848–1914*. Paris and The Hague, 1962.

Dupuy, Aimé. *1870–1871: la guerre, la commune et la presse*. Paris, 1959.

Duvaux, Jacques, and Weiller, Jean. "Economie française, échanges extérieurs et structures internationales." In *Cahiers de l'Institut de science économique appliquée*, series P, no. 1. Paris, 1957.

Duverger, Maurice. *Les partis politiques*. Paris, 1951.

Echard, William E. "Conference Diplomacy in the German Policy of Napoleon III, 1868–1869." *French Historical Studies* 4 (1966):239–64.

Edwards, Stewart. *The Paris Commune, 1871*. London, 1971.

Elwitt, Sanford. *The Making of the Third Republic: Class and Politics in France, 1868–1884*. Baton Rouge, La., 1975.

Farmer, Paul. *France Reviews Its Revolutionary Origins: Social Politics and Historical Opinion in the Third Republic*. New York, 1943.

Fohlen, Claude. "The Industrial Revolution in France." In *Essays in*

French Economic History, edited by Rondo E. Cameron. Homewood, Ill., 1970.

Gadille, Jacques. *La pensée et l'action politiques des évêques français au début de la IIIe république 1870/1883*. 2 vols. Paris, 1967.

Geuss, Herbert. *Bismarck und Napoleon III.: ein Beitrag zur Geschichte der preussisch-französischen Beziehungen 1851–1871*. Cologne and Graz, 1959.

Geyl, Pieter, *Napoleon, For and Against*. 2d ed. New Haven, 1963.

Geisberg, Robert I. *The Treaty of Frankfort: A Study in Diplomatic History, September 1870–September 1873*. Phildelphia, 1966.

Gille, Bertrand. *Histoire de la maison Rothschild*. 2 vols. Geneva, 1965–67.

_____. "Les emprunts de libération en 1871–1872." In *La France au XIXe siècle: mélanges offerts à Charles Hippolyte Pouthas*. Paris, 1973.

Girardet, Raoul. *La société militaire dans la France contemporaine, 1815–1939*. Paris, 1953.

_____, ed. *Le nationalisme français, 1871–1914*. Paris, 1966.

Girault, Jacques. *La Commune et Bordeaux, 1870–1871*. Paris, 1971.

Goguel, François. *Géographie des élections françaises sous la troisième et la quatrième république*. Paris, 1970.

_____. *La politique des partis sous la IIIe république*. 2 vols. Paris, 1946.

Goldschmidt, Hans. *Bismarck und die Friedensunterhändler 1871: die deutsch-französischen Friedensverhandlungen zu Brüssel und Frankfurt, März bis Dezember 1871*. Berlin and Leipzig, 1929.

Golob, Eugene Owen. *The Méline Tariff: French Agriculture and Nationalist Economic Policy*. New York, 1944.

Gonjo, Yasuo. "Le 'Plan Freycinet,' 1878–1882: un aspect de la 'grande dépression' économique en France." *Revue historique* 248 (1972):49–86.

Gorgues, André. *Les élections législatives et sénatoriales en Inde-et-Loire de 1871 à 1879*. Paris, 1973.

Gouault, Jacques. *Comment la France est devenue républicaine: les élections générales et partielles à l'Assemblée nationale (1870–1875)*. Paris, 1954.

Gould, J. D. *Economic Growth in History*. London, 1972.

Greenberg, Louis M. *Sisters of Liberty: Marseille, Lyon, Paris and the Reaction to a Centralized State, 1868–1871*. Cambridge, Mass., 1971.

Groote, Wolfgang von, and Gersdorff, Ursala von, eds. *Entscheidung 1870: der deutsch-franzöische Krieg*. Stuttgart, 1970.

Guilbert, Madelaine. *Les femmes et l'organisation syndicale avant 1914*. Paris, 1966.

Guillard, Jeanne. *Communes de province, Commune de Paris, 1870–1871*. Paris, 1971.

_____. "La Commune: le mythe et le fait." *Annales* 28 (1973):838–52.

Guillemin, Henri. *Les origines de la Commune*. 3 vols. Paris, 1954–60.

Haight, Frank A. *A History of French Commercial Policies*. New York, 1941.

Halévy, Daniel. *La fin des notables*. Paris, 1930.

————. *La république des ducs*. Paris, 1937.

Hallgarten, George W. F. *Imperialismus vor 1914: die soziologischen Grundlagen der Aussenpolitik europäischer Grossmächte vor dem Ersten Weltkrieg*. 2d ed. Munich, 1963.

Hammer, Karl. *Die französische Diplomatie der Restauration und Deutschland, 1814–1830*. Stuttgart, 1963.

Hanotaux, Gabriel. *Histoire de la France contemporaine (1871–1900)*. 4 vols. Paris, 1903–8.

Hartshorne, Richard. "The Franco-German Boundary of 1871." *World Politics* 2 (1949–50):209–50.

Hartung, Fritz. "Bismarck und Graf Harry Arnim." *Historische Zeitschrift* 171 (1951):47–77.

Harvey, Walter B. *Tariffs and International Relations in Europe, 1860–1914*. Chicago, 1938.

Herzfeld. Hans. *Deutschland und das geschlagene Frankreich 1871–1873*. Berlin, 1924.

————. *Die deutsch-französische Kriegsgefahr von 1875*. Berlin, 1922.

Hildebrand, Klaus. "Von der Reichseinigung zur 'Krieg-in-Sicht'-Krise: Preussen-Deutschland als Faktor der britischen Aussenpolitik 1866–1875." In *Das kaiserliche Deutschland: Politik und Gesellschaft 1870–1918*, edited by Michael Stürmer. Düsseldorf, 1970.

Hillgruber, Andreas. "Die 'Krieg-in-Sicht' Krise—Wegscheide der Politik der europäischen Grossmächte in der späten Bismarck-Zeit." In *Gedenkschrift Martin Göhring: Studien zur europäischen Geschichte*, edited by Ernst Schulin. Wiesbaden, 1968.

Hoffmann, Stanley, ed. *In Search of France*. Cambridge, Mass., 1963.

Hoffmann, Walther G. *Das Wachstum der deutschen Wirtschaft seit der Mitte des 19. Jahrhunderts*. Berlin, 1965.

Holborn, Hajo. *Bismarcks europäische Politik zu Beginn der siebziger Jahre und die Mission Radowitz*. Berlin, 1925.

Howard, Michael. *The Franco-Prussian War: The German Invasion of France, 1870–1871*. 2d ed. New York, 1969.

Joughin, Jean T. *The Paris Commune in French Politics, 1871–1880*. 2 vols. Baltimore, 1955.

Kayser, Jacques. *La presse en province sous la troisième république*. Paris, 1958.

Kehr, Eckhart. *Der Primat der Innenpolitik: gesammelte Aufsätze zur preussisch-deutschen Sozialgeschichte im 19. und 20. Jahrhundert*. Berlin, 1965.

Kemp, Tom. *Economic Forces in French History*. London, 1971.

————. *Industrialization in Nineteenth-Century Europe*. London and Harlow, 1969.

Kent, George O. *Arnim and Bismarck*. Oxford, 1968.

Keylor, William R. *Academy and Community: The Foundation of the French Historical Profession*. Cambridge, Mass., 1975.

Kindleberger, Charles P. *Economic Growth in France and Britain, 1851–1950*. Cambridge, Mass., 1964.

―――. *Foreign Trade and the National Economy*. New Haven and London, 1962.

Kocka, Jürgen. "Theoretical Approaches to Social and Economic History of Modern Germany: Some Recent Trends, Concepts, and Problems in Western and Eastern Germany." *Journal of Modern History* 47 (1975):101–19.

Kolb, Eberhard. *Der Kriegsausbruch 1870: politische Entscheidungsprozesse und Verantwortlichkeiten in der Julikrise 1870*. Göttingen, 1970.

―――. "Der Pariser Commune-Aufstand und die Beendigung des deutsch-französischen Krieges." *Historische Zeitschrift* 215 (1972): 265–98.

Kühn, Joachim. "Bismarck und der Bonapartismus im Winter 1870/71." *Preussische Jahrbücher* 163 (1916):49–100.

Kuznets, Simon. *Economic Growth of Nations*. Cambridge, Mass., 1971.

―――. "Quantitative Aspects of the Growth of Nations." *Economic Development and Cultural Change* 15, no. 2 (1967):96–111.

Lambert, André. *Le siège de Paris*. Paris, 1965.

Lambi, Ivo Nikolai. *Free Trade and Protection in Germany, 1868–1879*. Wiesbaden, 1963.

Lancelot, Alain. *L'abstentionnisme électoral en France*. Paris, 1968.

Landes, Davis S. "French Entrepreneurship and Industrial Growth in the Nineteenth Century." *Journal of Economic History* 9 (1949):45–61.

―――. *The Unbound Prometheus: Technological Change and Industrial Development in Western Europe from 1750 to the Present*. Cambridge, 1969.

―――. "Vieille banque et banque nouvelle." *Revue d'histoire moderne et contemporaine* 3 (1956):204–22.

Landou, Noël, and Landrevie, Jean-Paul. *De l'empire à la république: structures politiques et sociales du Tarn-et-Garonne (1869–1877)*. Paris, 1973.

Langer, William L. *European Alliances and Alignments, 1871–1890*. 2d ed. New York, 1964.

Latreille, André, et al. *Histoire du catholicisme en France*. 3 vols. Paris, 1957–62.

Laurentie, François. *Le comte de Chambord, Guillaume I et Bismarck en octobre 1870*. Paris, 1912.

Le Clère, Bernard, and Wright, Vincent. *Les préfets du second empire*. Paris, 1973.

Lévy-Leboyer, Maurice. "La croissance économique en France au XIXe siècle: résultats préliminaires." *Annales* 23 (1968):788–807.

―――. "La décélération de l'économie française dans la seconde moitié du XIXe siècle." *Revue d'histoire économique et sociale* 49 (1971):485–507.

Lill, Rudolf. *Die Wende im Kulturkampf. Leo XIII, Bismarck und die Zentrumspartei, 1878–1880*. Tübingen, 1973.

Linnebach, Karl. *Deutschland als Sieger im besetzten Frankreich 1871–1873.* Stuttgart, 1924.

Locke, Robert R. "A New Look at Conservative Preparations for the French Election of 1871." *French Historical Studies* 5 (1968):351–58.

————. *French Legitimists and the Politics of Moral Order in the Early Third Republic.* Princeton, 1974.

Lüthy, Herbert. *Frankreichs Uhren gehen anders.* Zürich, 1953.

Machlup, Fritz. "The Transfer Problem: Theme and Four Variations." In *International Payments, Debts, and Gold.* New York, 1964.

McManners, John. *Church and State in France, 1870–1914.* New York, 1973.

Maddison, Angus. *Economic Growth in the West.* London, 1964.

Malettke, Klaus. *Die Beurteilung der Aussen- und Innenpolitik Bismarcks von 1862–1866 in den grossen Pariser Zeitungen.* Lübeck and Hamburg, 1966.

Malo, Henri. *Thiers, 1797–1877.* Paris, 1932.

Marx. Karl. *The Civil War in France.* New York, 1969.

Mayeur, Jean-Marie. *Les débuts de la IIIe république, 1871–1898.* Paris, 1973.

Medlicott, W. N. *The Congress of Berlin and After: A Diplomatic History of the Near Eastern Settlement, 1878–1880.* London, 1938.

Micheu-Puyou, Jean. *Histoire électorale du département des Basses-Pyrénées sous la IIIe et la IVe république.* Paris, 1965.

Milward, Alan S. and Saul, S. B. *The Development of the Economies of Continental Europe, 1850–1914.* London, 1977.

Mitchell, Allan. *Bismarck and the French Nation, 1848–1890.* New York, 1971.

————. "Bonapartism as a Model for Bismarckian Politics." *Journal of Modern History* 59 (1977):181–209.

————. "German History in France after 1870." *Journal of Contemporary History* 2 (1967):81–100.

————. "Thiers, MacMahon, and the Conseil Supérieur de la Guerre." *French Historical Studies* 6 (1969):233–52.

Mitchell, B. R. *European Historical Statistics, 1750–1970.* London, 1975.

Mitchell, Pearl Boring. *The Bismarckian Policy of Conciliation with France, 1875–1885.* Philadelphia, 1935.

Mosse, Werner E. *The European Powers and the German Question, 1848–1871.* New York, 1958.

Naujoks, Eberhard. "Bismarck und die Organisation der Regierungspresse." *Historische Zeitschrift* 205 (1967):46–80.

————. "Rudolf Lindau und die Neuorientierung der auswärtigen Pressepolitik Bismarcks (1871/78)." *Historische Zeitschrift* 215 (1972):299–344.

Noland, Aaron. *The Founding of the French Socialist Party.* Cambridge, Mass., 1956.

Osgood, Samuel. *French Royalism since 1870*. 2d ed. The Hague, 1970.

Palmade, Guy P. *Capitalisme et capitalistes français au XIXe siècle*. Paris, 1961.

Palmer, Robert R. *The Age of Democratic Revolution*. 2 vols. Princeton, 1959–64.

Palou, Jean. *La franc-maçonnerie*. Paris, 1964.

Parker, William N. "National States and National Development: French and German Ore Mining in the Late Nineteenth Century." In *The State and Economic Growth*, edited by Hugh G. J. Aitkin. New York, 1959.

Paul, Harry W. *The Sorcerer's Apprentice: The French Scientist's Image of German Science, 1840–1919*. Gainesville, 1972.

Paxton, Robert O. *Vichy France: Old Guard and New Order*. New York, 1972.

Perrot, Michelle. *Les ouvriers en grève: France 1871–1890*. 2 vols. Paris, 1974.

Pflanze, Otto. *Bismarck and the Development of Germany: The Period of Unification, 1815–1871*. Princeton, 1963.

Pisani-Ferry, Fresnette. *Le coup d'état manqué du 16 mai 1877*. Paris, 1965.

Poidevin, Raymond, and Bariéty, Jacques. *Les relations franco-allemandes 1815–1975*. Paris, 1977.

Poidevin, Raymond, ed. *Metz en 1870 et les problèmes des territoires annexés*. Metz, 1972.

Pöls, Werner, "Bleichröder und die Arnim-Affäre." *Historische Zeitschrift* 211 (1970):65–76.

Pomaret, Charles. *Monsieur Thiers et son siècle*. 5th ed. Paris, 1948.

Ralston, David B. *The Army of the Republic: The Place of the Military in the Political Evolution of France, 1871–1914*. Cambridge, Mass., and London, 1967.

Rearick, Charles. "Festivals in Modern France: The Experience of the Third Republic." *Journal of Contemporary History* 12 (1977):435–60.

Reinach, Joseph. *La vie politique de Léon Gambetta*. Paris, 1918.

———. *Le ministère Gambetta: Histoire et doctrine (14 novembre 1881–26 janvier 1882)*. Paris, 1884.

Rémond, René. *La droite en France de 1815 à nos jours*. 2d ed. Paris, 1963.

———. *L'anticléricalisme en France de 1815 à nos jours*. Paris, 1976.

———. *La vie politique en France depuis 1789*. 2 vols. Paris, 1965–69.

Renouvin, Pierre, and Duroselle, Jean-Baptiste. *Introduction à l'histoire des relations internationales*. Paris, 1964.

Richardson, Nicholas J. *The French Prefectoral Corps, 1814–1830*. Cambridge, 1966.

Rich, Norman. *Friedrich von Holstein: Politics and Diplomacy in the Era of Bismarck and William II*. 2 vols. Cambridge, 1965.

Ritter, Gerhard. *Staatskunst und Kriegshandwerk: das Problem des 'Militarismus' in Deutschland*. 4 vols. Munich, 1954–68.

Rosenberg, Hans. *Grosse Depression und Bismarckzeit.* Berlin, 1967.

Rostow, W. W., ed. *The Economics of Take-Off into Sustained Growth.* New York, 1963.

Rothney, John. *Bonapartism after Sedan.* Ithaca, 1969.

Rougerie, Jacques. *Paris libre 1871.* Paris, 1971.

Roux, Georges. *La guerre de 1870.* Paris, 1966.

Roux, Marquis de. *La république de Bismarck: les origines allemandes de la troisième république.* Paris, 1905.

Saul. S. B. *The Myth of the Great Depression, 1873–1896.* London, 1969.

Schnerb, Robert. "La politique fiscale de Thiers." *Revue historique* 201 (1949):186–212; 202 (1949):184–220.

Schot, Bastiaan. "Die Entstehung des Deutsch-Französischen Krieges und die Gründung des Deutschen Reiches." In *Probleme der Reichsgründungszeit, 1848–1879*, edited by Helmut Böhme. Cologne and Berlin, 1968.

Schram, Stuart R. *Protestantism and Politics in France.* Alençon, 1954.

Seager, Frederic H. "The Alsace-Lorraine Question in France, 1871–1914." in *From the Ancien Régime to the Popular Front*, edited by Charles K. Warner. New York and London, 1969.

Seguin, Jean. *Les emprunts contractés par la France à l'occasion de la guerre de 1870.* Paris, 1914.

Shorter, Edward, and Tilly, Charles. *Strikes in France, 1830–1968.* London, 1974.

Sieburg, Heinz Otto. *Deutschland und Frankreich in der Geschichtsschreibung des 19. Jahrhunderts.* 2 vols. Wiesbaden, 1954–58.

Siegfried, André. *Tableau des partis en France.* Paris, 1930.

———. *Tableau politique de la France de l'oeust sous la troisième république.* Paris, 1913.

Silverman, Dan P. *Reluctant Union: Alsace-Lorraine and Imperial Germany, 1871–1918.* University Park, Pa., 1972.

Silvestre de Sacy, Jacques. *La maréchal de MacMahon, duc de Magenta (1808–1893).* Paris, 1960.

Siwek-Pouydesseau, Jeanne. *Le corps préfectoral sous les IIIe et IVe républiques.* Paris, 1969.

Smith, Michael S. "Free Trade versus Protection in the Early Third Republic: Economic Interests, Tariff Policy, and the Making of the Republican Synthesis." *French Historical Studies* 10 (1977):293–314.

Soulier, Auguste. *L'instabilité ministerielle sous la troisième république (1871–1938).* Paris, 1939.

Steefel, Lawrence D. *Bismarck, the Hohenzollern Candidacy, and the Origins of the Franco-German War of 1870.* Cambridge, Mass., 1970.

Steinbach, Christoph. *Die französische Diplomatie und das Deutsche Reich 1873 bis 1881.* Bonn, 1976.

Stengers, Jean. "Aux origines de la guerre de 1870; gouvernement et opinion publique." *Revue belge de philologie et d'histoire* 34 (1956);701–47.

Stern, Fritz. *Gold and Iron: Bismarck, Bleichröder, and the Building of the German Empire.* New York, 1977.

Stürmer, Michael. *Regierung und Reichstag im Bismarckstaat 1871–1880: Cäsarismus oder Parlamentarismus.* Düsseldorf, 1974.

_____. "Staatsstreichgedanken im Bismarckreich." *Historische Zeitschrift* 209 (1969):556–615.

Swart, K. W. *The Sense of Decadence in Nineteenth-Century France.* The Hague, 1964.

Thomson, David. *Democracy in France since 1870.* 5th ed. New York, 1969.

Tilly, Charles, ed. *The Formation of Nation States in Western Europe.* Princeton, 1975.

Trotsky, Leon. *The History of the Russian Revolution.* 3 vols. New York, 1932–34.

Valfrey, Jules. *Histoire du traité de Francfort et la libération du territoire français.* 12 vols. Paris, 1874–75.

Wahl, Alfred. *L'option et l'émigration des Alsaciens-Lorrains (1871–1872).* Paris, 1974.

Waller, Bruce. *Bismarck at the Crossroads: The Reorientation of German Foreign Policy after the Congress of Berlin, 1878–1880.* London, 1974.

Weber, Eugen. *Peasants into Frenchmen: The Modernization of Rural France, 1870–1914.* Stanford, 1976.

Wehler, Hans-Ulrich. *Bismarck und der Imperialismus.* 4th ed. Munich, 1969.

_____. "Das 'Reichsland' Elsass-Lothringen, 1870–79." In *Probleme der Reichsgründungszeit, 1848–1879,* edited by Helmut Böhme. Cologne and Berlin, 1968.

Whitcomb, Edward A. "Napoleon's Prefects." *American Historical Review* 79 (1974):1089–118.

White, Harry D. *The French International Accounts, 1880–1913.* Cambridge, Mass., 1933.

Wienefeld, Robert H. *Franco-German Relations, 1878–1885.* Baltimore, 1929.

Williams, Roger L. *The French Revolution of 1870–1871.* New York, 1969.

Winckler, Martin, "Der Ausbruch der 'Krieg-in-Sicht'-Krise vom Frühjahr 1875." *Zeitschrift für Ostforschung* 14 (1965):671–713.

Winnacker, R. A. "The French Election of 1871." *Papers of the Michigan Academy of Science, Arts, and Letters* 22 (1936):477–83.

Wolter, Heinz. "Die Anfänge des Dreikaiserverhältnisses. Reichsgründung, Pariser Kommune und die internationale Mächtekonstellation 1870–1873." *Die grosspreussisch-militärische Reichsgründung 1871.* 2 vols. Berlin, 1971.

Wright, Gordon. *France in Modern Times*. 2d ed. Chicago, 1974.
———. "The Anti-Commune: Paris, 1871." *French Historical Studies* 10 (1977):149–72.
Zeldin, Theodore. *Emile Ollivier and the Liberal Empire of Napoleon III*. Oxford, 1963.
———. *France, 1848–1945*. 2 vols. Oxford, 1973–77.
———. *The Political System of Napoleon III*. London, 1958.

Index

A

The Author

Allan Mitchell, author of *Revolution in Bavaria, 1918–1919*
(1965) and *Bismarck and the French Nation, 1848–1890* (1971), is
professor of history at the University of California, San Diego.

The Book

Typeface: Stempel V-I-P Bembo
Design and composition: The University of North Carolina Press

Published by The University of North Carolina Press